Feminist Readings/
Feminists Reading

Feminist Readings/ Feminists Reading

Sara Mills
Lecturer in Literary Linguistics, Strathclyde University, Glasgow, UK

Lynne Pearce
Lecturer in English Literature, Durham University, UK

Sue Spaull
Advisor and Trainer at SHAC, The London Housing Aid Centre, London, UK

Elaine Millard
Head of Communication Studies, Bilborough Sixth Form College, Nottingham, UK

University Press of Virginia 1989
Charlottesville

First published 1989 by Harvester Wheatsheaf

First published 1989 in the United States of America by
The University Press of Virginia
Box 3608 University Station
Charlottesville, Virginia 22903

Printed and bound in Great Britain

© 1989 Sara Mills, Lynn Pearce, Sue Spaull, Elaine Millard

Library of Congress Cataloging-in-Publication Data
Feminist readings/feminists reading/Sara Mills ... (et al.)
p.   cm.
Bibliography: p.
Includes index.
ISBN 0-8139-1242-3 — ISBN 0-8139-1243-1 (pbk.)
1. English fiction — History and criticism.   2. American fiction —
History and criticism.   3. Women in literature.   4. Feminist
literary criticism.   5. Feminism and literature.   I. Mills, Sara,
1954-   .
PR830.W6F46 1989
813.009'352042 — dc20   89-14818
                                          CIP

To Deirdre Burton and Gillian Skirrow
for all the inspiration and support they have given to so many
women

Contents

Acknowledgements

We would like to thank all those people who have given this book their support: our students, for whom it was written; Jackie Jones at Harvester Wheatsheaf for her enthusiasm and consideration through all stages of its production; our families and friends for providing us with the time and space necessary in which to meet and work; and especially the following individuals for their unfailing understanding, inspiration and care: Patrick Williams, Sarah Oatey-Shaw, Gordon Fairbairn and Les Millard.

The authors and publishers wish to thank the following, who have kindly given permission for the use of copyright material:

David Higham Associates Ltd. for extracts from *The Color Purple* by Alice Walker, published by The Women's Press, 1983.

André Deutsch Ltd. for extracts from *Surfacing* by Margaret Atwood, 1984, and for extracts from *The Wide Sargasso Sea* by Jean Rhys, 1968.

Yale University Press for extracts from *The Madwoman in the Attic* by Sandra Gilbert and Susan Gubar, 1979.

Virago and the Agents Rogers, Coleridge and White for extracts from *The Magic Toyshop* by Angela Carter, 1981.

Introduction

Sara Mills, Lynne Pearce, Sue Spaull and Elaine Millard

Since the early 1980s, there has been a great deal of writing on feminist literary theory. This has included several excellent 'introductory guides' which have attempted to supply a new generation of women readers with an overview of the major trends in feminist criticism since the re-launch of the modern Women's Movement in the late 1960s.[1] However, there are still those (both inside and outside academic institutions), who have heard of 'sexual politics' and 'images of women' criticism and erroneously believe that this is more or less all there is to feminist criticism. Unsympathetic academics continue to characterise feminist criticism as discontented women carping about the negative representations of themselves that they face when reading texts. A further simplification has been the characterisation of French feminism as too theoretical, and of Anglo-American feminism as too dependent on untheorised positions like New Criticism.[2] This book (following on from others like Toril Moi's *Sexual/Textual Politics*) aims to break down these monolithic categorisations, and show that they are far from accurate descriptions of *feminist literary practice*.[3]

There have been a number of publications which attempt to display a range of feminist readings of texts, but these collections have often been rather eclectic in their choice of theoretical position, so that for a reader new to feminist theory it is difficult to disentangle the various strands within particular positions.[4] For this reason, we have decided to limit the number of theoretical positions and the number of texts chosen so that the chapters can be seen to delineate very clearly one particular position, although, in practice, each one is often combined with others. It should also be noted that our theoretical texts all derive from the 1970s, in the belief that another book would be necessary to deal adequately with the multiplication and cross-fertilisation of reading practices that have emerged in the 1980s.[5]

In planning this book, we felt that it was vitally important for the reader becoming interested in feminist criticism for the first time to be aware of the range of possibilities available in feminist critical practice. It is worth noting, too, that historically we have moved into a new era, and that by the 1990s undergraduate students will literally be of another generation to the women who 'lived' the theoretical and political debates of the 1960s and 1970s. We feel strongly that it is important to recognise the potential alienation of younger feminists, who cannot possibly be expected to be conversant with the sum-total of the feminist literary criticism of the past 20 years. For many of us, our knowledge of past theoretical debates will be necessarily second hand. If we are to break new ground, we cannot bury ourselves in the work of our predecessors. And yet it is equally important that all that was useful and distinctive in the earlier readings is not forgotten; hence the pragmatic necessity of texts like Moi and Weedon, and of retrospective collections of essays like those of Showalter and Eagleton (see Bibliography).

Indeed, it is as a *complement* to these texts that we hope *Feminist Readings/Feminists Reading* will insert itself, extending feminist theories to feminist critical practice. A recent attempt to demonstrate 'theory in practice' was the Nottingham Critical Theory Group's collection of essays, *Literary Theory at Work*.[6] This collection comprises multiple theoretical responses to three preselected literary texts, and ranges over a wide spectrum of contemporary theoretical positions. While we do, of course, register our acknowledgement to this enterprise, the critical hindsight provided by the book's reception has been equally valuable in defining our own project and in helping us to negotiate certain problems. First, we are aware of the problems attending any simplistic notion of 'application' in our analysis of the relationship between theoretical model and literary text. We prefer to regard this book as supplying the reader with working examples of how particular theoretical positions appear in actual readings. Here the word example is used advisedly, since neither theoretical position nor 'reading' claim to be in any way prescriptive. Their function is merely to acquaint the new reader with a chosen aspect of that theoretical approach, and then to offer a reading based upon it. However, rather than being content with a reading of a literary text by a theoretical text, we have then gone on to read the theoretical text with/through/against the literary text in a concluding problem section in each chapter. In this way, we hope to ensure that the theoretical text is not privileged over the literary text in any absolutist or reductive way. We assume that the reading process carried out on the literary text is at the same time enacted on the theoretical text. We feel that our reading practice *is* affected by theoretical work – that we *engage with it* – and that particular positions are adopted as a result.

Response to the Tallack collection has also alerted us to the charges of political ineffectiveness that may be levelled at a collection which appears to offer the reader an arbitrary choice of reading positions. As a collective, we all feel very strongly that a theoretical position which does not inform a reading strategy or change the way that a reader approaches a text or, indeed, the way she thinks about herself and her life, has very little to offer us in this context. This is not to suggest that each of the positions can be adopted mechanically like a change of clothes, which would ignore the political foundations of the theories, since each of the theories involves a whole host of assumptions about the text, the reader and gender. However, in detailing the theories, we describe the assumptions which have to be made to formulate reading strategies. We also reveal the commitment of each of these theories to feminism in a broader context: to what Chris Weedon stresses is the unreservedly *political* purpose of all feminist writing: 'These political questions should be the motivating force behind feminist theory which must always be answerable to the needs of women in our struggle to transform patriarchy'.[7] In this respect, some of the theories proposed in this book will seem more politically engaged than others, with Marxist-feminism obviously claiming the most conscious materialism. However, because all feminist writing about literature has grown out of committed political consciousness – the Women's Movement – all of the positions discussed here are political to a greater or lesser degree. Therefore, the accusations of 'liberalism' that have attended the pluralism within literary criticism at large do not apply to feminist criticism, which does not compete with so much as *relate* to other positions within the greater commitment that is Feminism itself. For this reason, we urge the reader not to regard the six reading strategies offered here as either optional (take it or leave it) *or* dogmatic (this is the only possible reading), but both serious (committed) and flexible positions that can be practised as they stand, or revised, adapted or combined with others.

Indeed, this is already the criterion of several of the theoretical texts engaged with here: the evolution of Marxist-feminism has been intimately associated with psychoanalysis, for example. As we hope to show in the Conclusion, 'pluralism' in the received perjorative sense is in every way a misnomer for the ethos behind the collection of readings presented here. In contrast to the fierce arguments perpetuated by male theorists, as feminists we have preferred to develop and multiply our possibilities non-competitively. Theory for us is not fixed and essentialist, but shifting and mutable. It lives not outside, but inside critical practice. It is something to consider, digest and re-create for one's own purpose. It is, above all, something to *share*. Our hope, as feminist readers, in presenting you with these feminist readings, is not that you will merely agree or disagree, but read, discuss, then go forth and multiply.

It is largely a consequence of the co-operative spirit within feminist criticism that the work of the last 20 years can be regarded as an historical development or evolution, with feminists building on and re-defining themselves according to what has gone before. Using Julia Kristeva's framework, elaborated in her article 'Women's time', we can trace three major stages in the development of feminist literary theory: first, a critique of male canonical writing, complaining about the negative images of women; secondly, a concentration on the establishment and tracing of a female literary tradition, re-valuing those texts which had been written by women; and thirdly, a calling into question of gender difference.[8]

1. The concern of the earliest feminist critics was to scrutinise a

shared canon of literary 'greats' in order to try to account for the absence of a significant body of women's writing. Tillie Olsen's *Silences* catalogues the limitations placed on the creativity of both men and women, using testimonies from their letters and diaries.[9] She focusses particularly on the difficulty women have had in finding space and time for their work, including her own struggle to be a 'writing writer'. This struggle for space has been a consistent theme in accounts of writing women.[10]

Feminist literary criticism became a theoretical issue with the publication of Kate Millett's *Sexual Politics* in 1969.[11] This book concentrates on 'dis-covering' sexist assumptions in male-authored texts and can be credited with establishing 'patriarchal' as a valid critical term. As is recorded in Chapter One, it was the polemical nature of this text which distinguished it from equally provocative though more cautious studies that had gone before, such as Mary Ellman's *Thinking About Women* (1968), and situated it in the vanguard of a new public debate that linked women's fight for equality in the material world with the sexism inherent in both literature and literary criticism.[12] This book sparked off a great deal of public debate and interest in feminist literary criticism, and together with other texts such as Arlyn Diamond's collection *The Authority of Experience* (1977) aimed to criticise the images of women characters which were presented in male texts.[13] Shortly after this, critics began to make generalisations about feminist literary criticism as a whole, such as Josephine Donovan's collection entitled *Feminist Literary Criticism* (1975).[14] Cheri Register, in this collection, wrote an article entitled 'American feminist literary criticism' which also marked another turning point in its suggestion that feminist criticism should be *prescriptive*, that critics should suggest ways in which writers could produce 'literature which is good from a feminist viewpoint'.[15] A culmination of this trend of examining primarily male texts can be seen in Judith Fetterley's *The Resisting Reader* (1978) which suggests that much of American literature has been addressed to an exclusively male audience.[16] Inevitably, therefore, female readers when reading these texts have either had to position themselves as males, or have 'resisted' the reading position that they have been allocated. However, although the work which was done on male-authored texts became increasingly sophisticated, many feminists felt that rather than challenging the status of these texts, they were perhaps perpetuating some of the problems. Thus there was a moving away from analysis of male writing, and a move towards the reading and analysis of texts by women.

2. Elaine Showalter, in her book *A Literature of Their Own* (1977), and Ellen Moers, in *Literary Women* (1976), started a new phase in feminist literary scholarship, by turning their attention away from a critique of male writing and towards the establishment of a female tradition.[17] In one sense they continued the earlier work, since they restricted themselves to re-readings of 'classic' women writers, such as Jane Austen, the Brontës and Emily Dickinson, and attempted to argue for canonical status for a wider range of previously little-known women writers, such as Maria Edgeworth, Aphra Behn and many others. In these books, the aim was to show how much of a tradition of women's writing there has been in the past which has been consistently ignored in histories of British and American literature. They argued that rather than literary women being isolated exceptions, they formed, instead, communities of women writers, corresponding, exchanging manuscripts, reacting against and consciously referring to each other's work. In Dale Spender's recent book *Mothers of the Novel* (1986), this tradition of reclamation has been continued, for she also attempts to demonstrate both that there have always been women who wrote for their living, and that these women formed a close knit community inside which they supported and influenced one other.[18]

In an article entitled 'Feminist criticism in the wilderness' (1981), Elaine Showalter then went on to detail some of the work which was then being done in feminist criticism and argued that it could be divided into two categories: 'feminist critique' and 'gyno-criticism'.[19] Feminist critique she described as involving the woman as reader, often re-reading male texts, and offering different interpretations of the images of woman found there. Gynocriticism she described as a form of criticism which focusses specifically on women's writing – the woman as writer. The aim of such criticism was to establish the ways in which women's writing differed from men's and why.

Sandra Gilbert and Susan Gubar were also interested in examining the ways in which women's writing differed from men's. Their readings, in *The Madwoman in the Attic* (1979), of nineteenth century women's writing suggest that common themes found in those women's writing stem from their ambivalent relationship with their male predecessors and the fact that women writers in the nineteeth century had no *female* literary tradition to subscribe to; hence, they had to re-use male writing strategies to their own distinctly female ends.[20]

3. In France, during the 1960s and 1970s, many French feminists, such as Hélène Cixous, Julia Kristeva and Luce Irigaray, developed a system of analysis which was radically different to that which had been practised in the UK and the USA.[21] In these French works, theory has taken precedence over the selection and re-reading of specific literary texts. The writers construct a critique, not of the representation of women's experience in literature, but of the very nature of female subjectivity and the language through which it is symbolised. Through the related academic disciplines of linguistics, psychoanalysis and philosophy, each theorist moves towards a deconstruction of feminine and masculine modes of writing that tends to associate the feminine with the non-rational, disruptive modes of writing found in modernist fiction and *avant-garde* poetry. Central to all of the French feminisms is a knowledge of Saussurean linguistics and Lacanian theories of the subject as constituted in language. Language, they argue, in privileging the phallus, suppresses what is feminine, subjecting it to the symbolisation of a patriarchal system of naming and categorisation.[22] For Kristeva, the suppressed feminine emerges in both men's and women's writing of the modernist *avant-garde* which, by concentrating on language shows subjectivity in the process of construction. For Irigaray and Cixous, writing 'woman' is a more utopian quest to bring into being that which has not yet been written. They have employed the phrase 'to write the body' which, however, causes suspicion because of its suggestions of the kind of biological essentialism ('anatomy is destiny') that much feminism has seen as its major target. In practice, their writings work to unpick existing binary oppositions of male/female, rational/irrational, heard/silenced, using the symbolism of fluidity and female sexuality to confront the phallogocentrism of Western philosophical writings, rather than create an alternative women's sector. Their writing practices, though not in themselves readings of literary texts, can provide

literary theorists with categories for creating a post-structuralist feminist practice where texts are read as discursive constructs rather than reflections of an individual author's experience. These women use the sophisticated verbal and philosophical 'deconstructions' of Lacan and Derrida in order to destabilise the notion of gender positions within texts, and their methods have been further developed by the so-called 'deconstructive feminist critics' such as Peggy Kamuf, Alice Jardine, Gayatri Spivak and Shoshana Felman.[23]

Throughout these three phases of development in feminist criticism there have been other voices struggling to make themselves heard. Black feminist critics such as Barbara Christian and Barbara Smith have been mapping out the radical differences that exist for a feminist practice which concentrates on the factor of race in readings and text production, and in this way they have challenged the notion of gender as a unitary term.[24] They, along with writers such as Gayatri Chakravotry Spivak, have challenged white feminists' habit of referring to their own experience as universal and their refusal to acknowledge their own implicit or explicit racism.[25]

In a similar way, lesbian critics have attempted to make visible the particular interests of lesbian criticism, and have refused to be subsumed within a larger feminist criticism which does not take account of the differences in reading strategies and text production involved for lesbian women. Critics such as Lillian Faderman, Bonnie Zimmerman and Monique Wittig have written surveys of the state of the art of lesbian criticism, and have thus shown yet again that gendered experience is not unitary.[26]

Marxist-feminist criticism developed during the 1970s, when it became clear that Marxist criticism of all persuasions was not sufficiently aware of the question of gender in the analysis of texts, and was prone to subsume gender within the 'more important' concept of class. Many Marxist-feminist critics and groups began to question this assumption and developed readings which, in the Althusserian tradition, drew on psychoanalytic theory in addition to Marxist theory. As was indicated in the opening section of the Introduction, Marxist-feminism demonstrates the eclecticism inherent in the development of feminist theory and is perhaps best understood as a singular mutation of Marxism and gender issues raised by feminists of all kinds during the 1970s. The complications in actually defining Marxist-feminism (the hyphen is not unproblematic) will be dealt with in the first part of Chapter Six, but in this brief historical survey it should be noted that its effective practice in literary criticism (as opposed to the social sciences) is a phenomenon of the 1980s rather than the 1970s. Indeed, the Marxist-Feminist Literature Collective (whose article on women writers we have used as our key text in the Marxist-feminist chapter) was pioneering in relating the political debates of socialist feminists to literary critical practice, and the legacy of possibilities they unearthed has only quite recently found expression in the writings of Cora Kaplan and other works like Penny Boumelha's *Thomas Hardy and Women* (1982) and Judith Lowder Newton's *Feminist Practice and Social Change* (1985).[27] It is worth stressing here the point made in Chapter Six, that although most feminist theories owe a political allegiance to socialism, the practice of readings that are consciously Marxist-feminist is still relatively small. More recently, however, individual writers (such as Chris Weedon in *Feminist Practice and Post-structuralist Theory*) and groups of women working in education have recognised that the future for feminist theory must lie in a far more clearly articulated dialogue with materialism. Feminist theories of all denominations must embrace and be embraced by a broader materialist commitment.

Although in the above description the individual theories are outlined as if they were discrete entities, these various positions of feminist literary theory are constantly interacting with one another. Many instances of such hybridity will emerge in the following chapters, while its broader implications for today's feminist critic will form the focus of discussion in the Conclusion.[28]

Yet while this brief introductory survey of feminist critical theory has emphasised its complexity, it is nevertheless the responsibility of this collection to disentangle the threads and to reconstruct, as nearly as possible, the salient features of six historically specific theoretical approaches. Our aim was to produce readings that were purposefully sympathetic; both in their response to the original theoretical proponents, and to the extent that we were searching for what the positions had to offer the contemporary reader. For this reason, a substantial proportion of each chapter is concerned with a positive evaluation of the way these theories can work. When planning this book we had to decide if we should follow this opening section with naive or unproblematised readings: whether to work with a theory was to accept all of its rules. Some of the reasons why we thought this an untenable response should have already emerged, but in essence our feelings were that a prescriptive 'application' of this kind would not be anything more than a historical reconstruction. In many of the cases, these feminist theories have been attacked and criticised, and it would be unwise not to take that criticism into account as a way of moving on from these positions. Our practice was therefore to 'stretch' the positions in order to show how far it is possible to appropriate a theory developed at one particular historical conjuncture and use it in another. At the same time, we felt that it would have been impossible for us entirely to suppress the consciousness we have developed through the reading of recent theoretical texts, and the introductory and concluding sections of each chapter are written from what may be described as a broadly post-structuralist critical position. By 'post-structuralist position', we mean that we all share certain views on key issues in the theoretical debates of the present day, as worked on by theorists such as Roland Barthes, Louis Althusser, Jacques Derrida, Jacques Lacan, Michel Foucault, Mikhail Bakhtin and others. The key issues include language, the constitution of the subject, the social construction of gender, author intentionality and the position of the author and, as post-structuralists, we question certain liberal humanist assumptions about the nature of literature and texts in general. On this point it should also be noted that we do not see the use of male theorists as *necessarily* problematic, agreeing with recent writers like Toril Moi who argues for the appropriation of such texts as may usefully be enjoined to a feminist purpose.[29]

As the reader will already have gathered, the format of each chapter is tripartite: the actual reading of the literary texts is sandwiched between an introductory section (Part I) which offers a positive evaluation of the critical approach concerned, and a retrospective critique (Part III) which attends to problems that have arisen as a result of the reading. This final section also offers suggestions as to how the individual theories may be revised/appropriated for use by present-day feminists.

Our choice of both literary and theoretical texts has been necessarily selective. While acknowledging the problem of dealing with only token aspects of a theorist's/group of theorists' work, the parameters of the project made it inevitable that we concentrate on just one or two key texts per chapter, although the introductory sections make reference to the general theoretical context within which the reading is made. Our choice of literary texts has been similarly restricted to a total of seven. These are as follows: Emily Brontë's *Wuthering Heights*: Thomas Hardy's *Tess of the d'Urbervilles*; Jean Rhys's *The Wide Sargasso Sea*; Charlotte Perkins Gilman's 'The Yellow Wallpaper'; Angela Carter's *The Magic Toyshop*; Alice Walker's *The Color Purple*; and Margaret Atwood's *Surfacing*. In this selection we have tried to achieve a balance between established 'classics' (such as Hardy and Brontë), recently reclaimed 'feminist classics' (Rhys and Gilman) and popular contemporary writing (Walker, Carter, Atwood). Each chapter will focus on two of these texts, meaning that each one will be read or referred to by at least two different theoretical positions. In this way it is hoped that readers will begin to differentiate between the theories, and also to establish a sense of critical dialogue between them. It will be noted that all the literary texts are by women, with the exception of Hardy's *Tess*, which was included in the chapter on 'sexual politics', since Millett was herself primarily concerned with the critique of male texts. We are also well aware of the problems entailed in choosing 'literary' texts to analyse, given women's relative exclusion from 'literary status', and are all committed to the broadening and eventual removal of the canonical mechanism whereby certain texts are privileged over others and are considered to be of more value. We would hope that it would be possible in the not too distant future to discuss women's science fiction, romance, travel writing and political writing in a similar way, without losing sight of their specificity.[30] However, for the purposes of this book, we felt it necessary to choose texts which have been important within a women's tradition of writing, and ones which we feel women will have read.

In terms of style, our main aim has been clarity; some of the approaches we describe/engage with are notoriously difficult for new readers, and we have avoided using any academic terminology which is not fully explained. At the same time, we have endeavoured not to simplify the complexity of these arguments and, to assist the new reader, have supplied a Glossary at the back of the book. We believe, like Deborah Cameron, that, where possible, theoretical discussion should aim to avoid 'mystification' and should try to be clear.[31]

Conventionally books are produced by individuals working in isolation. This has not been the case with the production of *Feminist Readings/Feminists Reading*. This book was produced over a period of two years and although we live in very different parts of the UK – Birmingham, London, Glasgow and Nottingham – by frequent meetings and contact by post and telephone, we have managed to work together to produce a text which is genuinely co-written. We were inspired by the working model of the Marxist-Feminist Literature Collective and by the idea of co-operative writing which is often discussed in theoretical circles. However, this was the first truly collective writing project which any of us had experienced and we would like to draw attention to the cumulative and evolutionary quality of such writing. All of our work went through several draft stages and although writing in academic texts poses itself as springing up fully-formed, we feel that it is necessary to stress the process of the development of this book and this writing. Whilst collective work is more time-consuming and difficult than individualistic writing, it has been a valuable experience for us all, and, for us, is an important part of a feminist practice. Our discussions and criticisms have been enabling rather than competitive, and in this way have differed radically from the conventional reception of texts, where criticisms are marked in the margin: the blind spots of the argument are located. This is not to suggest that we have been uncritical, but that we have developed more useful ways of discussing the work that others have produced, aiming to create some positive contribution which can help to improve the theory. Whilst we would not wish to assert that co-operation is something inherently 'female', we have found it a very useful exercise in developing alternative forms to the conventional and, for us, essentially negative academic notions of research, criticism and publication. Similarly, it is our hope that the readers of these chapters will be encouraged to continue the discussions begun here; either as individuals, between friends, or as part of a larger student group. Literature, like food, is something best enjoyed when shared, and the point of this book has been to show that today's feminist is provided with a very full larder indeed.

NOTES

1. See, for example: Toril Moi, *Sexual/Textual Politics* (Methuen, London, 1985); Maggie Humm, *Feminist Criticism* (Harvester, Brighton 1987); Elaine Marks and Isabelle de Courtivron, *New French Feminisms* (Harvester, Brighton, 1980); Toril Moi (ed.), *French Feminist Thought* (Blackwell, Oxford, 1987); Chris Weedon, *Feminist Practice and Post-structuralist Theory* (Blackwell, Oxford, 1987); Mary Eagleton, *Feminist Literary Theory: A Reader* (Blackwell, Oxford, 1986).
2. Readers unfamiliar with any critical terms or denominations (e.g. 'New Criticism') should refer to the Glossary at the end of the book.
3. Toril Moi, *Sexual/Textual Politics* (Methuen, London 1985).
4. See, for example: Elaine Showalter, *The New Feminist Criticism* (Virago, London, 1986); Moira Monteith (ed.) *Women's Writing: A Challenge to Theory* (Harvester, Brighton, 1986); Sue Roe (ed.), *Women Reading Women's Writing* (Harvester, Brighton, 1987); Gayle Greene and Coppelia Kahn, *Making a Difference* (Methuen, London, 1985).
5. A resumé of more recent feminist criticism is provided by Marilyn Butler in the article, 'Feminist criticism, late 80s style', *Times Literary Supplement*, 11–17 March 1988, pp. 283–5.
6. Douglas Tallack (ed.), *Literary Theory at Work: Three Texts* (Batsford, London, 1986). This book is a collection of readings of three literary texts, using a range of literary-theoretical positions; for example, structuralist, Marxist, feminist. Elaine Millard was one of the contributors to the volume ('Feminism II: reading as a woman', pp. 135–57) and Sara Mills sat in on several of the discussion sessions for the book. We feel this book has served an extremely important function, since many students who feel intimidated by literary theory have felt enabled by an approach which gives concrete examples of reading practices: what literary theory can enable you to *say* about a literary text. Further forthcoming examples of this kind of book are Alan Durant and Nigel Fabb's *Following Theory* (Routledge) and *Theory and Poetry*, edited by Dave Murray (Batsford).
7. Chris Weedon, *Feminist Practice and Post-structuralist Theory* (Blackwell, Oxford, 1987) pp. 1–2.
8. Julia Kristeva, 'Women's time' in Toril Moi (ed.), *The Kristeva Reader* (Blackwell, Oxford, 1986); also see Moi's *Sexual/Textual Politics* for a discussion of these stages (pp. 12–13).
9. Tillie Olsen, *Silences* (Virago, London, 1980).
10. See, for example: Virginia Woolf, *A Room of One's Own* (Granada, London, 1977).
11. Kate Millett, *Sexual Politics* (Virago, London, 1977).
12. Mary Ellmann, *Thinking about Women* (Harcourt, New York, 1968).
13. Arlyn Diamond and Lee R. Edwards (eds), *The Authoirty of Experience: Essays in Feminist Criticism* (University of Massachusetts Press, Amherst, 1977).
14. Josephine Donovan (ed.), *Feminist Literary Criticism: Explorations in Theory* (University of Kentucky Press, Lexington, 1975).
15. Cheri Register, 'American feminist literary criticism: a bibliographical introduction' in Donovan (see note 14), p. 10.

16. Judith Fetterly, *The Resisting Reader: A Feminist Approach to American Fiction* (Indiana University Press, Bloomington, 1978).

17. Elaine Showalter, *A Literature of their Own: British Women Novelists from Brontë to Lessing* (Princeton University Press, Princeton, 1977); Ellen Moers, *Literary Women: The Great Writers* (Doubleday, Garden City, 1977).

18. Dale Spender, *Mothers of the Novel* (Pandora, London 1986). See also Jane Spencer, *The Rise of the Woman Novelist* (Blackwell, Oxford, 1987).

19. Elaine Showalter, 'Feminist criticism in the wilderness' in Elaine Showalter (ed.), *The New Feminist Criticism: Essays on Women, Literature, and Theory* (Virago, London, 1986).

20. Sandra Gilbert and Susan Gubar: *The Madwoman in the Attic: The Woman Writer and the Nineteenth-Century Literary Imagination* (Yale University Press, New Haven, 1979).

21. See Elaine Marks and Isabelle de Courtivron, *New French Feminisms* (Harvester, Brighton, 1980) and Toril Moi *French Feminist Thought* (Blackwell, Oxford, 1987).

22. An explanation of these terms and concepts is provided in Chapter Five; readers should also refer to the Glossary for brief summaries.

23. See Shoshana Felman, 'Women and madness: the critical phallacy', *Diacritics*, vol. 5, no. 4, 1975; Alice Jardine, *Gynesis: Configurations of Woman and Modernity* (Cornell, Ithaca, 1985). Although we have characterised this division as primarily French, Toril Moi has recently shown that there is a substantial amount of work being done in the UK and the USA by what she terms French Americans. See Moi, 'Feminism, postmodernism and style: recent feminist criticism in the US' (to be published in *Cultural Critique*).

24. Barbara Smith, 'Towards a black feminist criticism' (pamphlet) (Out-and-Out, New York, 1980); Barbara Christian, *Black Women Novelists: the Development of a Tradition* (Greenwood, London, 1980).

25. Gayatri Spivak, 'French feminism in an international frame' in *Other Worlds: Essays in Cultural Politics* (Methuen, London, 1987).

26. Lillian Faderman, *Surpassing the Love of Men: Romantic Friendship and Love Between Women from the Renaissance to the Present* (Junction, London, 1977); Bonnie Zimmerman, 'What there has never been: an overview of lesbian feminist criticism' in Gayle Greene and Coppelia Kahn (eds) *Making a Difference* (Methuen, London 1985); Monique Wittig, 'One is not born a woman', in *Feminist Issues*, vol. 1, no. 2, Winter 1981, pp. 41–8.

27. Penny Boumelha, *Thomas Hardy and Women: Sexual Ideology and Narrative Form* (Harvester, Brighton, 1982); Judith Lowder Newton and Deborah Rosenfelt, *Feminist Criticism and Social Change* (Methuen, London, 1985); Cora Kaplan, *Sea Changes* (Verso, London, 1986).

28. For an example of such hybridity, see Cora Kaplan and Alison Light's recent paper 'Framing feminism' at the ICA (London) called 'Feminist criticism in the 1980s'.

29. Toril Moi, *French Feminist Thought* (Blackwell, Oxford, 1987), p. 1.

30. See, for example, the following work on travel writing: Sara Mills, 'Alternative voices to orientalism', *Literature Teaching Politics*, no. 5 (1986), pp. 78–91; and '"Going native": women travel writers', in P.

Kowalewski (ed.), *Twentieth Century Travel Writing* (in press).
31. Deborah Cameron, *Feminism and Linguistic Theory* (Macmillan, London, 1985).

1
Sexual Politics

Lynne Pearce

Kate Millett: *Sexual Politics*
Thomas Hardy: *Tess of the d'Urbervilles*
Emily Brontë: *Wuthering Heights*

I

The 1977 Virago edition of Kate Millett's *Sexual Politics* has emblazoned across its cover the words, 'World Bestseller'. This, indeed, it was, and today, almost two decades after its original publication in 1969, it is sometimes easy for feminists to forget its initial impact: what Toril Moi has described as a 'powerful fist in the solar plexus of patriarchy'.[1] Reviews in the popular press conspired with the sensationalism of its marketing, proclaiming it, 'breathtaking in its command of history and literature' (*New York Times*) and 'One of those rare books that can change your outlook and force you to re-examine the way you live ...' *New Statesman*.[2] With Germaine Greer's *The Female Eunuch* (1971), *Sexual Politics* was the text that re-launched the modern Women's Movement in both its popular and academic manifestations. It was a manifesto for revolution whose challenge to patriarchy is implicit in all subsequent feminist writing.

The reason why *Sexual Politics* was instantly received as a revolutionary text is no mystery: it simply proclaimed itself as such. As recent critics like Toril Moi have observed, it was the polemical nature of Millett's text that distinguished it from other contemporary, more circumspect studies (such as Mary Ellmann's *Thinking About Women*, 1968: see Bibliography) and ensured its popular attention. *Sexual Politics* came waving its own red flag.

Any assessment of *Sexual Politics* consequently needs to account for not only its analysis of patriarchy, which has been severely challenged in recent years, but also the legitimacy of polemic as a critical genre. Most criticism of Millett's work by other feminists, in literary criticism in particular, has been essentially a quarrel with this one problem. Thus, while Moi begins by applauding Millett for the revolutionary impact of polemic on reading practice: 'The most striking aspect of Millett's critical studies ... though, is the boldness with which she "reads against the grain" of the literary text ... Millett's importance as a literary critic lies in her relentless defence of the reader's right to posit her own viewpoint, rejecting the received hierachy of text and reader', she subsequently condemns her for bias, inaccuracy and 'rhetorical reductionism' (pp. 24–5). Cora Kaplan, who concentrates in particular on Millett's selective misreadings of Freud, concludes: 'She looks for, and in most cases finds, a concrete reading, ties it to the text and heaves it over the side'.[3] The practical problems which can, indeed, be shown to result from a polemical approach will become manifest in the course of this reading. Here, however, I feel it necessary to defend the role of polemic both in Millett's text and in future feminist criticism. Polemic is by definition biased and controversial, and as Ann Jones has also recently observed, Millett's text never claims to be anything else: 'Millett's application of sexual political theory to texts was not designed to produce subtler or more complete readings of, for example, D. H. Lawrence. Instead it sought to highlight certain tendencies and assumptions within his work in the first wave of feminist consciousness raising'.[4]

In the remainder of this introductory section, I offer a summary and assessment of *Sexual Politics*. I shall describe the organisation of the book, its central theoretical premises and the main features of Millett's literary analyses. With respect to the latter, I shall pay special attention to her readings of Hardy's *Jude the Obscure* from what she has designated the period of the 'Sexual Revolution', and to her reading of Lawrence from the 'Counter-Revolution'. At all times, my reading will be directed towards revealing hypotheses and techniques that have a practical application in feminist criticism and which will hopefully be demonstrated in my own readings of *Tess* and *Wuthering Heights*.

Millett's text is divided into three main sections: 'Sexual politics', 'Historical background' and 'The literary reflection'. The first of these opens with a sub-section entitled 'Instances of sexual politics', where quotation of some of the most pornographic scenes from the work of Henry Miller and Norman Mailer could also have had something to do with the book's instant popular recognition. By selecting such overtly 'crude' and covertly misogynistic examples, Millett was able to demonstrate the fascist potential of heterosexual relations with little critical elucidation. Framed by a few ironic asides, Millett allows the texts to speak for themselves. This technique has been widely imitated by feminist critics since, especially in the realm of media studies. Numerous books and articles have exposed the sexism and pornography of images simply by reproducing them in a critical context.[5] While such an approach has not been without its problems, its central role in feminist consciousness-raising cannot be denied. Sexual political criticism is based on the principle of *exposing* patriarchal authority, and Millett's window on these bedroom scenes anticipates many famous 'naked apes'. Successful sexual political criticism begins with the art of incriminating quotation.

It is in the second section of the first part of the book that Millett outlines her 'theory of sexual politics'. This has already been summarised by other feminist readers who concentrate, rightly, on two key aspects of her argument: her definition of politics and her conception of patriarchy. The first of these is accounted for by the following oft-quoted sentence: 'The term "politics" shall refer to power-structured relationships, arrangements whereby one group of persons is controlled by another.'[6] Consequently, 'sexual politics' is to do with the potential oppression of one sex by another in the same way that racial politics is to do with the assumed authority of one racial group, or class politics with the ascendency of a particular class. Particularly important is the fact that politics in all these instances is an exercise of power which is not officially inscribed in state legislature. Those who govern have not been elected, and their 'subjects' are entirely without representation: 'For it is precisely because certain groups have no representation in a number of recognised political structures that their position tends to be so stable, their oppression so continuous' (Millett, p. 24). They are political institutions, in other words, which do not officially exist.

Yet although Millett aligns sexual oppression with racial and class oppression, her whole argument depends on the assumption that patriarchy comes first; that it subsumes all other categories of oppression: 'While the same might be said of class, patriarchy has a still more tenacious and powerful hold through its successful habit of passing itself off as nature' (p. 58). It is this view of patriarchy as a transcendent and monolithic force, the *origin* of all capitalist and class oppression, that has proved a central target for Millett's critics. While the exact relationship between patriarchy and the other forms of oppression is still far from being resolved, feminist critics like Kaplan and Moi have attacked Millett's thesis for being too simplistic. Millett does not, in Moi's words, allow that capitalism is itself 'a contradictory construct, marked by gaps, slides and inconsistencies' (p. 26), but conceives of it rather as a 'conscious, well-organised male conspiracy' (p. 28). Patriarchy, as the political institution by which one sex is oppressed by another, is the template for all forms of oppression. In a later section on the polemical manifestation of the sexual revolution, Millett underlines this point by invoking the similar conclusions of Marx and Engels, which she summarises thus:

> Under patriarchy, the concept of property advanced from its simple origins in chattel womanhood, to private ownership of goods, land and capital. In the subjection of female to male, Engels (and Marx as well) saw the historical and conceptual prototype of all subsequent power systems, all invidious economic relations, and the effect of oppression itself. (p. 121)

Yet if Millett's conception of patriarchy can be seen as monolithic (and her simplification of the Marxist analysis is undeniable), her enumeration of the *means* by which that patriarchy is manifested in modern society is not. In the chapter on the theory of sexual politics, she proceeds to examine eight ways in which patriarchy is both realised and sustained, namely: 'ideology', 'biology', 'sociology', 'anthropology', 'psychology', 'economics and education', 'force', and 'class'. These 'notes towards a theory of patriarchy', which draw upon a number of sociological and other texts, provide the reader with useful categories with which to produce a sexual political reading of a text, some of which will be employed in the following reading of *Tess* and *Wuthering Heights*. Most original is Millett's specification of the 'psychological', the omission of which she feels was crucial in earlier theories of patriarchy. To correct this deficiency, she draws parallels with the work done on racial minorities to argue that the ideology of patriarchy 'goes deeper' than economic oppression.[7] Supported by a biological determinism which regards the social dependency of the female as 'natural', patriarchy effects 'ego damage' on the female through subtle psychological pressure:

> When in any group of persons the ego is subjected to such invidious versions of itself through social beliefs, ideology and tradition, the effect is bound to be pernicious. This coupled with the persistent though subtle denigration women encounter daily through personal contacts, the impressions gathered from the images and the media about them, and the discrimination in matters of behaviour, employment, and education which they endure, should make it no special cause for surprise that women develop group characteristics common to those who suffer minority status and a marginal existence. (p. 55)

This notion of female inferiority is held by both sexes in a set of shared, but mostly unspoken, 'beliefs' that women (like Blacks) are intellectually inferior, emotional rather than rational, primitive and childlike, more sensually and sexually oriented. They are also assumed to have a 'contentment with their own lot', 'a wily habit of deceit, and concealment of feeling' (p. 57). These assumptions in turn force the victims into a number of 'accommodational tactics'; because they are thought to be weak, they can win attention only through 'ingratiating or supplicatory behaviour'; because they are thought to be ignorant, they have to appear it. We will see examples of such behaviour in the female characters in *Tess* and *Wuthering Heights*.

The second section of Millett's book records political, polemical and literary participation in the two historical periods Millett has designated 'The Sexual Revolution' (1830–1930) and 'The Counter-Revolution' (1930–1960). For the feminist literary critic, the most interesting aspect of this analysis is its reading of selected literary texts from the period of the Sexual Revolution. In contrast with polemical texts like Mill's *On the Subjection of Women* or Ruskin's 'Of Queen's Gardens' which 'had a definite stand to take for or against the sexual revolution', the literature of the period was 'confused in its response' (p. 29). Millett interprets this ambivalence as being due to the fact that writers were 'afraid, delighted and guilty' of the sexual revolution their works 'reflected', and, because their response was not properly formulated theoretically, they were able to 'explore sexual politics at an inchoate primary level' (p. 129). This recognition of indeterminacy on the part of the authors concerned prepares the way for her readings of Hardy, Meredith and Charlotte Brontë, whom she presents as enlightened, if confused and inconsistent, in their portrayal of relationships between the sexes. Consequently, Hardy's 'nervousness' in his treatment of Sue Bridehead in *Jude the Obscure* is put down to the fact that while he perceived, he did not fully understand, the combination of social and psychological forces at work in the New Woman:

> At the other pole [from Arabella] stands Sue – pure spirit. They [she and Arabella] are the familiar Lily and Rose, but Sue is a lily with a difference – she has a brain. Yet she is repelled by sense, for Sue is not only the New Woman, but a complex set of frequently unsympathetic defences, at times convincing, and at times only a rather labored ambivalence of Hardy's own – she is the Frigid Woman as well. Hardy is disgusted by Arabella, appalled, if intrigued, by her crude and terrible vitality. He champions Sue through a series of uningratiating maneuvers, but he is always slightly nervous of her. (p. 130)

It must be said that the confusion Millett accredits to Hardy here can as easily be seen as the result of her own reading method which, starting from the premise that literature is a 'reflection' of the real world, is unable to decide how much or how little responsibility to give the author. Hardy may well have been ambivalent about his own response to the sexual revolution, but this does not disguise the fact that Millett's own reading position – part intentionalist, part mimetic – is equally unsure. On the one hand, she is eager to praise Hardy for his 'insight' into Sue's character (as though she were an objectified 'real' person); on the other, she criticises some incredible or inconsistent twist in the plot ('This is not to say that the portrait is without flaws. Sue is broken by the arbitrary death of her children; Hardy's murder – their own suicide.' (p. 131)). I will return to these problems in my critique of Millett's theory in Part III. Here, however, I wish to offset these difficulties with a summary of the ways in which Millett's reading does constitute a significant feminist perspective on Hardy's novel. First, and perhaps most importantly, she reveals the way in which the mystery surrounding Sue's sexuality is *related* to her feminist opposition of 'a number of patriarchal institutions, principally marriage and the church' (p. 131). Her tragedy is the direct result of her inability to carry through the courage of her own convictions: she deplores the institutions oppressing her, but is unable to fulfil her sexual life outside them because she still fears them. She desires sexual revolution, but she cannot quite believe in it. As Millett writes:

> The moment her children are dead Sue breaks like a straw ... All her shaky but hard-earned faith in her own intelligence and the critical analysis it had accomplished on the society she had inhabited was assailed by collapses before what she confesses is her 'awe and terror of conventions I don't believe in. It comes over me at times like a creeping paralysis'. (p. 132)

Millett also uses her analysis of the psychological effects of patriarchy to note that both Sue and Isabella exhibit the 'self-hatred and contempt' common to all oppressed groups. This self-hatred is personal, but is also collective; like the majority of women in patriarchal society, they 'despise womanhood'. Indeed, it could be argued that one of the reasons Sue's rebellion failed was that, although it attacked patriarchy, it was not supported by any compensatory love or respect for women. Along with this general lack of self-respect, Millett also shows that Sue suffers from a specific sexual guilt. Her 'terror of conventions' (quoted above) is essentially the belief (product of the biological, anthropological and psychological tenets of patriarchy) that 'sex is female and evil' (p. 131). Her resulting masochism is, as we shall see, of a similar order to Tess's. Millett quotes the line; 'I cannot humiliate myself too much. I should like to prick myself all over with pins and bleed out the badness that's in me' (pp. 132–3).

Millett considers Meredith in a similar vein to her analysis of Hardy. *The Egoist*, like *Jude*, is a shrewd analysis of sexual political relations, but is similarly confused in its conclusion, in this case, marriage: 'This hardly seems satisfactory. It would be a splendid thing if the bitter generality of sexual politics were all to be solved in marrying the right person, and the sexual revolution confined and completed by a honeymoon in Switzerland' (p. 139). And it is for this very reason – that is, the resistance to a happy ending in marriage – that Millett singles out Charlotte Brontë's *Villette* as a true 'expression of revolutionary sensibility' (p. 147). This particular reading is one that has been repeatedly attacked by Millett's critics for its 'creative misreading'. Even what Millett reads as its resistance to conventional closure (i.e. marriage) is, according to Moi, totally unfounded, since: 'Brontë leaves the question of Paul's death unsettlingly open' (p. 30). Whether or not we accept Millett's reading thus returns us to the question of polemical discourse, and what limitations, if any, we seek to impose upon it. As long as we understand that she is not claiming her reading to be the only one, it may be considered liberating. By suggesting that Lucy Snowe actively resists the authority of M. Paul in this final manoeuvre, Millett posits an alternative to popular sentimental readings of the text. I shall engage a similar position in my own reading of *Wuthering Heights*, where the hero status of male characters does not absolve them of patriarchal tyranny.

In the following section of *Sexual Politics*, Millett describes how the incipient challenge of these nineteenth century texts was silenced by the reactionary forces of the Counter-Revolution (1930–1960). Apart from surveying the political events in Europe which supported this change (the aftermath of the revolution in the USSR and ascendency of the Third Reich in Nazi Germany), Millett mounts what Moi describes as a 'savage demolition' (p. 27) of Freud and psychoanalytic theory. This is the section of *Sexual Politics* that has probably been of most lasting influence on the development of feminism in the 1970s and 1980s. As Moi acknowledges: 'Millett's denunciation of psychoanalysis is still widely accepted by feminists both inside and outside of the women's movement' (p. 29). It is also the part of the study that has been most vigorously attacked by feminist psychoanalytic critics in recent years.

It should be remembered that at the time Millett was writing, Freudian theory had effected a major social revolution in the western world. Acknowledging that Freud's influence in the USA was 'almost incalculable', Millett was intent on exposing what she believed to be the pernicious sexual politics behind his theory: 'The effect of Freud's work, that of his followers, and still more, that of his popularizers, was to rationalize the invidious relationship between the sexes; to ratify traditional roles, and to validate temperamental differences' (p. 178). Although criticised by feminists like Kaplan, Mitchell and Rose for misreading Freud's work, Millett does (albeit in passing) pay tribute to his 'major contribution' to the understanding of the unconscious and infant sexuality, and she also acknowledges that 'vulgar Freudianism ...

exceeded the man's original intentions' (p. 178). Indeed, what her analysis does is attack this 'vulgar Freudianism'; what by 1969 had become the popular understanding of penis–envy in particular. In a series of subtle (her critics would say 'deceitful') manoeuvres, Millett represents Freudian theory as both descriptive and prescriptive. His most serious impact, she argues, was the implication that women were not only sexually disadvantaged, but that the only way for them to meet that disadvantage was to accept it, and to sublimate their desires in the alternative desire for children. Millett concludes that Freud had totally failed to recognise the *social* causes for the female's envy of the male:

> Confronted with so much evidence for the male's superior status, sensing on all sides the depreciation in which they are held, girls envy not the penis, but what the penis gives one social pretensions to. Freud appears to have made a major and rather foolish confusion between biology and culture, anatomy and status. (p. 187)

Ultimately, too, Freudian theory had the effect of supporting the easy association of 'masculinity and femininity with the genetic reality of the male and the female' (p. 203), which was particularly important in Millett's own readings of Lawrence, which we will now briefly consider.

In departments of English literature, *Sexual Politics* is known primarily for its readings of Lawrence. This, indeed, is how I first came across it, directed by a tutor who tactfully suggested I balance my own post 'A' Level 'mystical' readings of the texts with something more materialistic. Being placed in this context (i.e. as a 'reference' for students of Lawrence), has caused *Sexual Politics* to be identified primarily with twentieth century Counter-Revolutionary texts; the inference being that a sexual political reading is a strategy to be applied to male writers like Lawrence who were *consciously* promoting patriarchal oppression. Such a narrow interpretation of Millett's project in *Sexual Politics* is, as I hope I have shown, unwarranted. Many of the accusations of negativity levelled against the book would be mitigated if more attention had been paid to her readings of texts from the Revolutionary period cited above. The sensational exposés of Modernist sexism, for which *Sexual Politics* is famous, take place *alongside* enthusiastic, if confused, readings of Hardy, Meredith and Brontë.

Millett's reading of Lawrence, as already noted, is part of the third section of the book which also considers Miller, Mailer and

Jean Genet as part of 'The literary reflection'. Millett describes Lawrence himself as 'the most talented and fervid of sexual politicians' (p. 239). As she ranges through his oeuvre, Millett argues that Lawrence's patriarchal tendencies pass through five distinct phases: devotional, Oedipal, transitional, fraternal and ritualistic. This forms itself into a profile of increasing misogyny and homo-eroticism; a gradual exorcising of women to the point when they are no longer needed. Millett uses this thesis to link together her analysis of a number of key extracts. These episodes are carefully chosen and (to return to the importance of quotation discussed at the beginning of the chapter) expertly framed. Her readings of the sexual power-politics involved in, for example, the episode in *Sons and Lovers* when Paul Morel throws his 'pencil' at Miriam must now be ranked amongst the 'classics' of literary criticism. This particular analysis, like many of the others, is explicitly Freudian in its symbolic interpretation and, indeed, Millett's whole vilification of Lawrence depends, to a large extent, on *her* reading of Lawrence's reading of Freud. Millett is also particularly concerned with the way in which the misogyny of Lawrence's texts is expressed through force (one of her aspects of patriarchy listed earlier). Many of the power confrontations she cites are openly sadistic and brutal; a theme I will return to in my own subsequent reading of *Wuthering Heights*. According to Millett's thesis, this violence towards women moves inexorably through the patriarchal phases listed above until, in the late novels like *The Plumed Serpent*, it culminates in a sexual fascism that converts the earlier 'sacrificial' humiliation of women into their murder. In line with a great deal of contemporary pornography, Millett shows how Lawrence uses the erotic desire of women (for example, Kate, in *The Plumed Serpent*) as an invitation to abuse and, ultimately, murder. I quote here the conclusion to Millett's reading of *The Woman Who Rode Away*:

> All sadistic pornography tends to find its perfection in murder. Lawrence's movie priests themselves seem to understand the purpose of the rites and are 'naked and in a state of barbaric ecstacy', as they await the moment when the sun, phallic itself, strikes like a phallic icicle, and signals the phallic priest to plunge the phallic knife – penetrating the female victim and cutting out her heart – the death fuck. (p. 292)

This passage illustrates not only the way in which Millett's polemical hypotheses are brought to dramatic conclusions, but also many other features of her style. Typical is the unequivocal, provocative opening sentence: a statement which challenges, questions, but at the same time defies questioning. Typical, too, is the recourse to irony and ridicule; Millett undermines the sinister power of the Lawrentian male by describing him as a 'movie priest'. In a similar vein, she acidly parodies Lawrence's own style: his long cumulative sentences; his mystical repetition of the sanctified 'phallic'. Finally, she at once parodies and defies her subject with her own crudity. Millett, as her novels like *Flying* and *Sita* also show, is not afraid to meet male machismo on its own terms. Her text proclaims her 'knowledge' of the sexual practices she writes about and her vocabulary is similarly aggressive: 'street-wise'.

In conclusion, I would like to remind the reader of some of the features of Millett's text outlined here that would be of particular consequence in any sexual-political reading. First, there is her analysis of patriarchy itself, which, in the categories she invents for its articulation ('ideology', 'class', 'force' etc.), provides the reader with a framework with which to approach any text, whether or not overtly patriarchal. Secondly, there are her own distinctive techniques for revealing these features in texts, including a decisive use of incriminating quotation, 'creative misreading' and the unproblematic identification of fictional characters with their authors. Finally, and incorporating all these other features, is her use of polemical rhetoric, which, as in the reading of Lawrence just quoted, produces a style of writing that dazzles and damns without compunction. The limitations of such an approach as an effective feminist reading method I will return to in the final section. I offer next my own sexual political account of *Tess of the d'Urbervilles* and *Wuthering Heights*.

II

Both the texts chosen for this reading, Thomas Hardy's *Tess of the d'Urbervilles* (1891) and Emily Brontë's *Wuthering Heights* (1847), belong historically to the period of Millett's Sexual Revolution. This in itself registers something of an aberration in the expected target-area of Millett's theory since, as was suggested at the end of the previous section, the popular notion of sexual political readings is as a critique of twentieth century male authors. By focussing on these earlier texts (one by a woman), I therefore hope to redress the balance in the common perception of what Millett's text is about and thus emphasise its potential as a positive reading strategy. To this end, I will assess the contribution of both books to a 'deconstruction' (critical undermining) of patriarchy at the same time as elucidating the aspects of male authority and sexism they nevertheless 'reflect'. One of the problems with Millett's theory, to be discussed in Part III, is, of course, the fact that these two positions are not always easily separated. Whether a text is reflecting, condoning or criticising a particular social relation depends, in Millett's terms, on what one considers to be the 'intentions' of the author. The reason she approves of Hardy, Meredith and Brontë is that she identifies in these texts an authorial voice critical of the institutions being described. The reason she disapproves of Lawrence, Miller and Mailer is because she believes their author-narrators to be condoning the sexual politics they participate in. In my own readings, I have therefore combined explication of aspects of the texts which would seem to reflect patriarchy with others (through the working of plot, character, sexual relationships) which challenge it. The problems and difficulties of such major shifts in perception, supported only by an assumption of authorial intent, I will discuss at the end of the chapter.

I have organised my reading relatively simply by considering both texts simultaneously under four headings based on Millett's own analysis of patriarchy described in the previous section. These are images of women, force, class and socio-economic oppression, and the psychological effects of patriarchy.

Images of women

Sexual political criticism can be thought of most simply as an analysis of the images of women perpetrated by patriarchal culture. In this form, it has been the motivation behind all the readings of sexual and sexist representations of women: in the visual arts, in film and advertising, as well as in 'high literature'.[8] While 'images of women' is therefore a concept that could be used to describe the whole of Millett's enterprise, in this section I limit it to an analysis of specifically 'physical' representations of the women concerned.

A great deal has already been written on the physical characterisation of Tess, both by feminist and non-feminist critics. Indeed, in so far as Tess's tragedy is popularly read as the direct result of her appearance, a consideration of her physical attractions is central to any reading. From the start, readers realised only too clearly the connection between her sexual appeal and her fate, and Hardy had not even finished his first version of the text before he was attacked for the potential amorality of these implications. Mary Jacobus in her essay, 'Tess: the making of a pure woman', quotes the following indictment from Mowbray Morris, the editor of *Macmillan's Magazine*:

> Even Angel Clare ... has not yet got beyond a purely sensuous admiration for her person. Tess herself does not appear to have any feelings of this sort about her; but her capacity for stirring up and by implication for gratifying these feelings in others is pressed rather more frequently and elaborately than strikes me as altogether convenient ... You use the word *succulent* more than once to describe the general appearance of the Frome Valley. Might I say that the general impression left on me by reading your story ... is one of rather too much succulence.[9]

What is of most interest in this particular assessment is Morris's perception that Tess's sexuality is defined exclusively by the men who look at and desire her. He notes that she herself 'does not appear to have any feelings of this sort about her'. Often, it is true, Tess is seen specifically through the eyes of one of the male characters. In the scene where Tess is working on the rick at Flintcombe-Ash, for example, we are shown her body – its objectified appeal and its objectified vulnerability – through d'Urberville's appraising eyes:

> Of course you have done nothing but retain your pretty face and shapely figure. I saw it on the rick before you saw me – that tight pinafore-thing sets it off, and that wing-bonnet – you field-girls should never wear those bonnets if you wish to keep out of danger.[10]

What is particularly disturbing about d'Urberville's voyeurism is not only its objectification of Tess's body (note that he refers to her face and figure as 'it'), but the sexual threat it immediately arouses ('you field-girls should never wear those bonnets if you wish to keep out of danger'). Tess's body has been seen and approved from a distance with the eyes of a dealer. She is seen to comply with a certain critical standard, to have 'passed the test', and d'Urberville is prepared to 'put in a bid' (though, as his last sentence warns, such purchases can be made simply by force if necessary). Indeed, the class politics in d'Urberville's statement is (as elsewhere in the text) virtually synonymous with the sexual politics. His reference to 'field-girls' (socially as well as sexually 'inferior') establishes a distance between them which is the distance of power. It is d'Urberville's sex and class, though the first alone would be sufficient, that allows him to make this judgement of Tess. And it is patriarchy's psychological transference of sexual guilt to the woman that enables him to abdicate the responsibility of his sexism by blaming it on her: 'What a grand revenge you have taken! I saw you innocent, and I deceived you. Four years after, you find me a Christian enthusiast; you then work upon me, perhaps to my complete perdition!' (p. 377). In the previous chapter, d'Urberville transfers this blame even more unashamedly by referring to Tess as 'your dear damned witch of Babylon' (p. 370).

Elsewhere in the text, Tess is seen *indirectly* through the eyes of the male characters. In the erotic dawn meeting in the dairy, for example, Tess is described as Angel was seeing her as he held her in his arms:

> Tess's excitable heart beat against his by way of reply; and there they stood upon the red-brick floor of the entry, the sun slanting in by the window upon his back, as he held her tightly to his breast; upon her inclining face, upon the blue veins of her temple, upon her naked arm, and her neck, and into the depths of her hair. Having been lying down in her clothes she was as warmed as a sunned cat. (p. 210)

Once again, however, this intimate appraisal is preceded by a voyeuristic impression. Angel Clare is given his opportunity to enjoy the unsuspecting Tess, just as d'Urberville is:

> She had not heard him enter, and hardly realised his presence there. She was yawning, and he saw the red interior of her mouth as if it had been a snake's. She had stretched one arm so high above her coiled-up cable of hair that he could see its satiny delicacy above the sunburn; her face was flushed with sleep, and her eyelids hung heavy over their pupils. (p. 210)

Common to both these descriptions is the erotic concentration on specific *parts* of Tess's body: the reader is variously directed to her mouth, her arm, her neck, her hair. This is, of course, an aspect of the sexual representation of women that has received a good deal of attention in recent years, particularly in film and media studies where the fetishisation of the particular parts of the female body is obvious.[11] As other commentators have observed, Tess consists of a whole series of memorable anatomical details, some of which appear to have specific sexual-symbolic overtones. The most commonly quoted of these is the description of Tess's mouth (interestingly cross-referenced with the description just quoted) when she accepts the fateful strawberry from d'Urberville ('and in slight distress she parted her lips and took it in', p. 70).

Yet apart from being represented directly or indirectly through the gaze of the male characters, Tess is also 'reflected' in mirrors, through the women characters (in particular her mother), and by the narrator himself. The role of the narrator in this respect (who Millett would assume to be Hardy himself) poses something of a problem, since it will inevitably affect our final verdict as to whether *Tess* is a truly 'revolutionary' text in sexual political terms. Unfortunately, as Penny Boumelha has shown, the narrator of *Tess* would seem to share in the erotic voyeurism of the male characters. Her explanation for this is complex and stands outside a sexual-political reading, but her summary of narratorial involvement would seem persuasive:

> The phallic imagery of pricking, piercing and penetration which has repeatedly been noted, serves not only to create an image-chain linking Tess's experiences from the death of Prince to her final penetrative act of retaliation, but also to satisfy the narrator's fascination with the interiority of her sexuality, and his desire to take possession of her.[12]

The extent of narratorial collusion with the lust of the male characters does indeed make the theory that Hardy was merely 'reflecting' the patriarchal sexism of the age problematic. It is a question to which we will return in our final assessment of the sexual-political perspective of the novel, but it will already be realised that to claim for the text a more critical perspective would require a more sophisticated understanding of the relation between narrator and authorial intention than Millet's reading position allows.

Wuthering Heights, meanwhile, with its complex interchange of narrators, allows for a similar multi-perspective on the visual appearance of the female characters. Here the only overtly sexist (and sexual) descriptions come via the urbane gaze of Lockwood. His description of the second Catherine at the beginning of the novel is stereotyped and sentimental, and instantly rendered ridiculous by its subject, whose hostile rejection of compliments completely undermines his fanciful image of her:

> Her position before was sheltered from the light: now I had a distinct view of her whole figure and countenance. She was slender, and apparently scarcely past girlhood; an admirable form, and the most exquisite little face that I ever had the pleasure of beholding; small features, very fair; flaxen ringlets, or rather golden, hanging loose on her delicate neck; and eyes – had they been agreeable in expression, they would have been irresistible.[13]

Later in the same scene, Lockwood refers to Catherine even more ridiculously as the 'benificent fairy' (p. 55). Such compliment is ridiculous, not only because Catherine is herself indifferent to it, but because life at the Heights, entirely cut off from polite society, is oblivious to such gendered civilities. Indeed, when assessing the claims of *Wuthering Heights* to be a revolutionary text, this foil to the chivalry of ordinary middle class expectation could be accounted one of its major successes. Certainly, the permanent male residents at the Heights – Hindley, Heathcliff and Hareton – are more reticent in their compliments to the females. The only occasion on which Heathcliff considers Cathy's appearance with anything like objectivity is in his childhood description of her, seen through the window of the Grange:

> Afterwards, they dried and combed her beautiful hair, and gave her a pair of enormous slippers, and wheeled her to the fire, and I left her, as merry as she could, dividing her food between the old dog and Skulker, whose nose she pinched as she ate; and kindling a spark of spirit in the vacant blue eyes of the Lintons – a dim reflection from her own enchanting face – I saw they were full of stupid admiration; she is so immeasurably superior to them – to everybody on earth; is she not, Nelly? (p. 92)

There are two occasional references here to conventional standards of beauty – her 'beautiful hair' and 'enchanting face' – but the description is in no way sexually voyeuristic. What stimulates Heathcliff's admiration is not sensuous passivity as we see in the descriptions of Tess, but Cathy's 'kindling spark of spirit'.[14] While a shift from sexual to moral appraisal does not automatically absolve the speaker from sexism, Heathcliff's perception of Cathy would seem to be motivated by an esteem that is essentially asexual.

The same, however, cannot be said of Heathcliff's attitude

towards Isabella, whose sexual attractions he both acknowledges and repels with a misogynistic distaste as violent as anything Millett cites in Lawrence, Miller or Mailer:

> "And I like her too ill to attempt it [that is, take possession of Isabella]", said he, "except in a very ghoulish fashion. You'd hear of odd things, if I lived alone with that mawkish, waxen face; the most ordinary would be painting on its white the colours of the rainbow, and turning the blue eyes black, every day or two; they detestably resemble Linton's." (p. 145)

Heathcliff's sadistic hatred of all women apart from Cathy is inevitably one of the major problems facing anyone wishing to make a positive feminist reading of *Wuthering Heights*. This is, after all, violence against women carried to considerable extremes. As we will argue presently, *Wuthering Heights* exists on one level as a novel about wife-battering. In this description, however, we find a possibility for, if not excusing his behaviour, then at least aligning it to the radical position on gender adopted by the book as a whole. I propose that Heathcliff's hatred is not of the female, but of *femininity*. Throughout the text we find references to his distaste for the Linton characteristic of blue eyes and blonde hair. These genetic traits irritate him not only in the first generation (Edgar and Isabella), but also in his son and the second Catherine. They are represented as being co-terminous, indeed, with weakness and effeminacy; and this, we know, incites the hero to violence:

> It's odd what a savage feeling I have to anything that seems afraid of me. Had I been born where laws are less strict, I should treat myself to a slow vivisection of those two (Catherine and Linton) as an evening's amusement. (p. 301-2)

In terms of a critique of femininity, this may be regarded as either revolutionary or reactionary. On the one hand, it could be read as a simple repetition of the homosexual misogyny Millett found in Lawrence's writing; on the other (suspending the rather questionable degree of violence involved), it could be seen to advance the cause of the sexual revolution by championing the removal of the oppressive 'feminine', and proposing instead ungendered, equalised relationships based on the true sharing of power.

Heathcliff's distaste for gender difference is further evinced in the scene in which Cathy returns from the Grange, newly feminised. As other commentators have noticed, it is this rite of passage – social and sexual – that establishes the first (and fatal) difference between the two. Before this time, their relationship with one another was undefined in these terms, and possibly one way of understanding their subsequent relationship (which is puzzlingly ambiguous in sexual terms – that is, do they or don't they?) is an attempt to recover the asexual, ungendered equality of childhood. Cathy's famous pronouncements such as 'I *am* Heathcliff' (p. 122) and 'That is not *my* Heathcliff. I shall love mine yet; and take him with me – he's in my soul' (p. 196) could be read effectively in this light: love not as the union of male and female, but as a transcendence of sexual difference altogether.

The images contained in *Wuthering Heights* may thus be seen to be less reflective and more critical of patriarchal sexual politics than those found in *Tess*. The fact that neither text offers a consistent, ideological critique of these practices, however, makes their relative 'revolutionary' worth difficult to assess. This was, of course, the problem Millett herself encountered in her readings of Hardy and Brontë, and we will return to them at the end of the chapter.

Force

Several feminist critics have observed that, in *Tess of the d'Urbervilles*, there is very little essential difference between Clare and d'Urberville in their attitude towards Tess, despite their superficial characterisation as 'angel' and 'devil'. As we saw in the previous section, the apprehension of both men is primarily sensual: Clare's desire cannot be described as spiritual, it is simply a little more socially refined. There is no essential difference, either, in the power-politics of each relationship. Tess is always dependent: always subordinate. This power is exercised through all the various agencies of patriarchy that Millett outlines in her theoretical chapter, but the one I wish to focus on first is force.

Tess is full of episodes in which the heroine is seen to be in the physical control of her male suitors. Probably the most famous of these are the occasions on which she is forced to ride with d'Urberville; either on his horse or in his gig. The downhill gallop in which he first delivers Tess to Trantridge is a particularly vivid instance of male power-politics (p. 84). It is interesting to reflect with Penny Boumelha, however, that Clare, like d'Urberville, also drives Tess in traps and seduces her with berries:

> It is not only Alec who is associated with the gigs and traps that, on
> occasion, literally run away with Tess; it is during a journey in a
> wagon driven by Angel that he finally secures Tess's acceptance of his
> proposal ... It is noticeable, too, that during their wagon ride, Angel
> feeds Tess with berries that he has pulled from the trees with a whip,
> recalling the scene at The Slopes when Alec feeds her with
> strawberries. (p. 132)

On two other memorable occasions, Clare claims physical
possession of Tess by carrying her in his arms. The first is on the
walk to church when he carries her across the flooded road (p.
185); the second, on their wedding night, when, sleep-walking,
Clare carries her to the ruined abbey and places her in an empty
stone coffin.

Unlike *Wuthering Heights*, *Tess* contains few examples of this
exercise of force degenerating into physical violence (leaving aside
the rape itself, which is not described). It is continually *threatened*,
however, either by d'Urberville, or through the casual sexual
harrassment Tess suffers on her movement around the country.
D'Urberville's second seduction, moreover, includes a scene in
which this violence/violation is seen to be barely contained.
Mocking her position as a deserted wife, he feels once again in a
position to take advantage of her, and demonstrates this by
roughly seizing her hand:

> In an impulse he turned suddenly to take her hand; the buff glove
> was on it and he seized only the rough leather fingers which did not
> express the life or shape of those within.
>   'You must not – you must not!' she exclaimed fearfully, slipping her
> hand from the glove as from a pocket, and leaving it in his grasp. 'O
> will you go away – for the sake of me and my husband – go, in the
> name of your own Christianity!'
>   'Yes, yes; I will,' he said abruptly, and thrusting the glove back to
> her turned to leave. Facing round, however, he said, 'Tess, as God is
> my judge, I meant no humbug in taking your hand'. (p. 365)

Despite d'Urberville's parting reassurances, Tess's evident terror
betrays the fact that she knew exactly what the gesture had
meant; indeed, what it had been symbolic of.

Such threat of assault is mild, however, compared with what is
actually performed in *Wuthering Heights*. Isabella and the second
Catherine are ruled by Heathcliff through the perpetual threat of
physical violence, and even Nelly suffers her fair share of assault
in the course of duty. The instances of battering are too plentiful
to enumerate, so I will consider one particularly graphic example.

The marriage between Linton and Catherine is undertaken in imprisonment and under pain of death. Physically assisting Nelly through the door, Heathcliff locks his guests inside, and there ensues a bitter and violent fight between himself and the second Catherine. This struggle is significant, not only as an example of the blatant violence against women that Heathcliff perpetrates, but also for the way in which Catherine fights back. Although Heathcliff must inevitably win in physical terms, Catherine is prepared to fight equally physically, and, when that fails, to employ the arts of the oppressed (see discussion of Millett above) to win a reprieve:

> Regardless of this warning, she captured his closed hand and its contents again. 'We *will* go!' she repeated, exerting her utmost efforts to cause the iron muscles to relax; and finding that her nails made no impression, she applied her teeth pretty sharply.
>
> Heathcliff glanced at me a glance that kept me from interfering a moment. Catherine was too intent on his fingers to notice his face. He opened them, suddenly, and resigned the object of dispute; but, ere she had secured it, he seized her with his liberated hand, and, pulling her on his knee, administered with the other, a shower of terrific slaps on both sides of the head, each sufficient to have fulfilled his threat, had she been able to fall.
>
> 'I've given over crying; but I'm going to kneel here, at your knee; and I'll not get up, and I'll not take my eyes from your face, till you look back at me! No, don't turn away! *do* look! You'll see nothing to provoke you. I don't hate you. I'm not angry that you struck me. Have you never loved *anybody*, in all your life, uncle? *never*? Ah! you must look once – I'm so wretched – you can't help being sorry and pitying me.' (p. 307)

Although he reacts violently to this feminine appeal ('I'd rather be hugged by a snake. How the devil came you to dream of fawning on me?' – p. 307), Heathcliff is clearly knocked off guard by this intelligent appeal to his emotions. It is significant, moreover, that in their future relationship, while Heathcliff regains ultimate control over Catherine through the threat of physical violence, she continues to challenge and oppose his authority, both in words, and in her insolent reluctance to do what he tells her to do. We will return to this question of women's power in the novel later. Heathcliff's use of force is most extreme, however, in his treatment of Isabella. I have already quoted his pre-marital determination to paint her face 'the colours of the rainbow', and this he clearly proceeds to do. When Isabella eventually flees the Heights, it is, indeed, as a battered wife.

What, then, is the feminist reader to make of all this undisguised violence against women in the novel? Surely there is no way to claim that this is anything other than a manifestation of patriarchy by force at its most extreme? Indeed there is not; but the problems of authorial intention then re-assert themselves. By aligning Emily Brontë with the 'sane' disapproval of Nelly, we could perhaps make a case for the novel being a critique of such violence. We could also suggest, in line with the example quoted above, that the female characters also oppose this tyranny and exercise their own violence. Ultimately, however, it must be conceded that a sexual political reading, while exposing the utilisation of patriarchal force and violence as one of the key features of both novels, can come to no clear moral judgement about their meaning, since the 'authorial intention' is nowhere clear.

Class and economic oppression

Virtually all existing feminist readings of *Tess* acknowledge the very obvious connection that exists between sexual and economic exploitation. In a reference to the gig episode already discussed in the previous section, Mary Jacobus observes the way in which Tess's lack of physical control over her body is merely a factor of her total socio-economic oppression:

> Alec's gig ... is not simply the equivalent of a sports-car, his badge of machismo, wealth and social status. It is also a symbolic expression of the way in which Tess is to be deprived of control over her own body, whether by Alec himself or by the alien rhythms of the threshing machine at Flintcombe-Ash, in a scene where sexual and economic oppression are as closely identified as they had been in her seduction. (pp. 82–3)

At all points in the narrative we are reminded that Tess's treatment by both Clare and d'Urberville depends not only on the fact that she is a female, but a socially-inferior female.

I have already quoted d'Urberville's denomination of her as a field girl, and his inference there echoes many earlier reproofs, such as the occasion on which he first attempts to kiss her: 'You are mighty sensitive for a cottage girl' (p. 85). Similar assumptions undoubtedly influence Clare's treatment of her. Although he exercises what he considers to be respectful restraint in his behaviour, there is no doubt that their romance is more demonstrably physical than it would have been were Tess his social equal. All the passes he makes are made under the assumption that, as a milkmaid, Tess has literally 'no rights' to be offended. It is unthinkable, for example, that he would have presumed to carry Mercy Chant across a flooded road!

In terms of the plot, too, it is important to remember that the reasons for Tess going to Trantridge were economic. The family desperately needed money and her responsibility for the death of Prince – 'the bread-winner' – forced her to comply with her mother's plan against her own better judgement (see pp. 64–5). From this position of dependency, d'Urberville was able to blackmail Tess with his charity time and time again, and the various symbolic replacements for Prince haunt her through the narrative.

Another interesting mixture of sexual and economic exploitation appears in the person of Farmer Groby, Tess's master at Flintcombe-Ash. Groby knows about her history at Trantridge and recognises her on two subsequent occasions; once with Clare at an inn, and again, after her abandonment, on the road from Emminster. On this second occasion, his familiarity, which begins as mild sexual harrassment, quickly develops into something more malicious when he recognises her:

> She had reached the top of a hill . . . when she heard footsteps behind her back, and in a few moments she was overtaken by a man. He stepped alongside Tess and said –
> 'Good-night, my pretty maid', to which she civilly replied. The light still remaining lit up her face, though the landscape was nearly dark. The man turned and stared hard at her. 'Why, surely it is the young wench who was at Trantridge awhile – young squire d'Urberville's friend? . . . Be honest enough to own it, and that what I said in the town was true, though your fancy-man was so up about it – hey, my sly one? You ought to ask my pardon for that blow of his, considering.' (p. 322)

On this occasion Tess escapes what is clearly another sexual assault by taking to her heels. She is revenged alternatively, however, when she has the misfortune to end up in the employment of the same man. The blackmail he was unable to effect sexually, he now exacts through economic tyranny. Having bullied her for her slow work-rate he declares triumphantly: 'But now I think I've got the better of you' (p. 337). This invidious chain of events illustrates well Millett's formulation of the relationship between patriarchy and class. The two forms of oppression not only mirror, but collude with one another to render Tess, a working-class woman, liable to all manner of oppression, exploitation, abuse and blackmail.

According to Millett's thesis, the economic oppression of women is inscribed in marriage: the institution that antedated all other capitalism by reducing women to chattel status. In support of this analysis, there are several instances in Hardy's novel where Tess is referred to as a chattel quite blatantly. It is, moreover, a representation of herself in which Tess colludes. For while she actively resists becoming d'Urberville's 'creature' (p. 112), she submissively *desires* to be Clare's: 'I am so glad to think – of being yours, and making you happy!' (p. 231). Clare, himself, meanwhile, believes such a state of affairs to be equally natural and proper: 'It is in every way desirable and convenient that I should carry you off as my property' (p. 244). The degree of subjection Tess then seems willing to suffer within marriage, we will return to in the section on the psychological effect of patriarchy. It is worth noting in conclusion, however, that true to Millett's analysis, Tess's economic dependence is never free from her patriarchal oppression. Unmarried, her sexuality is a condition of service; married, she would merely have been expected to add housekeeeping to her prostitution.

Traditionally read as a love story, *Wuthering Heights*'s virtually feudal formulation of the institution of marriage has been generally overlooked. While we reflect upon the psycho-sexual power struggles taking place between the protagonists, it is easy to forget the economic reality of that power. The two households of the Heights and the Grange are best understood as mini-kingdoms, similar to those of the Gondal and Angrian sagas, and all sexual alliances – either marital or adulterous – exist to support, modify or undermine the existing order.[15] Both kingdoms are, moreover, unreservedly patriarchal. The only woman who stands to inherit any property in her own right is the second Catherine, and this Heathcliff quickly robs her of; first by marriage, and then, following his son's death, by the exploitation of her minority status (see p. 325). The first Cathy never had, or stood to have, any property of her own, since the Earnshaw inheritance passed automatically to Hindley. Consequently, like all women living under nineteenth century patriarchal law, her only exercise of economic judgement was through her marriage. This is another factor that has been seriously underrated in her reasons for marrying Edgar. In the conversation with Nelly in which she first reveals her decision to marry, she is quite unashamedly Machiavellian in her motives. She sees the move as expedient, not only for herself, but also for Heathcliff: 'Nelly, I see now, you think me a selfish wretch, but did it never strike you that, if Heathcliff and I married, we should be beggars? whereas, if I marry Linton, I can aid Heathcliff to rise, and place him out of my brother's power?' (p. 122). From the point of view of the plot, it is also worth noting that this explanation takes place *after* Heathcliff has already left the room. Therefore, despite Cathy's confidence that Heathcliff 'comprehends in his person my feeling for Edgar and myself' (p. 122), much of his later jealousy and torment ('*Why* did you despise me? *Why* did you betray your own heart ... ? – p. 197), could be traced to his belief that Cathy chose Edgar not for reasons of economics, but for reasons of *class*. As Nelly notes in her significant aside, Heathcliff left the room when 'he heard Catherine say it would *degrade* her to marry him' [my italics] (p. 121).

The relationship of class politics to gender indeed forms one of the novel's most complex responses to the patriarchal institution. Unlike *Tess*, which simply reflects the traditional prescription that class oppression colludes with patriarchy in the particular exploitation of working-class women, *Wuthering Heights* demonstrates that patriarchy does indeed *exceed* class in the exercise of power. For although the mystery of Heathcliff's birth exiles him to the kitchen during Hindley's tyranny, the fact that he is a man allows him to go out into the world, make his fortune and ultimately establish his own hegemony. Needless to say, a woman would never have been able to *earn* power in this way. Against his patriarchal authority, moreover, the class superiority of first Isabella and then the second Catherine is no defence. Both, in turn, suffer ridicule and humiliation when they attempt to use their status as 'ladies' to win respectful treatment. Just as Heathcliff was previously, so too are they banished to the servant's quarters. The supreme machismo of life at the Heights is well illustrated by Isabella's description of her first night there, on which she 'listened (in vain) to detect a woman's voice in the house' (p. 176). Both she and Catherine after her enter a kingdom in which the male reigns supreme, subsuming all other forms of authority.

In the second generation, the relationship between sex and class becomes more complex. Catherine, raised at the Grange, and with the advantage of education, *appears* to be of a higher social class than Hareton, who speaks and behaves like a servant. However, as Nelly keeps reminding her, they are, in fact, cousins, and their relationship can be seen as a coming to terms with that equality. Catherine has to learn to surrender her sense of class superiority; Hareton, the patriarchal 'birth-right' he uses to counter it: 'I'll see thee damned, before I be *thy* servant!' (p. 320). Thus, in the second generation, the sex and class differences which separated Heathcliff and Cathy are re-negotiated and ultimately trans-cended. One of the last impressions we have of Catherine and Hareton (witnessed by Lockwood), as the former teaches the latter to read, is as the two children Cathy and Heathcliff once were; blissfully forgetful of both class and gender difference. Thus a sexual-political reading, while acknowledging *Wuthering Heights* as a ruthless exposition of patriarchal inheritance, may nevertheless find, in the second generation, a possible critique of the institution that had (in Heathcliff's words), forced Cathy to 'betray (her) own heart'.

The psychological effects of patriarchy

I turn now to a consideration of the psychological internalisation of the effects of patriarchy on the female characters of both texts, contrasting the total self-abnegation of power in *Tess* with the resistance of the two Catherines in *Wuthering Heights*.

For the feminist reader, clearly one of the most distressing features of *Tess* is the heroine's unrelieved humility. Apart from a brief period towards the end of the novel in which she expresses slight bitterness at the injustice of her lot (pp. 404–5), Tess is never anything but a victim. She appears to be motivated only by guilt (activated, in the narrative, by the death of Prince), and all her actions are performed in the spirit of sacrifice, culminating in her last, symbolic 'offering' on the 'altar' at Stonehenge. This extreme passivity can, as Mary Jacobus has shown, be partly explained by Hardy's anxiety about her purity. To absolve her from any responsibility for her downfall, he was forced to render her naive and helpless, sometimes to the point of stupidity. She is denied, as Jacobus observes, 'the right of participation in her own life' (p. 78).

Tess accepts her role as victim from the very beginning of the novel. Indeed, her fatalistic view of life ('we live on a blighted star'), is philosophised even before the death of Prince. Her later outburst, 'Once victim, always victim – that's the law!' (p. 379) is therefore not something she has learnt through experience so much as a confirmation of what she already knew. There is no evidence, moreover, that Tess ever understood her oppression to be sexual and economic. Her unease at going to Trantridge is apparently based on pride (not wishing to beg), rather than any suspicion of the dangers of her own sexuality. Indeed, if we follow Jacobus's argument, it is expressively important that she *is* ignorant in these matters. Her conversation with her mother on her return to Marlott reassures us that she truly knew nothing of the 'danger in men-folk' (p. 117).

Tess's lack of education undoubtedly contributed to her own low opinion of herself and made her collude with the patriarchal assumption that women are of innately lower intelligence. Her relationship with Clare confirms all the popular Ruskinian beliefs that the female mind is intuitive and emotional rather than rational: a thesis brought to a truly sensational conclusion in her subsequent murder of d'Urberville. When Clare offers to teach her history, for example, her reply indicates that she knew intuitively all that there was to be known; that the lives of women like herself were always tragic: 'Because what's the use of learning that I am one of a long row only – finding out in some old book somebody just like me, and to know that I shall only act her part; making me sad, that's all' (p. 165). At the same time, she regards Clare's intellectual knowledge as altogether 'natural' and admirable: 'When I see what you know, what you have read, and seen, and thought, I feel what a nothing I am!' (p. 164).

Because of this almost pathological sense of her own insignificance, Tess's desire (were she not too guilty to admit it) is simply to abandon all her consciousness of herself in becoming Angel's wife. Unfortunately, the debasement she feels as the result of being a 'fallen woman' conflicts with this 'instinctive' feminine humility, making even the dream of skivvying for Clare seem beyond what she can honestly expect. The psychological consequences of this mixture of moral guilt and 'natural' humility are given their most nauseating expression in Tess's supplication to Clare after their marriage. She immediately accepts her rejection as just punishment, and only wishes to do what will be most convenient for him:

> I shan't ask you to let me live with you, Angel, because I have no right to! ... I shan't do anything, unless you order me to; and if you go away from me I shall not follow 'ee; and if you never speak to me any more I shall not ask why, unless you tell me I may ... I will obey you like your wretched slave, even if it is to lie down and die. (p. 272)

In the days that follow the marriage, Tess makes a laudable attempt to honour these vows. Quite beside herself as to how she should best discharge her wifely duty, she alternatively vacillates between the idea of killing herself, running away or getting Clare's dinner. The only thing that prevents her from taking her own life is the fear of the scandal it might cause to *his* name.

Tess's psychological assumption of patriarchal values is nicely corroborated by her male suitors. Various comments reveal that both d'Urberville and Clare considered her to be rather stupid. Reacting to her various suggestions for releasing him from the marriage, Clare exclaims: 'O Tess – you are too, too – childish – unformed – crude, I suppose! I don't know what you are. You don't understand the law – you don't understand' (p. 281). This charge of incomprehension would also appear to be corroborated by the narrator, who groups Tess with the lower animals when he remarks: 'To fling elaborate sarcasms at Tess, however, was much like flinging them at a dog or cat. The charms of their subtlety passed by her unappreciated, and she only received them as inimical sounds which meant that anger ruled' (p. 273). Later in the narrative, Tess receives similar contempt from d'Urberville. Aware of the irony of the situation, he mocks her for her parrot-like repetition of Clare's religious views, which put an end to his own 'conversion'. He remarks, scathingly: 'The fact is ... whatever your dear husband believed you accept, and whatever he rejected you reject, without the least reasoning or inquiry on your part. That's just like you women. Your mind is enslaved to his' (p. 368). And though he appears to accept the 'naturalness' of Tess's inferior intelligence on other occasions (for example, the references to cats and dogs quoted above), the narrator here chooses to share in d'Urberville's contempt by ridiculing her 'simplicity of faith in Angel Clare that the most perfect man would hardly have observed, much less her husband' (p. 368).

This apparent ambiguity in the narrational stance causes serious problems when we come to consider, once again, whether the novel is truly revolutionary in its prognosis, or merely a reflection of incontrovertible 'fact'. Could it be that the author-narrator is really as irritated by Tess's victimisation as we are? Is that why she is allowed the final existential action of murdering d'Urberville? Possibly; but then we are returned to the problem that her acts of retaliation are without consequence or, worse, give rise to even greater punishment. On the only other occasion on which she fights back by hitting d'Urberville with her glove, she awaits instant retribution as her just desert: 'Now, punish me! . . . Whip me, crush me . . . I shall not cry out!' (p. 370). As I will argue in my concluding remarks, Tess's attempts at retaliation merely compound her impotence. Her own diagnosis, 'Once victim, always victim' is never really challenged.

In *Wuthering Heights*, by contrast, a text which demonstrates a patriarchal ideology every bit as strict as that 'reflected' in *Tess*, the female characters do resist their psychological oppression. The fact that, like Tess, they cannot win, would seem to matter less than the fact that they try. The similarity in spirit between the two Catherines in the text is notable. One only has to examine the relationship Nelly has with each of her protegées to understand this: mother and daughter are equally wilful; each determined to get what they want.[16] Both women, too, make the most of their limited education. Cathy's education gives her a temporary advantage over Heathcliff as does Catherine's over Hareton. Both, moreover, are keenly articulate, and it is worth observing that the illusion of Cathy's power in her relationships with Linton and Heathcliff owes largely to her ability to match them verbally. Although without economic independence or physical strength, Cathy shares none of Tess's doubt in her own intellectual ability. Unsupported in other ways, words are her principal weapon. The rhetoric which she summons up on her death-bed reduces even the mighty Heathcliff to tears. Her wishes convert to threats and her threats to curses. Heathcliff, certainly, is aware that her words will live to haunt him: 'Are you possessed with a devil to talk in that manner to me, when you are dying? Do you reflect that all those words will be branded in my memory, and eating deeper eternally, after you have left me?' (p. 196). To condemn her husband and her lover to earthly damnation, therefore, is the realisation of Cathy's power. It will be seen as a pyrrhic victory, nonetheless, since her blackmail can only be properly effected through her death. Other feminist writers such as Sandra Gilbert and Susan Gubar have also commented on Cathy's recourse to illness and suicide as her only realisable means of protest and revolt.[17] In sexual-political terms, it is simply an inevitable factor in a power struggle between the master and the dispossessed. Having realised that she will never be allowed to have her own way and keep Heathcliff as a 'friend', she is quite prepared to give her own life in the cause of revenge: 'If I were only sure it would kill him ... I'd kill myself directly' (p. 159). Suicide, after all, is the only exercise of power left to those who have nothing, and Cathy, like Tess, has power over nothing but her own body. But whereas Tess's suicide is entertained as an acknowledgement of her own worthlessness, Cathy's is undertaken to re-establish superiority. Her decision is as calculated and as expedient as her reason for marrying Edgar. To Nelly she remarks coolly: 'Well, if I cannot keep Heathcliff for my friend – if Edgar will be mean and jealous, I'll try to break their hearts by breaking my own. That will be a prompt way of finishing all, when I am pushed to extremity!' (p. 155). This fundamental difference in the regard of self between Cathy and Tess is one of the main reasons why it would be easier for the feminist to proclaim *Wuthering Heights* a revolutionary text than *Tess*, and in the following section I will attempt some conclusions in line with this.

Revolution or reaction?

At the end of each of the preceding sections, I have tried to assess whether the texts' approach to the various agents of patriarchy would classify them as 'revolutionary' in Millett's terms. Usually, as we have seen, this will depend on our interpretation of the authorial intention: is the writer condoning or critical of the practices he or she describes? Is it implied that an alternative relationship between the sexes would be preferable?

The difficulty for the feminist reader looking for a revolutionary critique of patriarchy in *Tess* rests, as we have seen, with her victimisation. While it is easy to infer criticism of d'Urberville's exploitation or Clare's hypocrisy, we are still left with the sense that Tess's passivity, like her sexuality, is involuntary and 'natural'.

The censure of the book would seem to be aimed not at the patriarchal institution that constituted Tess and her unfortunate sexual appeal as a liability, but simply at the men who would take advantage of it. It is also implied, however, that such restraint is too much to expect. The responsibility is returned to Tess and her over-abundant charms. As Penny Boumelha has observed, Tess's sexuality is simply too provocative, and the implications are that her fate, if tragic, is inescapable:

> Tess ... is trapped by a sexuality that seems at times almost irrelevant to her own experience and her sense of her own identity. She is doomed by her 'exceptional physical nature' (p. 269) and the inevitability of an erotic response from men ... Her sexuality, provocative without intent, seems inherently guilty by virtue of the reactions it arouses in others. (p. 125)

By substituting the sensuous Tess with the more ethereal Liza-Lu at the end of the novel, Hardy seems to have been admitting not only that Tess's own fate was unavoidable, but that the only way to avoid similar tragedies was somehow to rid the world of such unfortunate sexual provocation. The adolescent, asexual Liza-Lu stands as an example of a new kind of woman who will engage men's devotion without arousing their lust. Read in this way, *Tess of the d'Urbervilles* would seem to come closer to the reaction of Ruskin than the revolution of J. S. Mill.

Written by one of the family of 'half-mad sisters' that, according to Millett, had sole claim to a 'revolutionary sensibility' among the women writers of the nineteenth century, *Wuthering Heights* has fair claim to be considered a book of the Sexual Revolution. My own reading here would seem to confirm this, though there is equal scope, as we have seen, to condemn it as one of the most violent and fascist representations of male tyranny ever written. Where the individual reader will finally decide to stand will depend, once again, on what she feels the author's position to be. While this is difficult in a book with so many different narrators (none of whom would appear to represent an objectified authorial viewpoint), there is the opportunity, as we have seen, for reading both character and plot as a powerful critique of patriarchal oppression. While it is true that Heathcliff establishes a patriarchal hegemony, the feminist reader can read his abuse of power as his revenge on the class difference that separated him from Cathy in the first instance. She can equally see his sadistic hatred of 'the feminine' as a desire to subvert traditional gender definition and return to his old, asexual relationship with Cathy. Both these hypotheses, moreover, would seem to have their justification in a second generation where, as we have seen, Hareton and the second Catherine learn to overcome their 'inherited' class and gender prejudice, and to form a new, equalised 'brother and sister' relationship of the kind Cathy and Heathcliff enjoyed as children.

Such a positive reading of a text is not what sexual-political criticism is famous for, and part of my purpose here has been to show how it might be engaged in that way. That quite opposite sexual political readings are possible for both these texts is one of the problems I now turn to in a closing critique on Millett's methodology.

III

Since I introduced most of the principal objections to the text of *Sexual Politics* itself in Part I, here I shall concentrate specifically on those problems raised by my own particular reading, most of which are themselves reducible to two main issues. Can the political position of a text be legitimately determined by the *implied* intentions of the author? Can the sexual politics of these texts be seen to directly mirror those existing in the 'real world'?

Millett's understanding of literary texts starts, as we saw in Part I, from the assumption that they 'reflect' the real world (hence her section title: 'The literary reflection'). 'To reflect' can, of course, mean 'to consider' as well as 'to mirror', but even on this basic point it is unclear what Millett's exact perception of the relationship is. Her confusion is most noticeable in her approach to the texts of the Sexual Revolution since, as we observed, she saw them as being only *partly* conscious of their mission. While she was able to present the texts of the Counter-Revolution as unproblematic 'reflections' (literally, 'mirrors') of male chauvinism, Hardy, Meredith *et al.* uncomfortably exposed the weakness of her hypothesis. The confusion she consequently accredits to Hardy as author (did Sue's behaviour really challenge patriarchy, or did her nervous recapitulation merely condone it?), is clearly her own. She is torn between implying that these novels *unconsciously* reflect patriarchal society and showing that they are *consciously* critical of it. She is unable to decide, in other words, the exact role of the author in relation to the text, and the exact role of the text to patriarchy it is engaged with. This, likewise, is the problem that my own readings of *Tess* and *Wuthering Heights* encountered. While it was relatively easy to describe the various workings of patriarchy in the texts, it was difficult to decide how to interpret them. Like Millett, I found myself faced with the choice of presenting the texts as proto-revolutionary (as conscious critiques of patriarchal oppression) or regarding their 'reflection' of that patriarchy as essentially conservative. And while for each text either position is equally tenable, I was also aware that I was more disposed towards a positive reading of the female text. Although one of the most significant aspects of Millett's theory is that it is not biologically determined in terms of author, I believe that she is likewise disposed in her own comparison of Hardy and Charlotte Brontë. In Millett's readings, the problem of authorial intention is made even more prominent by her transparent identification of author and narrator. Although I manage to avoid such a reduction in my own readings (which would, in the case of *Wuthering Heights*, be extremely difficult in any case), my moral conclusions (as outlined in the final section of Part II) depend on the construction of a particular *author position*, that is always only one step away from Hardy and Brontë. While I therefore side-step the worst excesses of the biographical fallacy by avoiding reference to the authors' own lives, I nevertheless conceive for them a particular position *vis-à-vis* the Sexual Revolution. My information may have come from the texts themselves rather than from anything I have read about Hardy's own erotic susceptibilities or Brontë's incestuous relationship with her brother and sisters, but my interpretations depend on the construction of an 'originating source' nevertheless. My concluding comments will now be directed to how I feel this reading position could be most usefully revised.

By shifting the parameters of my approach just slightly, I feel I could have avoided the intentionalism inherent in Millett's methodology, while retaining all that is useful in sexual political analysis. My suggestion is that the sexual politics of a text can be analysed quite adequately without necessarily calling the author into account. By admitting that it is the reader and not the author who is imposing the structure of analysis on the text, it is possible to make radical claims for it without implying that they are in any way definitive. Thus, my reading of the gender-class position adopted in *Wuthering Heights*, for example, need not be referred to a hypothetical authorial intention, but posited simply as a consciously adopted reader-position in line with much contemporary socialist-feminist criticism (see Chapter Six). Such a shift in theoretical perspective would also avoid all that has been regarded as most controversial in the polemic associated with sexual political criticism, that is, the assumption that the claims being made are definitive and based on only one possible reading of the text. Millett, as I noted in Part I, never claims absolute authority for her readings, but her repeated calls for the primacy of patriarchy, together with the way in which her readings of texts appear to reveal incontrovertible intentions, make it appear that she does.

My allusion to Marxist-feminism above will have revealed one of the ways in which I feel sexual political criticism can be most usefully appropriated by the feminist critic in the 1980s. A good example of such a synthesis is Penny Boumelha's book on Hardy from which I have quoted throughout this chapter. In her introduction, Boumelha also offers a suggestion as to how the relationship between literature and ideology may be modified. Instead of seeing the text as a simple 'reflection' of ideology as Millett does, Boumelha suggests that it: 'Produces, re-produces and transforms elements of ideology into its own literary effects. The "history" of a text is not a reflection or a doubling of real history, but it represents an ideologically constituted experience of real history' (p. 26). By thus shifting the responsibility for a sexual political reading from the author to the reader, and by acknowledging that the text 'produces, re-produces and transforms' ideology rather than merely reflecting it, we can pursue analyses of patriarchy at work in various texts without confronting the difficulties Millett created by regarding author-text-world as similar.

What I hope my readings here will have achieved above all, however, is a re-definition of sexual political criticism as a *positive* feminist reading method. Rather than a simple thesis with which to attack the sexism found in unlimited books, paintings or advertisements, we can use Millett's analysis to engage with all the texts that have *challenged* patriarchal oppression. For it would seem that Millett has been subject to the same selective reading that she herself has been accused of: everyone remembers her attacks on Freud and Lawrence, while forgetting her positive readings of writers from the Sexual Revolution. Despite the criticisms that have deemed *Sexual Politics* to be so monolithic in its conception of patriarchy as to make its oppression seem irreversible, the chapter on the Sexual Revolution does, I feel, offer many suggestions on how this power can be positively re-deployed by feminists.

NOTES

1. Toril Moi, *Sexual/Textual Politics: Feminist Literary Theory* (Methuen, London, 1985), p. 26. All further page references are given after the quotations in the text.
2. Quoted on the cover of the 1977 Virago edition. Reference given below.
3. Cora Kaplan, 'Radical feminism and literature: re-thinking Millett's *Sexual Politics'. Red Letters*, vol. 9. 1979, pp. 4–16.
4. Ann Jones, 'Feminism I: Sexual politics – Henry James, 'In the cage', in Douglas Tallack (ed.), *Literary Theory at Work* (Batsford, London, 1987), p. 85. All further references are given after quotations in the text.
5. See Rosemary Betterton (ed.), *Looking On: Images of Femininity* (Pandora, London, 1987). This is a collection of essays on images of women in the media and in the visual arts.
6. Kate Millett, *Sexual Politics* (Virago, London, 1977), p. 23. All further page references are given after quotations in the text.
7. Millett later indicates that it was failure to recognise this fact that caused the sexual revolution to fail in the Soviet Union. Although the revolution sought to remove patriarchy by redressing the economic dependence of women, it failed to set up a new psychic structure in its members to replace that of patriarchy (p. 173).
   Earlier sociological texts that Millett draws upon which exclude the 'psychological' factor include: William J. Goode, *The Family* (Prentice Hall, New Jersey, 1964) and Bronislaw Malinowski, *Sex, Culture and Myth* (Harcourt, New York, 1962).
8. See *Looking On* (Note 5 above).
9. Mary Jacobus, 'Tess: the making of a pure woman', in Susan Lipshitz (ed.) *Tearing the Veil: Essays on Femininity* (RKP, London, 1978), p. 80. All further page references are given after quotations in the text.
10. Thomas Hardy, *Tess of the d'Urbervilles* (New Wessex edition, Macmillan, London, 1974), p. 377. All further page references are given after quotations in the text.
11. See *Looking On* (Note 5 above).
12. Penny Boumelha, *Thomas Hardy and Women: Sexual Ideology and Narrative Form* (Harvester, Brighton, 1982). All further page references are given after quotations in the text.
13. Emily Brontë, *Wuthering Heights* (Penguin Classics, London, 1965), p. 53. All further page references are given after quotations in the text.

14. Penny Boumelha draws attention to the fact that Tess's sexuality is most exposed and vulnerable when she loses consciousness of herself, through sleep, or otherwise (see p. 121).

15. In 1826, Branwell Brontë was given a box of toy soldiers as a present from his father, and he allowed each of his sisters to choose a soldier for her own. The soldiers were named after popular heroes of the day such as the Duke of Wellington, and the explorer, William Edward Parry, and the children soon involved them in an elaborate saga of group games known collectively as 'The young men's play'. For these characters, the children invented imaginary kingdoms fraught with constant war and romance. The adventures were recorded in the form of poems, letters, magazines and newspapers, all produced on a miniature scale to correspond to the size of the soldiers themselves. The individual kingdoms the characters carved out for themselves were at first united in a confederation known as 'Glasstown', but after Charlotte's removal to school, the games fragmented and a schism occured when Emily and Ann developed their own independent saga based on the kingdom of 'Gondal', and Branwell and Charlotte created the new kingdom of 'Angria'. All these kingdoms were run as feudal monarchies and were essentially patriarchal, although Gondal was ruled for a while by a queen.

16. Compare Cathy's means of getting rid of Nelly when she wishes to entertain Edgar alone (pp. 110–11), and Catherine's wile in getting to see Linton at the Heights.

17. See Sandra Gilbert and Susan Gubar, *The Madwoman in the Attic: The Woman Writer and the Nineteeth-Century Literary Imagination* (Yale University Press, New Haven, 1979).

2
Authentic Realism

Sara Mills

Arlyn Diamond and Lee Edwards (eds): *The Authority of
Experience*
Alice Walker: *The Color Purple*
Emily Brontë: *Wuthering Heights*

I

For many feminists, authentic realism is distinguished as a critical
approach that, through an exchange of experience between author,
text and reader, can promise to 'change your life'. As such, it is less
a fully articulated theoretical position, but rather a reading
strategy, or a model of the relation between text and world. Its
proponents believe that women's writing can be usefully discussed
in terms of how texts relate to women's experience. Within this
perspective, literature is seen as a potential vehicle for change in
women's lives, since it can serve as a catalyst for consciousness-
raising, and a basis for constructing models for other ways of living.

There are several collections of essays which have been written
within this theoretical position: for example, Josephine Donovan's
Feminist Literary Criticism (1975), and the text which will be discussed
here in detail, *The Authority of Experience* (1977) edited by Arlyn
Diamond and Lee Edwards.[1] This collection can be broadly defined
as 'liberal feminist', since it attempts to demand equality of
treatment for women; for example, Maurianne Adams says: ' ...
women feel just as men feel; they need exercise for their faculties
and a field for their efforts as much as their brothers do' (p. 145).
The essays, although diverse in terms of subject matter – ranging
from the depiction of women in Chaucer and Shakespeare to

women in literature about the wilderness – share certain presuppositions which we can term authentic realism. In the following section, I will describe the development of this critical position and then attempt to detail its central tenets.

This critical approach developed at the time of, and in response to, the Consciousness Raising movement of the 1970s, where the statement 'the personal is political' originated. Women began meeting as groups to discuss their experiences, in order to demonstrate that these experiences were not peculiar to them as individuals, but were rather a part of larger scale patriarchal oppression. Listening sympathetically to each other's troubles led to a changing of consciousness, so that other women were seen as potential allies, as sisters, rather than as potential competitors for the attention of men. Women's literature played an important role in awakening them to an awareness of their oppression as women, since while dealing with the individual experiences of characters, literature could also be seen as having a wider reference. Many of the texts which were written at this time and which were read by women were used as part of a consciousness-raising process, and even now they are used for such purposes.[2] This process was designed to help women to use literature as a means of gaining some insight into their own lives, and into seeing the ways in which patriarchy limits women's possibilities. The texts were discussed in terms of how they related to individual women's lives, and how far women identified with the female characters. In the UK now, there are still many such reading groups, often consisting of women who have left education to have children, but who want to discuss and meet with other women within a feminist context.

Authentic realism also developed as a response to a growth in fictional writing by women which was positioned as highly autobiographical.[3] These texts may or may not be autobiographical, but the fact remains that they appear to have been written according to the conventions of such texts, in that, firstly, they are generally written in the first person as if confessing to the events in the character's life, and secondly, they often include events and information which bear striking resemblance to the author's life.[4] Given this type of text which positions itself as autobiographical, a critical position which draws on this link is, in many ways, invited. It is more difficult to discuss the text in the way one would a text which was positioned as a straightforward third person narrated novel, simply because the voice of the narrator/author seems so much at the forefront of the text. These texts address women readers in a different way to the way texts conventionally address the reader,[5] and they may affect our view of the world – the novels change lives.[6] Thus, women critics felt a different critical strategy was called for in the analysis of this type of text.

In the following section, I shall describe the following aspects of an authentic realist reading: firstly, its anti-theoretical nature; secondly, its treatment of the relation between female characters and women's experience; thirdly, its concern with the author; and finally, its emphasis on the pleasure of reading.

Authentic realism is used by many ordinary women when discussing literary texts, employed as if it were mere common sense and self-evidently the proper method for analysing women's texts; however, it is important to see it as a position which is historically situated and which is a *theoretical* position like any other.[7] Since many women, if not the majority of women, consider this a useful way to discuss texts, it must be treated seriously, and not simply discounted as unacademic and theoretically naive.

To a greater or lesser degree many of the critics adopting this position have stated that they are purposefully anti-theoretical, since they feel that theory is elitist and specifically prevents women from participating in debate. Because many women have been prevented through marriage, child-rearing, or through being actively discouraged, from continuing their education, theoretical issues around women's writing often do not address the very audience they are aimed at. Some groups, such as the Dalston study group, suggest that any feminist work should be written in such a way that all women will be able to understand it and put it into practice. Complex theoretical terms should not be used, since this type of language and approach to knowledge is typically patriarchal; in the way in which it excludes women, it has historically been one of the elements in their oppression. They say:

> The language used ... [has] the effect of making large numbers of women feel inadequate, stupid or angry ... the process we identify in education as a process of socialisation which often makes women, blacks, working class people, etc., unconfident and suspicious of intellectual work, and makes them doubt the strength and potential of their own language. It also perpetuates the split between the undervalued day-to-day language of such groups ... and the impoverished depersonalised analytical language of intellectuals.[9]

This anti-theoretical position can best be understood as arising for several reasons.[10] At the time when this position developed, New Criticism and Structuralism were becoming popular in university departments in Great Britain and the United States, and critics adopting these theories tried to look at the text as an object in itself without reference to the author or 'real life' in any form. Many women saw this professionalisation of English studies as yet another attempt to exclude women from jobs and discussion, and also an attempt to undermine the importance of so many texts by women which seemed to refer to the author's life and women's experience in general. To counteract this type of development, many of the feminist essays written at this time therefore attempt to write in a way which is easily accessible to other women who may not have had a university education, without patronising them.

The majority of women use this method when they are reading texts for pleasure, and thus it cannot and should not be dismissed lightly. If women find it useful to discuss texts in this way and they can gain solidarity and insight into their position through using it, then although an anti-theoretical stance should be problematised, it needs to be given credit for being a position which many women are able to put into practice. However, it should be remembered that one of the difficulties with this position is that it is sometimes difficult to encourage women to read in any other way. It is one theoretical position amongst many, and is politically useful in certain contexts, but should not necessarily be seen as a 'universal' reading strategy.[11]

The critics in *The Authority of Experience* collection attempt to write in a non-academic way: they write in the main with little reference to other critics, except to attack the misguidedness or prejudice of male critics when discussing female-authored texts. They use little jargon or technical terms, and write in a very personal, conversational manner. Lee Edwards, for example, instead of writing in a calm, academic way about the text she is discussing, describes the emotions she felt: 'Having reached these conclusions I can, even now, feel an inward churning of those emotions which the novel raised in me when I first read it, and flung the book away with expressions of dismay' (p. 175). In many ways, this is a challenging shift towards a new intimacy between critic and reader, moving away from conventional critical writing, with its careful academic footnoting practices and distinct 'objective', distanced position of the critic. Maurianne Adams states that when she read *Jane Eyre* she was surprised to come to the following conclusion:

> Now that the burden of trying to pretend to a totally objective and value-free perspective has finally been lifted from our shoulders, we can all admit, in the simplest possible terms, that our literary insights and perceptions come in part at least, from our sensitivity to the nuances of our own lives and our observations of other people's lives. Every time we rethink and reassimilate Jane Eyre we bring to it a new orientation. For women critics, this orientation is likely not to focus particular attention upon the dilemmas of the male, to whom male critics have already shown themselves understandably sensitive, but rather to Jane herself and her particular circumstances. (pp. 140–1)

Adams feels that other critics have written from the perspective of being male and simply not admitted that fact; she feels that it is now time for critics to admit how much their position is determined by their personal prejudices, their backgrounds and presumably, their gender. This self-revelation on the part of the critic also serves the purpose of stressing the solidarity which these feminists have with their women readers, and serves to break down the conventional distance and hierarchical relation between critic and reader.

A second element in an authentic realist reading is that it is necessarily concerned with the text's reference to experience. Many of the women who use this type of approach suggest that there *is* such a thing as women's experience which we can refer to: in that all women are oppressed by patriarchy, there are common experiences which women can draw on. There are certain biological functions such as menstruation, the menopause, potential child-bearing and child-rearing, which all women experience. All women suffer discrimination because of patriarchy, and experience oppression at the hands of men: for example, on the simplest level, women fear violence, rape, or sexual harassment by men. This results in women's freedom being curtailed, since we feel unable to walk or travel when we want to. We can all recognise these problems as ones which we share as women. Women's literary texts of the 1960s and 1970s often refer to women's experience, and give as much seriousness to depictions of women's lives as to men's, as much importance to the onset of menstruation, for example, as to the rite of passage of male puberty. It is this which can be discussed to give all women within a group an experience of sisterhood and a sense of belonging. It is this common denominator of events that are termed 'experience' which makes women's consciousness radically different to men's, and which makes certain women's texts demand a different treatment by the critic.

Some of the critics in this collection of essays examine the representation of female characters within male texts, since, as Arlyn Diamond says: 'The parts we play in literature are not unconnected with the parts we are permitted to play in life' (p. 2). They look at these women characters and attempt to redress the balance of negative male criticism of these characters.[12] For example, Marcia Lerenbaum tries to recuperate Moll Flanders and show that she is a truly 'feminine' character, in that she can be seen to undergo many female biological changes, such as child-birth, the menopause and so on. Other critics consider female characters and ask whether they are feminist or not, as Fries does in her essay on Chaucer's Criseyde. This character is described as a 'would-be feminist, and as victim of her ... society' (p. 45). In this way, characters are discussed as if they were real people existing in the time in which the text was produced. As Lerenbaum says, characters are 'created out of everyday fact and human psychology' (p. 102).

There is a sense in which characters are judged according to an ideal of female representation: for example, Katherine Rogers compares Samuel Richardson's representation of women characters to that of Henry Fielding, and she finds that Richardson is more sympathetic to women: 'Genuinely convinced that women's minds were as worthy of development as men's, Richardson praised qualities that most of his contemporaries either could not see or did not value in women' (p. 118). She shows that Richardson is in fact remarkable for his 'conclusion that women are better off unmarried' (p. 128), which she considers a pro-feminist position. In his texts he presents female characters who are 'equal or superior to their male counterparts' (p. 130). In this account Richardson is seen to 'identify with women, to see things from their point of view' (p. 134). Thus, male writers are judged as to whether they are sympathetic to women or not, by the way they portray female characters in their text. A more subtle approach is that of Judith Fetterley who, in considering Ernest

Hemingway's *A Farewell to Arms*, shows how much of a male point of view is presented, and she suggests that this leads to the implied reader of the text being constructed as male. She says, 'All our tears are ultimately for men because in the world of *A Farewell to Arms* male life is what counts' (p. 262); the female characters do not elicit our sympathy as readers because of the way the text is written.

Female characters are considered important in authentic realist criticism, because they are thought to affect the female reader's self-image.[13] Since women read and identify with characters, these characters should, according to authentic realist critics, be strong and resourceful to serve as role-models. Marcia Landy says: ' ... the image of herself in literature she has been asked to appreciate, is that of silence, receptivity, and responsiveness to the needs of the man' (p. 20). Landy draws attention to the image of women as silent and passive which men have constructed, because she feels it needs to be challenged and replaced by another which is closer to reality. Indeed she says: 'we expect affirmation ... in a work of art' (p. 17). By affirmation she means that our feelings about ourselves and others are ratified by representations. This position can be reduced to absurdity, where, as Toril Moi says: 'Instead of strong happy tractor drivers and factory workers [which is the supposed requirement of socialist realism], we are now presumably, to demand strong happy *women* tractor drivers', simply because women readers would like strong representations.[14]

However, there is some truth in the assertion that there was a need at this time for strong representations of females, to counteract the effect of the weak, emotional representations that were common in both male and female writing. Not only are the texts' images important for women's experience in general but for the reader as an individual woman; many of the critics discuss themselves as individuals and, more particularly, the lack of 'fit' between the images they are offered in male texts and the image they have of themselves. Arlyn Diamond, when discussing criticism of Chaucer's *Wife of Bath*, disagrees with many critics who feel that the wife of Bath offers insight into the female character in general. She says: 'My disbelief is based on my inability to recognise myself, or the women I know, or have known in history, in this figure compounded of masculine insecurities and female vices as seen by misogynists' (p. 68).

This is the central tenet of authentic realist criticism. The most extreme version of this type of character criticism is perhaps Cheri Register's article, in which she states that feminist criticism should be prescriptive, that is, it should tell women writers what type of characters women readers would like to have.[15] The reason for this is so that texts are produced which contain depictions of women which are positive, and which have inspiring role-models to follow.

Thus, authentic realist critics share a notion of what women are *really* like, and representations are measured against this, and judged deficient or accurate accordingly. If the representation seems to accord with our notions of what women are like, then the characters and the writing are deemed authentic or true to life. Male writers have portrayed women as stereotypes or as mythical figures in the past, and authentic realist critics demand a change to figures which are closer to the way women are in real life. This position has led to demands for a reform in the way women are portrayed in children's books and in advertisements, so that women, instead of being represented simply as housewives and sex objects, are seen as individuals who can have a range of occupations and modes of being. For some, the notion of authenticity is problematic, but this group of critics has highlighted the way women have been portrayed by men in the past, and the changes which women writers have brought when portraying women characters themselves. Thus, if we were to approach Thomas Hardy's *Tess of the d'Urbervilles* from this perspective, we would discuss the degree to which we thought that the central character Tess and other female characters approximated to our notion of an authentic female experience and to our own experience.[16]

Some authentic realist critics turn from an analysis of male texts to the work of male critics on women's writing, and they attempt to defend such writing from male neglect or attack. Lynn Sukenick makes this point clearly when she says: 'Elements of women's writing which have been unappreciated or denigrated by male critics may appear in a different light once the prejudices of these critics have been named as such' (p. 44). Reaction to such treatment by male critics can result in statements like that of Dale Spender, who believes that women should not respond to each other's work in a negative way, since at this particular historical moment, women should only say positive things about other women's work.[17] The fact that women's writing has been described in negative terms is seen as a result of the negative views of critics about women in general. Thus, the feminist critic's role here is to point out the partiality of the view of male critics. For example, Priscilla Allen devotes her article to a discussion of the negative male criticism of Kate Chopin's *The Awakening*. For her, it is a case of showing how the critics have 'misread' the text because of their gender (p. 225); they have tended to sympathise with the male characters and have therefore been unsympathetic towards the central character Edna. Allen shows that women reading this text read it in quite a different way. She asks: 'Is the novel about *men* coping with Edna, one might ask, or are Edna's problems with them central?' (p. 228). An authentic realist reading shows that in such a woman-centred text, it is a misreading to concentrate on anything other than the problems of the central character, Edna.

Although some of the critics analyse the work of male writers and criticise the work of male theorists, there is a sense in which the central aim of this approach is a turning away from 'images of women' criticism, since merely attacking literary representations seemed to them to be 'barren' and not 'fruitful'.[18] In turning from men's texts, many found that they could not apply the usual critical terminology to women's writing. It was no longer interesting to talk about the structure of the text, the narrative technique and so on. Many women felt and still feel split when talking about women's texts: they use a theoretical position for men's texts, and yet they feel uncomfortable using such a model for women's texts, and some of them turn to a more untheorised model.[19] Taking a gendered position foregrounds some of the problems of male texts, and shows the elements which have been ignored throughout literary criticism. Attention is moved to considering the representation of women characters in women's writing and how authentic the content of such texts appears to readers. Having seen that men writing about women are often unsuccessful in portraying women characters, there is a move to consider the women characters in women's texts. As Mary Cohen says: 'It is vitally important that the protagonists in Lessing's longest and most significant works ... are women, women whose personal lives have been painful and at times even debilitating

(p. 179). The reason it is so vitally important is that, for Cohen, this depiction reflects women's experience in the real world and is thus authentic. Very frequently these characters are discussed as if they were people, and when they are convincing as people, they are seen as authentic.

The reason that these critics discuss the relation between female characters and women's experience is that they believe that literature has a very close relationship to life in a broad political sense. Literary representations have some effect on what people do in the real world; as Arlyn Diamond says, literature embodies: '... a society's most deeply held convictions, sometimes questioning these values, sometimes disguising an artist's ambivalence with regard to these matters, but never disengaged from the claims of time or social order' (p. 1). She goes on to say that a simple shift of attention from male characters to female characters is not enough: 'The critics represented here do not rest with the description of an author's techniques or the stance of a particular work, but instead point constantly to the need to measure literary reality on the one side against historical and personally felt reality on the other' (p. 2). Reality is seen as something which is 'reflected' in literature, and since reality is different for women and for men, the 'reflection' of this in literature must be equally different.

Many of these critics weigh literature against their own experience; for example, Lee Edwards says, when discussing Virginia Woolf's *Mrs Dalloway*: 'Let me note that Virginia Woolf, Clarissa Dalloway, and I share two common characteristics: our sex and, in the broadest sense, our class' (p. 196). She then goes on to discuss what these characteristics have meant for all three – character, author and critic – in terms of the limitations on what they have been able to do. She refers to the three as 'we' throughout this discussion, again breaking down the distinction between text and reality. All three have felt the limitations of their class and gender and all have tried to break free from these restrictions. In another essay in the collection, Dawn Landy also refers to her personal history and her reasons for writing the article:

> I suppose I began to compose this essay on women in the wilderness long ago, when I was a girl living in the desert and dust of Southern Arizona and later in the irrigated central valley at Phoenix, and I

suppose that now I am not in the beginning of consciousness, but somewhere in the middle, and am only elaborating upon an earlier response to the flat landscape and coarse uninhabited mountains. (p. 194)

She goes on to describe her life in this area, and her experience at university, where she studied literature which dealt with the wilderness: 'Repeatedly, however, I could find no place for myself and for my pleasure in the wilderness in the traditionally recorded images of women on the frontier ... I did not see myself in this image and could not believe that it fully communicated the character of the frontier woman' (pp. 195–6). This involvement of the critic and self-revelation is important for criticism, since, in conventional criticism, the critic as a person is notably absent. These interventions by the critic change the nature of criticism from a dry scientific report to something which affects women as individuals.[20]

A third element in an authentic realist reading is a concern with the author and her relation to the text. For many of the critics in this collection, it is important to discuss the author's life, especially when the text is written by a woman. The author is seen to have a close relationship with her characters, and with the content of the text. Often author and character are conflated. Adams relates the content of Charlotte Brontë's texts to the author's life, and shows how the limitations which the characters suffer in Brontë's texts are ones which Brontë herself suffered in real life. She says: 'Some women's lives have always pursued this course [education], likely enough with similar sacrifice, in Brontë's time and earlier; Charlotte Brontë is herself an instance, in her life, if not in her fiction' (p. 157). The distinction between author and character becomes, in many of the essays, almost insignificant.

A final element in authentic realist criticism is that these women critics discuss their pleasure in the texts, something which is notably lacking from male theorising of the time. All of the theorists state what they found most enjoyable or most traumatic in the text, sometimes recounting a particularly exciting episode in the plot. And whilst pleasure is discussed in an untheoretical way, it is important that the pleasure in reading is not pushed into the background when analysing texts, since many of the texts considered in this collection are ones which have been read compulsively and repeatedly by many women. This approach takes reading and the effects of reading seriously in terms of female identification. Some of these texts offer potential models of fantasy for women readers, offering alternative ways of living, and ways of experiencing. Very little work had been undertaken at this time on the notion of pleasure and the reasons for certain texts moving their readers so forcefully.[21]

To sum up, the central features of an authentic realist reading of a literary text consist of relating elements of the text to women's experience in order to make women more aware of their oppression as a group; literature is seen as a powerful vehicle for changing women's self-image. In this type of analysis, female characters are described as successful if they are seen to depict women's lives in an authentic way, and if they seem to reflect the experience of the author. Literature and life are thus seen to be connected in the most intimate of ways.

II

The books which will be used for this analysis are *The Color Purple* by Alice Walker and Emily Brontë's *Wuthering Heights*.[22] Both of these books have been read and re-read by many women. They are obviously important books in the formative years of many women's lives and later. They are books which women have used in discussion groups and which have been of fundamental importance to women individually and also as a group, in terms of constructing a tradition of women's writing. In the course of this analysis, I sent a questionnaire to a range of women, from academic and non-academic backgrounds, to ask them what it was they liked about these books and why they felt the books were important to them; I will draw on their responses in this section.[23]

Both of these texts seem to be written for a female audience and women have claimed them as part of a female tradition. *Wuthering Heights* has been claimed as part of the mainstream canon, and *The Color Purple* has been awarded the Pulitzer Prize and been made into a feature film by Spielberg, and thus they have both a male and female audience; however, they are primarily women's texts, i.e. it is women who read and re-read them. Many women remarked on the importance of *Wuthering Heights* to them in adolescence, and *The Color Purple* seemed important for its overtly feminist content. Many of the women readers remarked on the fact that they felt deeply involved by these texts to the extent that they cried when they read them, even when they had re-read them several times. Some also felt that these were texts which 'changed your life'. Even Anne, who did not like *Wuthering Heights*, 'because I couldn't identify with any of the characters', said that she had still read it several times.

Beginning with *The Color Purple*, I shall therefore offer some suggestions for the popularity of these texts among women readers and relate the experience of my interviewees to the recurrent features of authentic realist criticism, which many of them seem to be using. There are several elements in *The Color Purple* to which an authentic realist reader would respond. The most important of these are the depiction of sexuality, strong female characters, the form and language of the novel, and the relation of the text to the author and to experience, and I will deal with these in turn.

The Color Purple attempts to look at women's sexuality in a different way to that in which it is conventionally seen, since it gives very negative portrayals of heterosexual love, and very positive portrayals of lesbian love, both sexual and non-sexual. In comparison to female sexuality, the depictions of heterosexual love-making are often presented as disgusting. The first event which confronts the reader in the text is the fact that Celie has been sexually abused by her step-father; his sexuality is seen as indiscriminate and violent, and the reader is shocked that a 14-year-old girl is subjected to incest. However, this is not portrayed as an isolated instance of aberrant sexuality, since Sophia also admits that she had to become physically strong as a girl in order to ward off such attacks from male members of her family. Because of her experiences, Celie consequently becomes revolted by male sexuality and admits finally that men's sex organs remind her of frogs (p. 215). She likens sex to going to the toilet and refers to her husband 'doing his business' (p. 68). Again, this is not an isolated response to male sexuality, since Sophia becomes bored by Harpo's mechanical love-making, and he does not notice her lack of response; she says: 'He git up there and enjoy himself just the same. No matter what I'm thinking. No matter what I feel. It just him. Heartfeeling don't even seem to enter into it' (p. 59). Shug attempts to convince Celie that sex with men does not have to be

unfeeling and unpleasurable; however, Celie remains uncon-
vinced, and it is her point of view which dominates the text – it is
with Celie that the reader identifies. It is interesting therefore that
the relationship which Celie has finally with Mr — is more like the
relationship of brother and sister; we assume that it is not a sexual
one.

In stark contrast to this negative portrayal of heterosexual love,
relationships between women are portrayed in a very positive
way. Lillian Faderman shows how lesbianism has been portrayed
in men's literature through the ages, and the misconceptions there
have been about what women actually *do* together.[24] Even in
lesbian novels like *The Well of Loneliness*, by Radclyffe Hall, the
actions of lesbians are confined to vague embraces and yearnings,
and lesbianism is described as 'inversion' – a medical term for a
genetic predisposition which is viewed as an illness.[25] In the past,
there have been frequent depictions of lesbianism as a problem,
and this is one of the few occasions where lesbianism is
celebrated.[26] Here it is seen as a liberating experience which does
not entail guilt; instead, Celia's love-making with Shug is described
as:

> Little like sleeping with mama, only I can't hardly remember ever
> sleeping with her. Little like sleeping with Nettie, only sleeping with
> Nettie never felt this good. It warm and cushiony, and I feel Shug's
> big tits sorta flop over my arms like suds. It feels like heaven is what
> it feels like, not like sleeping with Mr — at all. (p. 98)

It is interesting that lesbianism is described not in terms of how
it is similar to heterosexuality; there is little mention of
penetration, but instead, Shug tells Celie that, 'Lot of sucking go
on, here and there she say. Lot of finger and tongue work' (p. 69).
Lesbianism is also described in terms of the way it is similar to
other forms of female love: Celie's love for her mother and her
sister, as in the above quotation, or as similar to her love for her
children: 'Then I feels something real soft and wet on my breasts,
feel like one of my little lost babies mouth. Way after while, I act
like I a little lost baby too' (p. 97).

It is also one of the few texts where lesbianism is portrayed not
as something which is necessarily biologically determined, but as a
choice women can make as an alternative to oppressive sexual
relations with men. Lesbianism is described in a direct way, and
not in a voyeuristic way as in men's literature. Faderman notes

that much of the portrayal of lesbians in literature has been for a male audience and for male sexual stimulation. This depiction at least shows lesbianism as an alternative to the unfeeling and aggressive sexuality of the males in the text. Shug and Celie make love in a very caring way, and Shug initially makes love to Celie to show her about clitoral stimulation, which Celie had not discovered.

The love between women is not seen as primarily sexual, although that plays an important part in their relationship, but they are seen to love one another and care for one another in the manner of 'romantic friendship' as described by Faderman. The strength of their emotional involvement is of greater importance than their sexual relationship. Shug dedicates a song to Celie and helps her when she needs to set up her own business; she is also aware enough of the problems in male/female relationships not to allow Celie to become her maid. At certain points the sexual side of their relationship becomes less important: 'Us sleep like sisters, me and Shug' (p. 124) and they find enjoyment in hugging and cuddling. The fact that Shug sleeps with Celie's husband is almost irrelevant; Celie does not feel jealousy about this because it does not seem very important. I found this emphasis on female friendship in the face of oppressive male relations very heartening, and among the interviewees, Sandra said: 'Despite being heterosexual I felt I could really relate to it – and felt very moved by it'; Kay also described the love scenes as 'very moving'. It is the emotional side of the relationship between Shug and Celie which is of importance, and their love-making is seen as an expression of this love; their relationship is seen to be of the same order as the relationship Celie has with her sister Nettie. The important permanent sexual and non-sexual relations are those between women; all of the other male-female relationships are seen as temporary. In this respect, I feel *The Color Purple* is a significant realignment of many women's worlds, which are often centred around relations with men.

However, some of the women readers found the depiction of sexuality between women to be slightly problematic. I, like some of the interviewees, felt it was good to have a representation of female sexuality in terms of other women, rather than in terms of penetration by men, and it was also important that the representation is of clitoral rather than vaginal stimulation.

However, Linda said: 'I can't honestly say I liked the bits where Celie "discovers" her sexuality. I found the emphasis on experimentation – all the references to "magic buttons" etc. – rather whimsical and irritating'. The depiction of sexuality in the text is weighed against readers' notions of what they feel female sexuality is like, and found either to be accurate or deficient.[27]

A second element in an authentic realist reading of this book is the fact that this is a woman-centred or 'womanist' text; the focus of interest is not only on one Black woman character but it is on the relations between women characters.[28] The women are not defined in terms of their relationships with men, i.e. as sister, mother, wife of a man. Relationships with men are seen as temporary and almost as incidental. You may have had children by a man, but in this text the important relationship is with the children and not with their father. The central relationships for Celie are those she has with her sister and with Shug; her marriage and her traumatic childhood relationship with her father are not the focus of attention. Further, when Celie learns that her 'father' is in fact her step-father, she is not particularly moved by the news. She is far more concerned, as are the other women in the text, with her relationship with her children and women friends. She loves Nettie so much that she is prepared to offer herself to the man she thinks is her father, rather than have him abuse Nettie. Despite the fact that she does not see or hear from her sister for 20 years, they send letters to each other regardless; and even though Shug leaves her to have an affair with a man, Celie still continues to love her.

Men are mentioned as oppressors, lovers, deceivers and, like Grady, disappear once the relationship is finished; but the real focus of interest is on the women. Few of the women characters are shown in a negative light. The women support each other through trouble and help each other to cope. For example, Mr —'s sister, Kate, gets him to buy Celie clothes and forces Harpo to do more work around the house. Celie makes Harpo call his new girl-friend by her real name Mary Agnes, rather than by a nickname which belittles her. Shug will not consider leaving Celie 'until I know Albert won't even think of beating you' (p. 67). Mary Agnes sleeps with the prison warden so that Sophia is let out of prison. When one of the women needs to leave home or is forced to leave, the other women look after her children.

There is even a shift in the text so that Celie's letters, which were at first written to God, are, in the later section of the book, addressed to Nettie, when Celie realises that God is a part of white patriarchy, which reveals the shift within the text from living within and being oppressed by a male-dominated society, to a position where women make their own choices and discover sisterhood. When the solidarity of women is betrayed, it is presented in a negative light: for example, Celie tells Harpo to hit Sophia to make her obey him, and she becomes ill as a consequence. It is only when she admits this to Sophia and begs her forgiveness that Celie recovers (p. 37).

There are depictions of strong women throughout the text; the women are seen to do all the work: Sophia mends the roof of their house, and Celie chops cotton single-handedly on the farm when her husband is too obsessed with Shug to work. Sophia is described as very physically strong: 'Arms got muscle. Legs too. She swing that baby about like it nothing' (p. 32). Sophia and her sisters are described as Amazons, and they carry her mother's coffin to her funeral. Sophia has to be so aggressive because she was brought up amongst aggressive males, and this was the only way she could survive. Irene commented that: 'Sophia's statement about women in her family needing weight to ward off male members of the family is ... close to many women's experience'. However, her physical strength and aggression is seen to be, at least in part, the cause of her own downfall: strength has to be tempered. Kay said: 'I will *never* forget the woman who is imprisoned for striking out. She stands up to her husband and patriarchal white society and is dealt with accordingly. I could weep everytime I think about that big, strong independent woman being crushed'. Several of the readers mentioned how important Shug was for them; she is portrayed as so powerful as to be almost frightening. Naima said how much she enjoyed seeing: ' ... a woman full of life who lives her passions as *she* likes and not as the conventions suggest she should (these are of course to men's benefit). She is a woman, free, strong, generous *and* full of talent'.

Celie shows another type of strength – not the physical strength which we associate with men, but a strength of will. She is not a strong character at the beginning of the novel, and generally does as she is told by the male characters. Shug scolds her for being so subservient to her husband and finally Celie gains enough self-confidence and power to stand up to Mr —; she faces him with the fact that he has treated her badly, by withholding the letters from her sister. Naima says about Celie: 'She seems to have achieved a certain awareness, a certain consciousness through her own experience, nothing drawn from a theory or indoctrinating of some kind. It made me feel respect for this woman who becomes aware of her identity as a woman through a hard life'. When Celie leaves her husband, she manages to achieve financial independence from men by setting up her own small-scale clothing firm. Irene commented on this: 'Mainly it is the women's capacity to *survive* the subjugation by men that makes the novel enjoyable'.

The reader sees another element of Celie's power in the scene where she confronts her husband with having withheld letters from her sister, since she curses him: 'Until you do right by me, everything you touch will crumble' (p. 176). Her strength is supernatural, since a miraculous dust devil springs up at her words, and the reader is led to believe, because of Shug's rather frightened intervention, that Celie's curse would really have had an effect on Mr —, if it had not been stopped.

In contrast to the strength of the female characters, the men are described in terms which are essentially negative. When they are not straightforwardly evil, they are shown to be weak. Celie's step-father and Mr — are portrayed as cruel, selfish and unfeeling in their treatment of Celie and other women. Shug calls Mr — 'a weak little boy' (p. 43), since he did not have the strength to disobey his father and marry her. Instead he marries Celie as his father wishes, whilst continuing to see Shug. Harpo is described as equally weak: when he wants to make his wife Sophia obey him, he decides to hit her; Celia notes: 'Next time us see Harpo his face is a mess of bruises' (p. 35). On another occasion, Celie sees Harpo and Sophia 'fighting like two mens' (p. 36). Harpo cannot conceive of any relationship with a woman which does not involve the woman obeying her husband completely. Finally, he eats massive amounts of food so that he will be as big as Sophia, and he is surprised to find that this has no effect either. He cries to Celie like a baby. This bears comparison with Shug, since all the men she has affairs with are weak: Grady does not work and she has to keep him, and she pays for Germaine, her young lover, to go to college.

None of the men stand up for the women when they are in

trouble: for example, in church, Mr — does not defend Shug when the preacher calls her a slut. Celie says: 'Somebody got to stand up for Shug, I think. But he don't say nothing' (P. 40). Men treat women as property, as, for example, in the scene where Mr — is given Celie as a wife instead of Nettie; he refers to her as 'that one' and she is made to turn around for him, as if she were livestock. Her father even throws a cow into the bargain to induce him to take Celie, and this seems to be one of the major elements which makes Mr — decide to marry her.

Although these male characters are weak as individuals, the power of patriarchy makes them strong and enables them to behave in a way which disadvantages others. We are presented with a depiction of the power of men to prevent women from fulfilling themselves: Celie is the victim of incest and her children are taken from her by her step-father, her sister leaves her because of her husband's sexual harassment; even Nettie's letters are kept from Celie by her husband.[29]

It is only towards the end of the book that Celie's husband comes to some realisation of how badly he has behaved, and he is then presented as a reasonable character with whom we can imagine Celie continuing to live. For Irene, this reconciliation is important, as she says: 'It presented us with women who suffer because of their relationship with men and yet ends with a friendship being formed between a man and a woman'.

A third element which an authentic realist reader would draw attention to is the form and language which are used, since they lead the reader to feel close to the characters and the events in the text. Linda drew attention to the special intimacy created by the novel's epistolary form. The second person singular is by definition the most intimate form of address, opening itself to the reader as well as to the addressee. Linda observed that letter-writing, along with diaries and other 'confessional' forms, represent the crucial 'sub-genres' of the female literary tradition, and had been central to her own life-experience: 'Letters have played a major – the major? – role in my relationships, and this seems to have been generally true for women throughout history'. Letters *between* women, in particular, have often (as in *The Color Purple*) assumed the nature of, as Linda puts it:' a secret conspiracy against men', and become a 'symbol of faith and promise between women'. This is why Albert's act of concealing Nettie's letters is perceived by women readers as such a despicable betrayal. Linda remarked: 'I shared in the murderous instinct – absolutely! I suppose it's because the episode is symbolic of the absolute power of the male in keeping women apart'.

The letters do not have the structure of a conventional letter or of conventional chapters – they are based around anecdotal events in the life of Celie, and in this way one can imagine the character of Celie writing these letters late at night before going to sleep. The events are not narrated in the conventional way of situating the narrator at a particular point in time describing the events in chronological order: here the narrator is situated at the same point in time as the events – they are described as they happened with the lack of hindsight and foreshadowing which letters or a diary would have. For example, when Celie's baby goes missing, she at first thinks that 'God took it', and it is only in the next chapter that she finds that it is her father who has abducted the baby. Celie has the same knowledge as the reader, and this makes us empathise more with her as a character.

The language in the text is also very important in this type of reading. The fact that Walker has decided to use Black American as the language of Celie's letters also makes the novel seem more authentic. The text is full of conversations rather than the narration of events; for example, in the early parts of the book, in one of her letters to God, she writes: 'Dear God, Harpo want to know what to do to make Sophia mind. He sit out on the porch with Mr —. He say, I tell her one thing, she do another. Never do what I say. Always backtalk' (p. 34). In this way, conversations are reported through the medium of Celie's writing, and even the narrative voice is based on the model of spoken language: the sentences are short, and reflect the way sentences are constructed in conversations, rather than being filtered through a standard narrative voice. Thus, the novel is less like a series of letters, but rather like a series of conversations. The reader is aware of the voices of the characters throughout the text; there seems to be a reflection of the speech patterns of certain people in reporting conversations with the repeated 'I say', and 'he say'. For example: 'I tell her she can't be all the time going to visit her sister. Us married now, I tell her. Your place is here with the children. She say, I'll take the children with me. I say, Your place is with me. She say, You want to come?' (p. 34).

This conversational tone is added to by the fact that Celie writes words as they would be pronounced, for example 'kine' for kind (p. 3), 'git' for get, 'ast' for ask, etc. The fact that she uses certain words such as 'titties', 'thing', 'pussy', which would normally only be used in intimate settings or in jokes, also draws the reader to the figure of Celie; she uses the words of intimacy, because this writing is constantly addressed to an interlocutor – she does not have to use the impersonal terms of written forms.

On the first page there is an added element which makes us feel that this is an authentic depiction of a diary written by an adolescent, since it begins: 'Dear God, I am fourteen years old. I ~~am~~ have always been a good girl' (p. 3). The fact that the 'I am' is crossed out in the text means that we read this to be a depiction of the type of error a young girl would make in writing a diary. The events are described with the limitations that a 14-year-old's consciousness would have; for example, she is unable to articulate her father's assaults on her, and when she is pregnant, she is surprised when the baby appears; 'When I start to hurt and then my stomach start moving and then that little baby come out of my pussy chewing on it fist you could have knock me over with a feather' (p. 4).

A fourth element which authentic realist readers remarked upon is that they felt that the book related to women's experience. Kay said that she wept openly as she read this book: 'I did feel it reflected women's experience, *all* women's experience because it was about suffering, humiliation, degradation *and* joy, love, strength and celebration'. The fact that the novel related to experience also made a strong impression on her: 'For me, Celie's emergence from her terrible life as a strong and intelligent woman inspired me and saddened me at the same time'. For some of the women, the question of race was important, although as Lizzie said: 'Sometimes I was aware that Celie was a black woman, sometimes just that she was a woman'. And Irene said that she felt it 'reflected the experience of lots of women – white as well as black'.

An authentic realist reading is also concerned with the author and her life and the relation to the text; in this case, it is important that *The Color Purple* was written by a woman of colour.[30] On the last page of the book is written: 'I thank everybody in this book for coming, A. W. author and medium.' (p. 245), which leads the reader to assume that Alice Walker feels that she has composed the book in a less structured way than most novelists; she has almost written by allowing voices to be heard. This supposed lack of conscious control makes the text less of an artefact, more of a 'confessional'. The fact that she has included this comment also leads one to assume that the author feels she has a close relation to her text. She also describes, in an article entitled 'Writing *The Color Purple*', the way in which the characters in the story invaded her life: the characters of Shug and Celie would tell her what to do in her life, and would refuse to appear when she wanted to start writing.[31] For example, she writes:

> Just as summer was ending, one or more of my characters – Celie, Shug, Albert, Sofia or Harpo – would come for a visit. We would sit wherever I was sitting, and talk. They were very obliging, engaging, and jolly. They were, of course, at the end of their story but were telling it to me from the beginning. Things that made me sad often made them laugh. Oh, we got through that; don't pull such a long face, they'd say. (p. 455)

Because Alice Walker is herself Black, the depiction of Black American characters has a more authentic feel than if they had been depicted by white writers, male or female. The authentic realist reader assumes that Walker must know more about Black people and therefore she must be qualified to discuss them and portray them. The fact that this text was written by a woman is important; that it was written by a woman of colour is even more so. Much structuralist and post-structuralist work, in particular the work of Roland Barthes and Michel Foucault [32], has attempted to show that the author is of no importance in the discussion of texts; the author is effectively 'dead'. However, many feminists would disagree with this type of theoretical position, since the gender of the author is of vital importance, both in terms of the way the text is received by male critics and the way it is read by female readers. This text, in particular, is read in a different way because it was written by a woman of colour than if it had been written by, for example, a white male. Written by a female, it is an attempt at a redefinition of women's experience, and a celebration of that experience. But written by a man it would be yet another attempt to take over radical positions and neutralise them. There would also be the charge of potential racism and voyeurism, if the book had been written by a white male. Many proponents of authentic realism would also say that only women can write effectively about women's experience, because only they have undergone such experience[33]. Thus, within this type of reading, because Walker is Black, she can write about Black characters in a way which convinces the reader that they are like people in real life.

To sum up, this novel has served as a vehicle of consciousness-raising for many women, white and black; many ordinary women, when reading this book, find that they can relate the experiences of the female characters to their own lives, and enjoy the depiction of strong characters. In reading such texts in this way, they become aware that the problems they face are not simply individual problems, but are ones faced by other women.

Wuthering Heights is a novel which has also been extremely important for women readers. Most women have read it at some time in their lives, and many have re-read the novel several times. In this authentic realist reading of the text, the following elements will be concentrated on: strong female characters, identification with the characters, the depiction of love, and language and form.

Beginning with strong female characters, we find, just as in *The Color Purple*, that they are limited by their male oppressors: Cathy is as wild and adventurous as Heathcliff as a child, and Kay remarks that 'Cathy's wildness was exciting'. Cathy runs across the moor with Heathcliff and stays out with him; as Nelly Dean says: '... from the hour she came downstairs, till the hour she went to bed, we had not a minute's security that she wouldn't be in mischief. Her spirits were always at high-water mark, her tongue always going – singing, laughing and plaguing everybody who would not do the same' (p. 83). She is an extremely wilful child, and after her father's death, she spends her time on the moors with Heathcliff despite the punishment which ensues. However, her freedom is gradually curtailed, especially after an incident where she goes to Thrushcross Grange with Heathcliff to torment the Linton children. On running away, she falls and is bitten by the Lintons' dog. The Lintons look after her, and when she returns from Thrushcross Grange, she has changed:

> ... instead of a wild, hatless little savage jumping into the house, and rushing to squeeze us all breathless, there lighted from a handsome black pony a very dignified person, with brown ringlets falling from the cover of a feathered beaver, and a long cloth habit which she was obliged to hold up with both hands that she might sail in. (p. 93)

This feminisation of Cathy is seen as a limit on her as a person, because: ' . . . while her eyes sparkled joyfully when the dogs came bounding up to welcome her, she dare hardly touch them lest they should fawn upon her splendid garments' (p. 93). It is in this way that Cathy's wildness is tamed, and she is also weaned away from the person she loves most, because Heathcliff is not of the same social class. When Heathcliff reluctantly comes to shake her hand: 'She gazed concernedly at the dusky fingers she held in her own, and also at her dress; which she feared had gained no embellishment from its contact with his' (p. 95). From this moment onwards in the text, the relationship with Heathcliff is discouraged, and Cathy's wildness is subdued, in an attempt to make her a perfect wife for Edgar Linton.

Her daughter Catherine is also strong and wilful; she forces Nelly to let her go out on the moor alone. However, she is tricked by Heathcliff, and lured into his house. Once there, she is forced to marry Linton against her will. Catherine's first reaction to Heathcliff's threat is to consider burning the door down, for she knows that her dying father will be worried by her absence. Gradually, she realises that she must comply with his wishes, and marries Linton, who says to Nelly:

> Papa. . .says I'm not to be soft with Catherine; she's my wife, and it's shameful that she should wish to leave me. He says, she hates me and wants me to die, that she may have my money; but she shan't have it; and she shan't go home! She never shall! – she may cry and be sick as much as she pleases! (p. 311)

In this way, by being forced into a feminine role and by being forced to marry, the strong women characters in the text are tamed by male characters, and this taming is sanctioned by society.

Many of the readers said that they identified with characters within the text; surprisingly some of them identified with Heathcliff – which may be because he feels so strongly. Linda said: 'My identification with the thwarted tormented relationships which comprise the book is simply *as* thwarted tormented relationships!' She also remarked that she felt a 'perverse attraction to Heathcliff's jealousy and Catherine's selfishness' and explained this by saying that it was the result of 'being brought up in a society where absolute love is regarded as single, exclusive, obsessive etc.'. Linda also mentioned that she had read the book as analogous to her own relationship with a woman and saw the obstacles thrown in the path of Cathy and Heathcliff as similar to the obstacles imposed on lesbian relationships; she remarks: 'I wonder if other lesbians have responded to the text in this way, or whether they are unable to transcend the fact that Cathy and Heathcliff are male and female'. She stated that for her the book's enduring fascination lay in its *transcendence* of sexuality: 'the ancient Romantic idea that there is a "higher spiritual soul-communion " (I suspect lots of women are attracted to this book for this reason)'. She also acknowledged, however, that the appeal of such transcendence was clearly a form of wish-fulfilment ('romance' in the popular sense of the word), co-terminous with the limitations placed upon relationships in real life. She admitted to seeing the predestined yet socially impossible relationship between Cathy and Heathcliff as an analogy to her own repressed friendship with another woman, and observed that for this reason *Wuthering Heights* probably had a special meaning for lesbians and other groups (mistresses, partners-in-incest, etc.) whose love would never be sanctioned by the society in which they lived. For Sandra, the gender implications were also problematic: 'I experienced conflicting emotions. I was both attracted to and repelled by Catherine and Heathcliff; they are so impressively yet terrifyingly powerful. Perhaps what I felt most was sympathy for Catherine; her rejection of Edgar's conformity and her attraction to freedom and equality with Heathcliff'.

The third issue which many of the interviewees drew attention to in their appraisal of this book was the fact that love is of such intensity that it survives even death. As in much romance, love is seen to be of central importance both to the female and male characters.[34] Here, it is Heathcliff who suffers from love, arguably far more than Cathy. He is driven to deceitful and violent acts by his love for her, to the point where he is likened to a 'devil'. The love between Cathy and Heathcliff is not like other earthly loves; Heathcliff describes his love for Cathy and compares it to Edgar's love for her:

> ... every thought she spends on Linton, she spends a thousand on me ... I was a fool to fancy for a moment that she valued Edgar Linton's attachment more than mine – If he loved with all the powers of his puny being, he couldn't love as much in eighty years, as I could in a day. And Catherine has a heart as deep as I have; the sea could be as readily contained in that horse-trough, as her whole affection be monopolised by him. (p. 186)

Such is his love for Cathy that on her death he prays that she will
haunt him:

> 'I pray one prayer – I repeat it till my tongue stiffens – Catherine
> Earnshaw, may you not rest as long as I am living! You said I killed
> you – haunt me, then! The murdered *do* haunt their murderers, I
> believe – I know that ghosts *have* wandered on earth. Be with me
> always – take any form – drive me mad! only *do* not leave me in this
> abyss, where I cannot find you! Oh God! it is unutterable! I *cannot* live
> without my life! I *cannot* live without my soul!'
>
> He dashed his head against the knotted trunk; and lifting up his
> eyes, howled, not like a man, but like a savage beast getting goaded to
> death with knives and spears. (p. 204)

Many women remarked on how attractive they found the
prospect of a man loving them with such intensity. They
remarked on how this often contrasted starkly with their own
lives. As Mandy described the book: 'All pash and nothing about
the rent'. And Sandra described the feeling of 'the fantastically
intense and passionate atmosphere of the whole book'. Other
readers also mentioned the appeal of the emotional depth
portrayed in the novel; for example, Lizzie said: 'I loved this book
both times I read it, first as a schoolgirl and then more recently.
Both times what impressed me was the whole range of emotions
expressed and the vividness of the turmoil the characters were
plunged into. This book still haunts me'. Linda suggested a reason
for this: 'Probably what appeals to me (and other women) in a love
that defies present circumstance, survives the grave etc. etc., is
that it gives this transcendent reality to what is impossible on
earth'.

The language and form of the text are also important for the
feeling of authenticity that the reader develops. The text is
written as if told by a variety of characters: Mr Lockwood is
related the tale by Nelly Dean, who on occasion hears gossip from
other characters such as Zillah. In this way the text is, like *The
Color Purple*, a form of reported conversation rather than
straightforward narrative prose. The reader receives information
that is reported through conversations, rather than being
presented with 'facts' and the information is given only in a
piecemeal fashion. The reader is also engaged in the text, since she
soon realises that the main source of information, Nelly Dean, is
not reliable; the reader is involved and has to be astute and to
weigh up Nelly's judgements on events. The sources of

information are all women, who have to attempt to find out what has happened without the men discovering. Nelly passes notes to Cathy from Heathcliff, and is given information by Zillah; all this has to be kept secret from the male figures.

To sum up, an authentic realist reading of this text finds the depiction of love of great importance to women readers; this is the element which gives readers pleasure and makes them re-read the text, and which involves them most in the events of the novel.

III

The central problems of authentic realism have been described in detail by Toril Moi in her discussion of this position.[35] Firstly, there is a problem with any position which supposes that it is untheoretical, since this is in fact a theoretical position, whether one is aware of it or not. Many of the critics writing within an authentic realist framework claim not to be holding a theoretical position at all, but this is obviously an illusion; theory cannot be escaped in this way, and the theoretical origins of authentic realism have been traced convincingly by Toril Moi. However, it must be said that an avoidance of jargon and addressing one's writing to a non-academic female audience has great advantages for feminist discussions, though that in no way rules out *explicit* theoretical positions.

A further serious shortcoming of this approach is one which I have drawn attention to in the first section: the notion of women's experience. Experience is clearly not the same for all women: even our biological similarities are not constructed in the same way by society. Menstruation might be roughly the same physical process for all women, but the way it is constructed and treated within each society and social group differs radically. In a similar way, our expectations and the limitations on our behaviour differ according to social class: no-one can fail to be aware that upper class women have been less restricted than working class women.[36] Any experience that we share as women is a changing heterogeneous concept. Discussions of experience by many of these critics veers dangerously close to prescriptivism: that is, because a novel does not seem to deal with *my* experience, it is not authentic. There is the related problem that the demand for realism, truth to life, clashes with the demand for role models, since the reader cannot ask for a reflection of reality, if at the same time she is asking for something idealised.

In terms of race it is certainly not the case that the way experience is constructed by different racial groups is the same – many women of colour resent the way in which white middle class feminists assume that they share sisterhood simply through the fact of being women. Cora Kaplan in her article on *The Color Purple* has noted this factor and stressed that it is a mistake to read it as a text which refers to women's experience in general; instead it must be read with reference to its historical background and specificity, as a Marxist-feminist reading would.[37] In this case it is the history of Black people and their literature in the United States which must be addressed, and it would be a mistake to read it as referring to women's experience as a whole, or women's sexuality as a whole. In order to discuss *The Color Purple* as relating to women's 'experience', for white women, it is necessary to leave out the whole section on Nettie's travelling to Africa, which is central for its depiction of the roots of Black Americans, and the continued exploitation of Africa by Whites.[38]

A further related problem which Cora Kaplan points to, is that if we refer texts to our experience, we have to ignore the whole question of textuality, of novels as textual entities which refer to other writing and are constructed within the conventions of other books.[39] She shows that *The Color Purple* was written in reaction to novels by Black male writers, such as Eldridge Cleaver and James Baldwin, who portrayed the life of Black American men without reference to Black women. Leaving out the textual history of a novel involves us in omitting a major textual determinant. Thus the text is seen as a simple reflection, and language is seen as a simple transparent medium through which meanings pass. More recent post-structuralist criticism questions this 'transparency' of language, and suggests that the textual determinants, like genre, are more important in the production of the text.[40]

Although this method can be readily used in the discussion of books which are written within the realist tradition, it is rather more difficult to apply it to texts like those of Christine Brooke-Rose, Monique Wittig or Gertrude Stein (although that does not stop critics from trying). Modernist and post-modernist texts cannot be referred to an 'experience' which we all share, since it is textuality rather than 'reality' which is the focus of attention. Even when discussing novels written within the realist tradition, the textual nature of literature is not addressed.

A related problem is the fact that although literature is important for determining how people conceive of themselves as individuals, it is not the only element, and perhaps not even the most important. Books like *Wuthering Heights* and *The Color Purple* are obviously central for many women but they are only elements in a larger social enterprise which is much more powerful; for example, education, parenting and the media define women's roles much more pervasively than literature. Perhaps the problem here is giving literature a centrality which in real life it does not necessarily have. Women critics who work in literature departments often find it difficult to see literature in perspective, as *one* element which provides role models for women. Linda also remarked upon the dangers of this type of criticism if it is taken too seriously, since women readers can begin to identify and perhaps emulate disenabling characters; she noted the 'perils of giving adolescent girls D. H. Lawrence to read' for this reason.

However, despite these shortcomings, the importance of authentic realism lies in the fact that it can be a useful political stage in the changing of women's consciousness and hence women's position in society. Gayatri Spivak has suggested that perhaps this type of reading strategy is a temporary position that might be taken up in certain circumstances,[41] and she notes that in certain circumstances it is necessary to 'take the risk of essence'.[42] The problem with this is that it *is* a risk; Black writing, both male and female, is very frequently read as autobiographical, as is women's writing in general, and re-appropriating positions which have been assigned to you by society runs the risk of reaffirming you in your subjected position.[43] However, if authentic realism can be considered a strategic type of reading, suited to some circumstances, and not to others, it can be used very effectively.

NOTES

1. Arlyn Diamond and Lee R. Edwards (eds) *The Authority of Experience: Essays in Feminist Criticism* (University of Massachusetts Press, Amherst, 1977). Since it is a tendency rather than a position, there

are many feminist positions which draw on the assumptions of authentic realism.

2. Texts such as Marilyn French, *The Women's Room* (Sphere, London, 1977); Erica Jong, *Fear of Flying* (Granada, Frogmore, 1974); Kate Millett, *Sita* (Virago, London, 1977); Doris Lessing, *The Golden Notebook* (Granada, Frogmore, 1962).

3. For example, Doris Lessing, *The Golden Notebook* (Granada, Frogmore, 1962); Dorothy Richardson, *Pilgrimage* (Virago, London, 1915–35); Sylvia Plath, *The Bell Jar* (Faber, London, 1963); Agnes Smedley, *Daughter of Earth* (Virago, London, 1977).

4. A good example of this is Agnes Smedley's *Daughter of Earth* (Virago, London, 1977), which has striking resemblances to her autobiography, *Battle Hymn of China* (Pandora, London, 1974).

5. Given that many texts address us as males; see J. Fetterley, *The Resisting Reader: A Feminist Approach to American Fiction* (Indiana University Press, Bloomington, 1978).

6. See Rosalind Coward, 'This novel changes lives', in Mary Eagleton (ed.) *Feminist Literary Theory: A Reader* (Blackwell, Oxford, 1986), pp. 155–60. By realising, through literature, that an event in their lives was not unique, many women changed their view of their lives and radically re-structured their relationships.

7. By seeing it as a theoretical practice, and tracing the history of its development, we at least partly eliminate the troubling 'naturalness' or 'common sense' which this approach assumes for itself.

8. Criticism of this position will be discussed in the final section of this chapter.

9. Dalston study group, 'Was the patriarchy conference "patriarchal"?', in *Papers on Patriarchy*, cited by Deborah Cameron, *Feminism and Linguistic Theory* (Macmillan, Basingstoke, 1985), p. 135.

10. By the term anti-theoretical I mean not that the approach is un-theoretical but rather that it is working against the idea of theoretical knowledge. See Glossary for terms.

11. It is often taught in schools, and for those who have no further literary training, it is the only way they have to read.

12. Other critics who do this are discussed in Chapter Four.

13. In this, it is very similar to the work of John Berger, *Ways of Seeing* (Penguin, Harmondsworth, 1972); and Judith Williamson in her work on reader positioning, *Decoding Advertisements: Ideology and Meaning in Advertising* (Boyars, London, 1978). See also, for a full discussion of the relation between representations and self-image, Rosemary Betterton, *Looking On: Images of Femininity in the Arts and Media* (Pandora, London, 1987).

14. Toril Moi, *Sexual/Textual Politics* (Methuen, London, 1985).

15. See Cheri Register, 'American literary criticism: a bibliographical introduction', in Josephine Donovan (ed.) *Feminist Literary Criticism, Explorations in Theory* (University of Kentucky, Lexington, 1975), pp. 1–28.

16. In all of these examples, we have in our teaching, in various educational contexts, found that this type of reading strategy evokes very strong reactions from students. In reading *Tess of the d'Urbervilles*, female students refer to similar emotional crises they have

undergone or to the emotions they experience when 'identifying' with Tess.

17. Dale Spender, *Women of Ideas and What Men Have Done to Them* (Ark, London, 1982). Toril Moi, in *Sexual/Textual Politics*, has shown, however, that this is an extremely dangerous stance, since it can lead to women producing second-rate work, and being praised for it patronisingly. Constructive criticism is the only way for feminist criticism to progress.

18. 'Images of women' criticism analyses the negative portrayals of female characters in male texts, and demands changes. See Chapter One.

19. This may be because 'theoretical' implies 'critical', but it may also be that women readers feel that these texts address them in a different way to male-authored texts. It is difficult to analyse them using theoretical models which pay no attention to gender difference, or the way the reader is positioned as male or female.

20. Other feminist critics such as Toril Moi and Deborah Cameron also give elements of personal history so that the reader is aware of the political position within which the writing is produced.

21. See for example Roland Barthes, 'The pleasure of the text', in S. Sontag (ed.) *Barthes: Selected Writings* (Fontana, London, 1982), pp. 404–14. This is, however, considered by many feminist film theorists: see for example, Annette Kuhn's *Women's Pictures* (Routledge and Kegan Paul, London, 1982), and Laura Mulvey, 'Visual pleasure and narrative cinema', *Screen*, 1975, vol. 16, no. 3, pp. 6–18.

22. Alice Walker, *The Color Purple* (Women's Press, London, 1983); Emily Brontë, *Wuthering Heights* (Penguin, Harmondsworth, 1982).

23. I would like to thank all of the women who replied to the questionnaire, especially the following whose comments I have used in this chapter: Anne, Mandy, Linda, Naima, Kay, Irene, Lizzie, Sandra. The interviewees were chosen to display a range across race, class, and sexual preference.

24. Lillian Faderman, *Surpassing the Love of Men; Romantic Friendship and Love Between Women from the Renaissance to the Present* (Morrow, New York, 1981). Authentic realism is drawn upon by many lesbian critics; see, for a discussion of this, B. Zimmerman, 'What has never been: an overview of lesbian feminist criticism', in Gayle Greene and Coppelia Kahn (eds) *Making a Difference* (Methuen, London, 1986).

25. Radclyffe Hall, *The Well of Loneliness* (Virago, London, 1982).

26. Even in contemporary texts, there are still examples of lesbianism being depicted as a painful and unhappy experience. Notable exceptions, however, are Ellen Galford's *Moll Cutpurse* (Stramullion, Edinburgh, 1985) and *The Fires of Bride* (The Women's Press, London, 1986) and also Barbara Burford's *The Threshing Floor* (Sheba, London, 1985).

27. It is interesting that lesbian sexuality was one of the elements which was significantly played down in the Spielberg film and reduced to coy embraces; see Darryl Pinkney, 'Black victims: Black villains', *New York Review*, 29 January 1987, pp. 17–20, for a discussion of the relation between the film and the book.

28. Alice Walker developed the term 'womanist' to refer to a Black feminist writing practice and criticism which did not have the racism implicit in the term feminist (see Glossary).

29. This 'man-hating' nature of the book is often remarked upon by critics; see Pinkney, *op. cit.*

30. I use both the term 'woman of colour' and 'Black'; some women prefer to use the former since it refers to women from a wide range of racial origin; however, since Alice Walker identifies herself as 'Black', this term has also been used.

31. 'Writing *The Color Purple*', in Mari Evans (ed.) *Black Women Writers* (Pluto, London, 1985), pp. 453–7.

32. Michel Foucault, 'What is an author', in J. V. Harari (eds.) *Textual Strategies: Perspectives in Post-structuralist Criticism* (Methuen, London, 1980); Roland Barthes, 'Death of the author', in *The Rustle of Language* (Blackwell, Oxford, 1986), pp. 49–55.

33. This can clearly be seen from the recent Virago controversy when it was discovered that a book which was supposedly written by an Indian woman, was in fact written by a white male.

34. In writings by men, love is often seen to be the preserve of women. Many feminist critics see this as one of the important aspects of pleasure in the romance. See, for example, Rosalind Coward, *Female Desire: Women's Sexuality Today* (Paladin, London, 1984).

35. Toril Moi, *Sexual/Textual Politics* (Methuen, London, 1985).

36. See Janet Radcliffe-Richards, *The Sceptical Feminist: A Philosophical Enquiry* (Routledge and Kegan Paul, London, 1980), for a discussion of this problem.

37. Cora Kaplan, 'Keeping the color in *The Color Purple*', in *Sea Changes* (Verso, London, 1986), pp. 177–187.

38. Most of the interviewees in fact did this.

39. In Chapter 4, Elaine Millard writes about *The Color Purple* specifically as a text in relation to other texts.

40. See for example the work of Michel Foucault in *The Order of Things: An Archaeology of the Human Sciences* (Vintage/Random, New York, 1973).

41. Gayatri Spivak, 'Imperialism and sexual difference', in *Sexual Difference Conference Proceedings* (Oxford Literary Review, Southampton, 1986), pp. 225–240.

42. Gayatri Spivak, *In Other Worlds: Essays in Cultural Politics* (Methuen, London, 1987).

43. I am indebted to Zoe Wicomb for making this point to me; this is the subject of her forthcoming article about Black women's writing. Peggy Kamuf also makes this clear in her article, 'Writing Like a woman', in Sally McConnell-Ginet (ed.). *Women and Language in Literature and Society* (Praeger, New York 1982), pp. 284–97.

3
Gynocriticism

Sue Spaull

Elaine Showalter: 'Feminist criticism in the
wilderness'
Jean Rhys: *Wide Sargasso Sea*
Margaret Atwood: *Surfacing*

I

In 1986, Dale Spender offered the following evaluation of her
university education: 'A grossly inaccurate and distorted view of
the history of letters'.[1] No doubt many women would now accept
her statement as a just description of their own education, for her
book *Mothers of the Novel* is a recent addition to a fairly well-
established mode of feminist criticism. Spender identifies 100
women novelists before Jane Austen and yet, she says, her
introduction to the 'greats' was an introduction to great men. 'I
left university with the well-cultivated impression that men had
created the novel and that there were no women novelists (or
none of note) before Jane Austen' (p. 115). With so many women
writing during the 1700s, and achieving recognition amongst
contemporary audiences, Spender questions the disappearance of
all but a few of these women since the eighteenth century. She
concludes that 'in order to be great, one must be a man' (p. 119).

In an attempt to redress the balance, Spender devotes her book
to the examination of those, now 'obscure' eighteenth century
women novelists. She claims that it was women who 'mothered'
the novel and, moreover, that their novels act as a 'record of
women's consciousness, a documentation of women's experiences

as subordinates in a male-dominated society'. She asks: ' ... what have the men done with all the women, and why?' (p. 3).

Spender is clearly not the first to address herself entirely to a *female* literary tradition, nor is she the first to question the validity of the canon of 'great' literature. My aim in this chapter is, first, to trace the move to establish such a female literary tradition. In doing so, I shall focus on those critics working in the 1970s who, noting the absence of a female perspective within the literary canon, sought to focus on women's writing and women's lives. Specifically, I shall be examining critics whose aim was not only to read women's literature for its portrayal of women's experience (as in 'authentic realist' criticism – see Chapter Two) but who sought to identify an authentic female voice in women's writing: a style and genre which were distinctly female. I shall draw on the work of Ellen Moers, Patricia Meyer Spacks and Nina Baym[2] but concentrate on the work of Elaine Showalter, who coined the phrase 'gynocritics' to describe what is commonly known as 'woman-centred' criticism.[3] I hope that my explication of the work of these women will then serve as a useful background for my own readings of *Wide Sargasso Sea* and *Surfacing*, which I shall carry out using Showalter's gynocritical model.

Elaine Showalter describes gynocritics as 'the psychodynamics of the individual or collective female literary tradition' (p. 201). She assesses the task confronting feminist critics as identifying 'the unique difference of women's writing' (p. 186). And, indeed, this is how many feminist critics have structured their readings of women's writing. Their aim is to seek out a feminine aesthetic, or 'essence', which differentiates women's writing from men's. That feminine aesthetic is often identified with language: a language specific to women's writing, whose 'difference' is guaranteed by the 'femaleness' of the author. The critics further focus on other aspects of literature: its genre or form, its style or themes, character portrayal or subject matter and so on. At each stage, they return to their original premise: that the language and textual strategies of women's writing are a result of the author's experience of everyday life. Thus, their analyses of the qualitative 'difference' of women's writing are carried out with regard to the female author's biological, psychologial and historical differences from men. But most importantly, that 'difference' is shown as a result of women's social and economic position within patriarchal society: a society so repressive that at times (as Dale Spender argues) it has barely allowed women a voice at all.[4]

Examining women writing in the USA between 1820 and 1870, Nina Baym describes the fiction of the period as 'profoundly oriented toward women' (p. 11). She argues that women were writing specifically for female audiences using a genre rarely used by men. Concentrating on plot as the common factor amongst the novels – 'The many novels all tell, with variations, a single tale' – Baym compares the various female protagonists' journeys towards self-fulfilment with Jungian rites of passage (p. 11).[5] She argues that '... the failure of the world to satisfy either reasonable or unreasonable expectations awakens the heroine to inner possibilities' (p. 19). Read in their context – as a response to nineteenth century society – the novels express women's capacity for personal change and endeavour. They represent 'a moderate, or limited, or pragmatic feminism' (p. 18). Baym sees the form and content of these novels as a direct expression of their authors' positions within nineteenth century American society. She reads them as a reflection of women's repression under patriarchy, but also as a subtle and limited resistance to that patriarchy.

Similarly, most of the critics writing within gynocriticism offer an analysis of women's writing both as a response and as a challenge to patriarchy. Ellen Moers argues categorically that '[There] is no such thing as *the* female genius or *the* female sensibility'.[6] And further: 'there is no single female style in literature'. Yet in her readings of women writers from the eighteenth century onwards, she too identifies common factors in their work, examining those factors in relation to women writers' experience, their social setting and audiences, and importantly, their mutual influence upon one another. And she too sees much women's literature as a challenge to the male tradition and to the silencing of women effected by patriarchy:

> Each of these gifted writers had her distinctive style; none imitated the others. But their sense of encountering in another woman's voice what they believed was the sound of their own is, I think, something special in literary women – perhaps their sense of the surrounding silence, or the deaf ears, with which women spoke before there was such an echo as women's literature. (p. 66)

Moers sets out to establish 'the echo of women's literature', the female literary tradition which men have destroyed; to retrace the connections between women writers which were often so difficult for them to forge during their own lifetimes. She identifies common themes in the wealth of literature she examines, and frequently the common handling of those themes. Whilst throughout her book she relates her findings back to women's experience itself, she moves beyond 'authentic realist' criticism to assess *why* women's perspective differs from that of their male contemporaries; to pinpoint those aspects of women's experience which generate the style and content of their writing; and to examine the means by which women offer some resistance to patriarchy through their writing.

Just as Nina Baym noticed the different portrayal of female characters by men and women writers respectively – '[men's] good women were far more passive than the female protagonists created by women themselves' (p. 13) – so Moers focusses on their different handling of similar subject matter. Moers is particularly interested in the strategies women have used to resist patriarchy. For example, she assesses women's handling of the subject of adultery (traditionally fertile ground for men's writing), describing it as 'part of a feminist outburst against the institution of marriage as created not in heaven but on earth by unjust, man-made laws' (p. 154). And she continues: 'The adultery novel after Rousseau became the woman writer's vehicle of attack on the economic and social-class realities that make a mockery of love; as well as a vehicle of demonstration that woman has a capacity to think, feel and act for herself'.

Throughout *Literary Women*, Moers finds similar evidence of women's expression of their frustration at the constraints society has placed on them. Examining women's language, she focusses on their use of metaphors as one technique by which they encapsulate both their powerlessness and their resistance to patriarchy. Moers notices the frequency with which women use metaphors involving birds – greatly adaptable due to the species' many forms. Examining their use in *Jane Eyre*, she asks: 'Is the bird merely a species of the littleness metaphor? Or are birds chosen because they are tortured, as little girls are tortured. ... Or because bird-victims can be ministered by girl-victims' (p. 245). Continuing her analysis, Moers suggests that '[The] more feminist the literary conception ... the larger, wilder and crueller come the birds' (p. 246). She illustrates the point with an extract from Willa

Cather's novel *The Song Of The Lark* (1915), where after the female protagonist has been made an unwanted offer of 'cosy' marriage by her lover, a golden eagle appears overhead. Cather writes: 'O eagle of eagles! Endeavour achievement, desire, glorious striving of human art! From a cleft in the heart of the world she saluted it . . .'[7] Moers also observes the absence from women's writing of a bird metaphor frequently used by men – that of the nesting bird traditionally associated with motherhood. She notes that it 'seems striking by its absence from women's literature, or by the bitterness with which it is used to imply rejection of the maternal role' (p. 247).

Moers' analysis of the 'monstrous' also informs her discussion of the 'Female Gothic' – a phrase which she coined and which has been used to classify an important tradition in women's writing ever since. Her discussion begins with an assessment of Mary Shelley's *Frankenstein* in the light of Shelley's own experience of life. She compares the birth of the monster with Shelley's traumatic experience of the birth and death of her own child, thereby aligning women's writing with their biological and psychological experience. Taking this further, she examines the whole 'Female Gothic' tradition in relation to 'the savagery of girlhood . . . also the self-disgust, the self-hatred and the impetus to self-destruction that have been increasingly prominent themes in the writing of women in the twentieth century' (p. 107). Quoting Mary Wollstonecraft, Moers equates the 'terrors, restraints and dangers' of the Gothic novel with 'the realities of a woman's life' (p. 134).

Like Moers' *Literary Women*, Patricia Meyer Spacks' book *The Female Imagination* (1975) is an examination of the similarities of experience and response of women writers across the centuries. Spacks endeavours to assess the feminine essence of women's writing: an aesthetic unchanging through time. She asks: 'What are the ways of female feeling, the modes of responding, that persist despite social change? Do any characteristic patterns of self-perception shape the creative expressions of women?'[8] Drawing on the reactions of her students to women's writing, she focusses on the similarities between the experiences of the woman reader and the woman writer even when divided by 100 years or so.

Spacks describes the 'difference' of women's writing as a 'delicate divergence' (p. 315). Like Moers, she examines women's handling of subject matter traditionally used by men. She identifies a female literary tradition working within a male tradition. 'The books do not destroy or even seriously challenge the old, man-created myths about women, but they shift the point of view' (p. 315). But although Spacks assumes that there is something in women's writing and female creativity which transcends historical boundaries – a female voice unaffected by differing social contexts – her study also identifies subtle changes in women's modes of expression from the eighteenth and nineteenth centuries to the twentieth century. Whilst in eighteenth and nineteenth century novels by women, Spacks argues that female protagonists sometimes offered 'at least subterranean challenges to the vision they appear to accept', she sees an increasing propensity amongst twentieth century women writers to express feelings of powerlessness, of frustration and anger (p. 315). She says: '[they] dramatize the heroism of suffering, irony and self-pity' (p. 152). Even depictions of rebellion frequently end in madness or nervous breakdown.

Spacks offers the 'female imagination' as the only possible outlet for women's true aspirations, the means by which they can 'affirm in far-reaching ways the significance of their inner freedom' (p. 316). An important 'difference' of women's writing is that for many women imagination remains a significant dimension of reality. As far as their writing is concerned, Spacks sees this as a positive result of women's social alienation, encouraging unique forms of expression. Spacks' description of the 'female imagination' bears a close resemblance to Elain Showalter's notion of the 'wild zone' which is central to her theory of gynocritics. Having examined the background to that theory, I shall devote the following section of this chapter to an analysis of Showalter's work itself.

Most of Elaine Showalter's own attempt to assess the 'unique difference of women's writing' is contained in two essays: *Towards a Feminist Poetics* (1979) and *Feminist Criticism in the Wilderness* (1981).[9] Since the second of these two essays contains – and expands on – much of the material of the first, I shall concentrate my discussion on the latter, which also incorporates Showalter's in-depth explanation of her 'gynocritics' theory.

Showalter begins her discussion by analysing the position feminist literary criticism had reached before the 1970s. She argues that its main feature was its unwillingness to take on any theoretical basis. This could be accounted for partly by the diversity of different methodologies aligning themselves to feminist criticism. But it was also due to many feminists' suspicion of the predominantly male critical schools, which were seen as 'arid and falsely objective' (p. 181). In contrast, feminist criticism was rooted in the subjective: 'the authority of experience' (p. 181). But, like the criticism discussed above, Showalter's approach was different from those feminist critics practising 'authentic realism'.

In an attempt to offer some form of classification of the many diverse forms of feminist criticism, Showalter divides them into two modes. The first she labels 'the feminist critique'. This involves the feminist as a reader, usually in re-reading male texts: offering different interpretations of the images of women found there, or questioning misconceptions about women in other forms of criticism (see Chapter One). Showalter argues that the role of such criticism is limited. At best it can only compete with different readings of the same text and, further, it relies on the male critical theory it attempts to revise. It must always work within an androcentric model – one which accepts male experience to be universal. Feminist criticism is thus halted in its attempt to establish its own theoretical base. Showalter identifies the need for a form of criticism that is woman-centred, independent of men, and seeking 'to find answers to the questions that come from *our* [women's] experience' (p. 184). She argues that feminist criticism must find 'its own subject, its own system, its own theory and its own voice' (p. 184).

This brings her to her second mode of criticism: the woman as a writer, or 'gynocritics'. By concentrating specifically on women's writing, Showalter argues that feminist critics immediately 'leap to a new conceptual vantage point' (p. 185). Their concern henceforth is to examine the *difference* of women's writing, and it is this central premise that marks the boundary between authentic realism and gynocriticism.

Drawing together a variety of gynocritical theories, Showalter divides them into four specific groups or 'models of difference' – biological, linguistic, psychoanalytical and cultural – each of which she sees as a development from the one before. She evaluates them in turn, but concentrates on the fourth, the model of cultural difference, which incorporates elements of the other three and which, she argues, constitutes the most sophisticated analysis of women's difference. Below is a brief summary of each of the models.

Biological criticism

This analyses the difference between women's writing and men's as a result of the difference of their bodies. Showalter points to the allegiance between this form of criticism and Victorian theories about women's physiology, which justified women's inferiority by describing the adverse effects of their physiology on the functioning of their brains. Although biological feminist criticism rejects these theories of inferiority, Showalter notes that some critics have accepted their 'metaphorical implications'. For example, Gilbert and Gubar in *The Madwoman in the Attic* claim that since creativity has been defined as a 'male' activity – 'the writer fathers his text' – there are enormous problems for female creativity.[10] Showalter argues that as well as metaphors of literary paternity, metaphors of literary maternity predominated in the eighteenth and nineteenth centuries (although often to describe the work of male authors). She describes attempts by feminist critics to reclaim these metaphors, to show how women's use of the body as a source of imagery is an assertion of the strength of her difference, not its weakness. Showalter therefore acknowledges the importance of the study of biological imagery in women's writing. But she concludes that biological criticism can only be effective in conjunction with the study of linguistic, social and literary theories, since '... there can be no expression of the body which is unmediated by [these] structures' (p. 189).

Linguistic criticism

Showalter identifies the debate over language as 'one of the most exciting areas in gynocritics'. Language is seen as a system that structures and shapes our perception and understanding of reality. Furthermore, it is seen as a male-constructed classification system into which women must force their experience. Many French feminists argue that this linguistic debate is central to the discussion of women's difference. They argue for the creation of a female language as an appropriate expression of female experience.[11] Within masculine discourse, woman is 'forced to speak in something like a foreign tongue, a language with which she may be personally uncomfortable'.[12] It is with the French feminists that Showalter locates the overlap between her 'biological' and 'linguistic' models of gynocritics. The creation of a feminine language, they claim, will involve creating a language system whose first allegiance will be to the natural rhythms of the female body. Showalter, however, disapproves of a theory that divorces feminist criticism from the intellectual and academic world, dispensing with academic or official discourse and thereby alienating itself. She claims that women will be forced to remain silent unless they can communicate with their male counterparts. In a similar way, Mary Jacobus argues for a women's writing that works within male discourse but works 'ceaselessly to deconstruct it: to write what cannot be written'.[13] But Showalter stresses the need to improve women's access to language, to remove the hidden censorship which denies women the 'full resources of language'. Until that is done, she claims, 'it ought not to be in language that we base our theory of difference' (p. 193).

Psychological criticism

Much psychoanalytically-oriented feminist criticism takes its lead from Freudian notions of the Oedipal phase and Lacan's application of that theory to the acquisition of language and entrance of the child to the 'Symbolic Order'.[14] Freudian theories concentrate on women's 'castration complex': their difference is centred on their lack of a penis and the psychological effects caused by that lack. Referring back to her analysis of biological criticism, Showalter demonstrates how a feminist criticism based on such a Freudian analysis is continually confronted by problems of women's disadvantage and consequent inferiority. Certainly Gilbert and Gubar argue that women's difference is characterised by their struggle to overcome the disadvantages inherent in their gender.

Lacan argues that the entrance of the father or Phallus in the Oedipal phase coincides with a child's entrance to the Symbolic Order and their entry into language. At this point they become aware of gender difference, and also the difference inherent in language itself. Whilst for the male child the entrance into the Symbolic Order is characterised by his identity with the father or Phallus, for the female child the experience is a negative one and characterised by her identification with lack.

Showalter identifies some feminists who have made positive use of this theory. She cites Nancy Chodorow's work *The Reproduction of Mothering: Psychoanalysis and the Sociology of Gender*.[15] Chodorow offers an alternative interpretation of Freud's theory. Concentrating on the pre-Oedipal phase, she suggests that it is in fact the female child who positively identifies with the mother, and the male child whose experience is negative – an experience of being 'not female'. After the Oedipal phase, women experience difficulties with feminine identity *vis-à-vis* the masculine Symbolic Order, but their unity with other women remains. Showalter finds instances of a similar analysis in other feminist critics (critics who include Ellen Moers, Nina Baym and Patricia Meyer Spacks). These women focus on relationships between female characters in women's novels, and on the relationships amongst women writers themselves. She concludes that psychoanalytic feminist theory can offer some explanation of 'similarities between women writing in a variety of cultural circumstances' (p. 197), but that other factors are left unexamined. For a gynocritic theory that covers all aspects of women's writing, Showalter turns to an examination of theories of 'cultural' difference.

Cultural criticism

By using a model of women's cultural difference, Showalter argues that feminist critics can also incorporate ideas about their language, bodies and psyche, but they will 'interpret them in relation to the social context in which they occur' (p. 197). She argues that a cultural theory identifies women's 'collective experience within the cultural whole', whilst simultaneously acknowledging important differences amongst women writers.

Showalter quotes Gerda Lerner in suggesting 'the possibility of the existence of a female culture *within* the general culture shared by men and women' (p. 198). She then goes on to examine a model for this female culture, devised by two anthropologists, Shirley and Edwin Ardener. The Ardeners analyse society in terms of 'muted' and 'dominant' groups. They argue that: 'Whilst every group in society generates its own ideas about reality at a deep level, not all of these can find expression at a surface level because the ... communicative channel is under the control of the dominant group'.[16] Women are in this relatively inarticulate position; they constitute a 'muted group' whose reality does not get represented. The Ardeners stress that women are not 'silenced', however: 'The muted structures are "there" but cannot be "realized" in the language of the dominant structure. Where society is defined by men, some features of women do not fit that definition'.[17] 'The important issue is whether they [women] are able to say all they would wish to say, where and when they wish to say it' (p. 20).

The Ardeners suggest that muted groups almost have to 'translate' their thoughts into the dominant mode of communication; they require an 'extra step' after the thought is conceived before it can be realised in speech. They stress that this probably works at an unconscious level, and extremely rapidly. The Ardener's theory extends beyond linguistics to more fundamental notions of culture and its relation to nature. The symbolic stress between the two was first observed by Levi-Strauss:

> The contrast of nature and culture would be neither a primeval fact, nor a concrete aspect of universal order. Rather it should be seen as an artificial creation of culture, a protective rampart thrown up around it because it only felt able to assert its existence and uniqueness by destroying all the links that led back to its original association with the other manifestations of life.[18]

Likewise, the Ardeners argue that men have been in the position of having to define themselves in relation to women and to nature in order to accommodate 'the two logical sets which classify human beings by different bodily structures: male/female and the two sets: human/non-human' (Edwin Ardener, p. 5). Since the model for 'mankind' is based on that for *man*, their opposites – women and non-mankind – tend to be ambiguously placed. The Ardeners refer to the non-human as 'wild'. Consequently, those elements of female experience which fall outside the dominant structure, as defined by men, are also seen as features of the 'wild'.

Showalter concentrates on the Ardeners' notion of the 'wild zone' of women's culture, a zone spatially, experientially and metaphysically outside the dominant boundaries. Spatially it is a 'no-man's' land, forbidden to men, and experientially, it includes parts of female lifestyle unlike those of men: in both these areas there are corresponding male zones, not open to women. Metaphysically, however – in terms of consciousness – there is no corresponding male experience alien to women. All male consciousness is within the boundaries of the dominant structures and thus accessible or structured by language. Although they have never experienced it first hand, women may know what male experience is like, since it has been the subject of myth and legend. But man can never know what is in the wild. It is always imaginary.[19] 'In their texts it becomes the place for revolutionary women's language – the language of every thing that is repressed' (Showalter, p. 201).

Showalter argues that the 'wild zone' represents the true arena for an examination of women's difference. It is here that she locates the essence of femininity. A cultural model of feminist criticism and women's difference establishes the female tradition as a 'positive source of strength and solidarity' as well as a 'negative source of powerlessness' (p. 204). Since women are inside two traditions simultaneously, feminist critics must address themselves to both dominant and muted structures. Women's fiction should thus be seen as a 'double-voiced discourse, containing a dominant and a muted story' (p. 204). It is with this model in mind that I shall carry out my readings of Jean Rhys's *Wide Sargasso Sea* and Margaret Atwood's *Surfacing*.

II

Using Showalter's cultural model of gynocritics for my reading of Jean Rhys's *Wide Sargasso Sea*, I shall be examining the novel for Rhys's two different perceptions of reality corresponding to 'dominant' and 'muted' groups.[20] Within the text, it can be argued that Rhys creates these two axes in a variety of different forms. The most obvious is the male/female dichotomy. But there is also a racial divide, primarily between the British and Jamaican communities (obfuscated by the novel's protagonist's white Creole origin of mixed European and Negro descent). There are frequent references to the differences between the naturally wild landscape of the Jamaican countryside, and memories of the cultivation and urbanisation of England, representing the conflict between nature and culture. And, perhaps most importantly, there is the contrast Rhys draws between madness and sanity.

Collating the 'negatives' from all the above oppositions, Rhys concentrates on a portrayal of 'Otherness', of cultural negativity as defined by Western civilisation's system of signification – the 'muted' group. But she also challenges the classification system itself by depicting cultural negativity as a source of power and strength. *Wide Sargasso Sea* can be seen as Rhys's attempt to find a matriarchal and 'natural' female discourse. Metaphorically, we can trace the 'wild zone' of the Jamaican landscape and lifestyle as a platform for that discourse, a space within which the muted groups can speak. Yet the dominant culture is ever-present, embodied in British imperialism, personified by Rochester. Hence the importance of the concept of madness in the novel, which must immediately become a relative term in its position at the centre of the debate about alternative perceptions of reality.

Wide Sargasso Sea is based on Charlotte Brontë's novel *Jane Eyre*.[21] Using Brontë's depiction of Rochester's first wife, Rhys vividly portrays a young woman's struggle against male dominance (as well as her personal confrontation with British imperialism). Returning her to the lush Jamaican landscape of her childhood, Rhys traces the story of Antoinette Cosway (later renamed Bertha by her husband) through her marriage to Rochester to 'madness' in the attic at Thornfield Hall. The novel is concerned to depict the gulf, due both to cultural and gender differences, between the experiences and lifestyle of its young Creole heiress – her perception of 'reality' – and that of Rochester: the British, male imposter.

In their commentary on *Jane Eyre*, Gilbert and Gubar in *The Madwoman in the Attic* describe Bertha as Jane's 'hunger, rebellion and rage'. This too corresponds to Rhys's portrayal of Antoinette's madness: a madness that epitomises her difference from Rochester, and her refusal to accept his perception and values as the norm. By displacing Brontë's Rochester into an alien culture, Rhys attempts an inversion of the dominant ideology in order that she may allow the muted group to speak.

Wide Sargasso Sea falls into three parts, the first of which is told by Antoinette. In the second, Rochester describes his arrival in the West Indies, his marriage and its disastrous consequences. And the final part is again narrated by Antoinette, this time from her imprisonment in her husband's English attic.

The novel is initially concerned with Antoinette's insecurity (and that of her whole family), due to their racial origin. Neither Antoinette nor her mother have either 'money or blackness to secure themselves an identity'.[22] It is largely through her use of sensuous imagery that Rhys vividly depicts the ambivalent relationship of the young Creole heiress with the lush Jamaican landscape – in much the same way that Charlotte Brontë had done in *Jane Eyre* and Emily Brontë in *Wuthering Heights*. Due to her lack of identity, Antoinette suffers first at the hands of her own society – a 'white nigger', resented by the recently freed slaves – and, later, as Rochester's wife, subject to his western, male desire for imperialist domination. Thus, Antoinette feels alternately secure and afraid, free and imprisoned; feelings powerfully evoked in her dreams, but also in the pervasive atmosphere of the whole novel.

In the first section of the novel, Rhys evokes, both dramatically and sensually, the cultural barriers between English and Jamaican communities. The relationship between Antoinette's mother and her second (English) husband, Mason (as well as Antoinette's own relationship with her step-father), reinforces this cultural divide, and prefigures the marriage between Antoinette and Rochester around which the novel is centred. Many of the themes introduced in the first section, together with the imagery and symbolism supporting them, form the background to the ensuing struggle of wills between the novel's Creole heiress and her domineering English husband. The struggle is as much about the conflict between two opposing 'realities', however, as about that between two incompatible personalities. And each reality is multifaceted, increasing the complexity of the struggle. There is the obvious opposition between the recently freed slaves and the British community – who were once their masters (a position for which Rochester must accept responsibility, despite his more recent arrival in the country). But Rhys delves more deeply. Rochester clearly embodies the imperialism which brought his forefathers to the West Indies, and it is the attitudes that characterise this nationally inherited trait which seem to have become naturalised in him to form part of his 'maleness'.

From the first abrupt sentences of the novel, we are made aware of Antoinette's alienation, belonging neither to the white community of slave owners, nor to the country's Black community: 'They say when trouble comes close ranks, and so the white people did. But we were not in their ranks' (p. 15). It is this lack of identity which constitutes the basis of Antoinette's insecurity. She longs to become part of the Jamaican culture epitomised by Christophine (the Cosway's Black Jamaican housekeeper; a powerful woman who possesses the magical powers of 'obeah'). But her desire is thwarted by her heritage, and by her mother's aspirations to become part of the middle class white community. The disappearance of the old order – the collapse of the Coulibri Estate, once owned by Antoinette's father, with the release of the slaves – results in a threatening chaos verging on anarchy '... why should anybody work?' (p. 17): an anarchy threatening the security and stability of the whole white community. Rhys uses the family's garden as a powerful metaphor for the collapse of that old order:

> Our garden was large and beautiful as that garden in the Bible – the tree of life grew there. But it had gone wild. The paths were overgrown and a smell of dead flowers mixed with the fresh living smell. Underneath the tree ferns, the light was green. Orchids flourished out of reach or for some reason not to be touched. One was snaky looking, another like an octopus ... (p. 16)

Instead of the beautiful, cultivated land of a wealthy estate, the garden has returned to its natural wildness. The metaphor is central to the novel as a whole, contrasting the 'unnatural' orderliness of the British community with the natural, more primitive community of Jamaica. It is important that the 'wildness' of the gardens should appear to have triumphed. But whilst the garden has retained its beauty, Rhys's imagery is mixed – the orchids are like snakes and octopuses, there is the smell of dead flowers mixed with that of the living. Rhys thus conveys the threat lurking in this beauty, a threat which is to remain an inherent part of Antoinette's experience of both her childhood and adult worlds.

Throughout Charlotte Brontë's *Jane Eyre*, we see Jane continually gathering strength from her friendships with other women: with the servant Bessie at Gateshead, with Helen Burns and Miss Temple at Lowood, and with Diana and Mary at the parsonage where she eventually seeks refuge, having fled Rochester and Thornfield Hall. So, too, Antoinette's greatest support is from the Black woman Christophine, but also from her faltering friendship with Tia.

Tia is Antoinette's closest (indeed, only) 'play-mate' during this period of her childhood, yet whilst the bonds linking them are obviously strong, there are marked differences between them. Tia is closely associated with the magical qualities of the native

Jamaican women, with the 'secret' which is to become central to Rochester's experience of an alien world. And it is this mysterious, sometimes inhuman, quality which simultaneously attracts Antoinette to Tia, and yet prevents the fruition of their friendship. 'Then Tia would light a fire (fires always lit for her, sharp stones did not hurt her bare feet, I never heard her cry)' (p. 20). Despite their mutual need for camaraderie and their apparent compatibility, the cultural and social barriers between them are so strong as to make any egalitarian, envy-free relationship impossible. Antoinette's fall in social status owing to the collapse of the Coulibri Estate, rather than breaking down the social divisions between them, allows Tia to give vent to her bitter resentment of the other girl's former position: to express her own recently-gained superiority: 'Real white people, they got gold money. They didn't look at us nobody see them come near us. Old time white people nothing but white nigger now, and black nigger better than white nigger' (p. 21).

Antoinette's mother's second marriage to an Englishman marks their reinstatement in the white community. Or so it appears. The marriage foreshadows that between Rochester and Antoinette. Both matches are initially materialistic, and in both an attitude of British imperialism evolves – the need to conquer and control. Mason's inability to understand the Blacks, or indeed the Creole race into which he has married, is also later reflected in Rochester's uneasiness amongst his wife's friends and servants, his ceaseless but fruitless attempt to unveil the 'secret' of the place and its natural inhabitants.

Antoinette is aware that Mason's arrival will have given rise to a renewed threat from the Jamaican people. Yet her feelings towards both races remain ambivalent. Whilst she recognises Mr Mason's insensitivity and short-sightedness: '... my mother knows but she can't make him believe it. I wish I could tell him that out here is not at all like English people think it is. I wish...' (p. 29), she is drawn to the sense of comfort, security and solidity offered by his resolute 'Englishness'. The picture of the Miller's Daughter remains for her a symbol of all that is 'England', contrasted with the mystical, often threatening, strangeness of her Jamaican contemporaries. She is comforted by the sense of being dominated and controlled, content not to have to question, not to have to work out her own identity, and not to have to think about her

'destiny' – a question answered more easily by the Christian, God-
fearing English people than by the more 'realistic' (and fatalistic)
Jamaicans:

> There are more ways than one of being happy, better perhaps to be
> peaceful and contented and protected, as I feel now, peaceful for
> years and long years, and afterwards I may be saved, whatever Myra
> says. (When I asked Christophine what happened when you died, she
> said, 'You want to know too much'.)(p. 31)

The climax of the first section of the novel is the burning of the
Coulibri house, leading to Antoinette's brother's death and her
mother's madness. In a fast-moving display of sensual impressions, the fire focusses many of the tensions and anxieties,
insecurities and misunderstandings experienced by Antoinette and
the whole Cosway family in relation to the native Black
community. The incidents associated with the fire are to prove
Antoinette's apparent peacefulness ill-judged. Against a mirage of
sense-impressions – the noise of the crowd outside ('like animals
howling'), smoke, the smell of Antoinette's burning hair, flames as
the bamboo catches – Mason's words of comfort are hollow
rhetoric: 'They will repent in the morning. I foresee gifts of
tamarinds in syrup and ginger sweets tomorrow' (pp. 32–3). The
horror and confusion is vividly evoked in the flurry of activity and
emotions – Annette in hysterics, Pierre lifeless in her arms,
Christophine, Mannie and Sass rushing to and fro with water-
pitchers, the anonymous, menacing crowd staring up at them
from the outside. And again, Mason's rhetorical prayer to God
falls cold and insignificant, with the added irony that it appears
initially to be responsible for subduing the crowd. But Jamaican
superstition is shown to be stronger than any Christian belief. The
plunge of Coco, the parrot, to its death, wings clipped and aflame,
finally disperses the hating Black people, poignantly prefiguring
Antoinette's own fall to death – hair burning, figurative wings
clipped – from the balcony of Thornfield Hall.

Antoinette's final clutch at the relative happiness of her Coulibri
childhood re-emphasises the divide between herself and the
Jamaican identity she longs for. Seeing Tia after the chaos and
terror of the fire, Antoinette reaches out to her as her only
remaining link with the cultural community who have risen
against her and her family. The final image of the scene freezes
the impasse between the two girls in a static moment of attraction

and repulsion, of like and unlike – perhaps the most powerful image in the novel:

> When I was close I saw the jagged stone in her hand but I did not see her throw it. I did not feel it either, only something wet running down my face. I looked at her and I saw her face crumple up as she began to cry. We stared at each other, blood on my face, tears on hers. It was as if I saw myself. Like in a looking-glass. (p. 38).

The search for self-identity is a theme common to much women's writing, and the mirror is constantly used to symbolise this search due to its ability to trap an image of the self. Yet that image is not always an obvious likeness. Showalter's analysis is again pertinent here. Her notion of women writer's 'double-voiced discourse' can usefully be transposed to their portrayals of female characters in their novels. Hence Antoinette is simultaneously inside and outside the Jamaican culture of her homeland. Again, Jean Rhys has extracted her symbolism from her source-text, *Jane Eyre*, where mirrors also play an important part. Jane is constantly confronting her 'truest and darkest double' in reflections of herself. Perhaps the most significant of these encounters is the first one, which occurs in the 'red room' after her conflict with her step-brother, John Reed:

> Returning, I had to cross before the looking-glass; my fascinated glance involuntarily explored the depth it revealed. All looked colder and darker in that visionary hollow than in reality: and the strange little figure there gazing at me with a white face and arms speckling the gloom, and glittering eyes of fear moving where all else was still, had the effect of a real spirit... (p. 46)

And it is the 'real spirit' which is later released through its embodiment in Bertha, Rochester's mad first wife.

Jean Rhys, then, is using the looking-glass for similar purposes. At the end of *Wide Sargasso Sea*, Antoinette is deprived of a mirror, just as she has also had her name taken from her. Rochester has attempted to destroy her identity as completely as possible – and certainly to destroy her affinity with the 'muted group'. She says:

> Names matter, like when he wouldn't call me Antoinette, and I saw Antoinette drifting out of the window with her scents, her pretty clothes and her looking-glass.
> There is no looking-glass here and I don't know what I am like now. I remember watching myself brush my hair and how my eyes looked back at me. The girl I saw was myself yet not quite myself. (p. 147)

As I have suggested, Antoinette's is a constant search for her self-identity and her insecurity is carried through from her childhood. Her final confrontation with Tia is really the climax of her struggle to locate herself in the Jamaican 'order' where Tia already has a place. Antoinette's position *vis-à-vis* the two main opposing cultures, Jamaican and British, is to remain ambivalent. Her marriage to Rochester separates her still further from the Jamaican, yet at the same time, she finds herself still more in need of its strength and support. It is not until her suicidal jump into the flames at Thornfield Hall that she would seem to have finally found that strength herself – to have found her true identity which seems to consist, in some sense, of her union with Tia; perhaps her union with other women: 'But when I looked over the edge I saw the pool of Coulibri. Tia was there. She beckoned to me and when I hesitated, she laughed. I heard her say, You frightened? And I heard a man's voice, Bertha! Bertha! . . . I called "Tia!" and jumped . . .' (p. 155)

Just as the symbol of the mirror reappears at frequent intervals throughout the novel, so many other incidents and much of the imagery from the first section of the novel are carried through to form its basic structure. Despite Antoinette's ambivalent position, there is significant structural differentiation between the two opposing cultures – or the two opposing 'realities' – in the novel. Thus, in the first section we have seen Mason's Englishness as it appears to Antoinette, carrying with it the apparent security of a stable father-figure. It is the longing for similar security and stability that would seem to underlie Antoinette's acquiescence in her arranged marriage with Rochester. Contrasted with this solidity and its accompanying insensitivity is the mystery and magic associated with Christophine and Tia: Christophine's powers of obeah, Tia's ability to light fires and her inability to feel pain. In her endless search for identity and security, Antoinette finds sympathy and innate understanding in these people, fulfilling the lack created by her rejection by her mother. Similarly, she shares their almost pantheistic relationship with the Jamaican countryside, although it is clearly no benevolent natural world: 'And if the razor grass cut my legs and arms I would think "It's better than people". Black ants and red ones, tall nests swarming with the white ants, rain that soaked me to the skin – once I saw a snake. All better than people. Better. Better, better than people' (p. 24).

Through the Jamaican women's affinity with the natural world, Jean Rhys would seem to emphasise what Levi-Strauss described as the symbolic stress between society and nature; the association of women with a more primitive, 'uncivilized' way of life – with all that is 'not man'. The idea is also central to Showalter's cultural model of gynocritics. Rhys shows this 'otherness' in a positive light. Just as the symbol of the mirror is carried over from *Jane Eyre*, so the recurring image of fire is extracted from the earlier novel. Jean Rhys' depiction of Jamaica is one of an intense, sensuous and emotional experience. Thus, fire is important for its destructive qualities, but also for the vivid colours which link it with the lush Jamaican landscape. These colours can again be traced back to *Jane Eyre*, as can the importance of fire itself. And those elements of the novel which Gilbert and Gubar have described as Jane's own 'hunger, rebellion and rage' are transposed by Jean Rhys onto the passionate, powerful women of the Jamaican community. The destruction of the Coulibri house by fire confirms the power of the Jamaican world, symbolically acknowledging its triumph over British imperialism. The former association of Tia with fire and Antoinette's final act of defiance against Rochester in her suicidal destruction of Thornfield Hall could be seen to reinforce this enigmatic link between the magical powers of a 'primitive' cultural community and those of all women in their attempt to evade male repression.

The fire kills Pierre (Antoinette's 'idiot' brother), and sends Annette (her mother) 'mad', a madness which finally sets a seal on her rejection of her daughter and causes her husband to desert her. After a brief interval of refuge in a convent, Antoinette is forced back 'outside' into the dangerous insecurity of the real world. Her subsequent nightmare is ominously like a premonition. It is the same dream she had had on the eve of the changes leading to her mother's marriage – walking through a forest, followed by an enemy, paralysed. This time she is clad in white, again followed by a hating man, and again terrified. Both dreams remain unexplained. Antoinette says, 'I dreamed I was in Hell' (p. 51). The disjointed stumbling sentences of the description evoke a nightmare world of powerlessness, and it is this world that is further evoked through the depiction of her marriage to Rochester.

The central section of *Wide Sargasso Sea* is narrated by Rochester, with a brief passage from Antoinette's viewpoint. The relationship between author, narrator, and characters, and particularly that between their viewpoints and that of the reader, is complex. The novel is narrated by the two main characters alternately – Antoinette, Rochester, Antoinette (briefly), Rochester and finally Antoinette. Consequently, the reader is presented with two different versions of 'reality' – those of the muted and dominant groups (although rarely two different accounts of the same event). Because of the way the novel is structured, because it is Antoinette's perception which frames the narrative and because of the setting of this narrative, the reader is directed to sympathise with Antoinette, not with Rochester. It could be argued that Rhys uses irony to stage a critique of Rochester's version of 'reality' by allowing him to 'speak for himself'. And because of the style and setting, the acute and vivid evocation of the pervasive atmosphere of Jamaica – and particularly of its matriarchal community – the muted group can even be seen to make itself heard through Rochester's own confused incomprehension. It is Rochester's insecurity, his inability to make sense of his new life, that completes our disbelief in his perception.

Thus, the novel is constructed around these two conflicting 'realities'. The conflict is presented both contiguously – through the juxtaposition of Antoinette's and Rochester's respective narratives – but also within each narrative itself; Antoinette experiences both British and Jamaican cultures (which, I suggest, correspond to masculine and feminine discourses respectively), and Rochester's narrative is constantly at odds with the world he is portraying. His acknowledged inability to relate to that world reaffirms this disparity.

The conflict Rochester experiences in many respects resembles Antoinette's earlier feelings of beguilement and repulsion in her relationship with her Jamaican landscape and community. His fluctuating emotions are apparent from the wavering, divided opening sentence of his description: 'So it was all over, the advance and retreat, the doubts and hesitations. Everything finished, for better or for worse' (p. 55). The entire novel is centred on this movement between contraries, exchanges between primary images – light and darkness, day and night, sun and moon, heat and cold, fire and ice – all of which somehow coalesce on Antoinette's honeymoon island: 'Desire, Hatred, Life, Death, came very close in the darkness. Better not know how close. Better not think, never for a moment' (p. 79). By collapsing these opposites together, Rhys is perhaps trying to 'express the inexpressible'; to reach that point of female experience which is beyond the bounds of patriarchal discourse.[23] It is at these enigmatic, evocative moments that the writing is at its most poetic. And it is through this poetic writing that Rhys seems to 'work within "male" discourse' but 'works ceaselessly to deconstruct it' (Jacobus, p. 12). Whilst Rhys is clearly drawing sharp distinctions between male and female perceptions of reality, and hence expressing difference in male/female terms, the novel could be seen to be focussed on female experience, and it is within this experience that notions of 'difference-as-opposite' are brought into question. (As I have suggested, this female world is the main subject of the narrative even when Rochester acts as narrator.) It is in this way that Rhys allows 'feminine values [to] penetrate and undermine the masculine structures which contain them' (Showalter, 1981, p. 28). Rochester is here the outsider in an alien culture and community, and it is his ideology and perception which are at odds with the dominant world-view.

Thus, whilst it is the blurring of boundaries and indistinct plurality of vision which characterise the whole atmosphere of Jamaica in the novel and enhance the beauty and magic of the honeymoon island, for Rochester this is 'unreal', and it is also distressing. He dislikes and distrusts Antoinette's ambiguous racial background. Unable to 'place' her within a race, he implies that there must be impurity in her dual national heredity – a criticism carrying heavy moral overtones including that of sexual promiscuity: '... her eyes ... are dark and can be disconcerting. She never blinks at all it seems to me. Long, sad, dark alien eyes. Creole of pure English descent she may be, but they are not English or European either' (p. 56). From the outset, Rochester describes Antoinette in these terms: as an alien, a stranger, sometimes almost sub-human. Antoinette's world is not Rochester's world, her 'reality' is not his. Rochester says: 'But the feeling of something unknown and hostile was very strong. "I feel very much a stranger here" I said. "I feel that this place is my enemy and on your side."' (p. 107). He cannot accept the disjunction between his previous experience and the 'reality' now confronting him. Consequently, he consistently attempts to impose his own views onto Antoinette: 'Reality might disconcert her, bewilder her, hurt her, but it would only be a mistake, a misfortune, a wrong path taken, her fixed ideas would never change. Nothing that I told her influenced her at all' (p. 78).

The ironic treatment of Rochester is at its height here: clearly, this description could equally fit his attitude to Antoinette's 'reality'. For Antoinette, Rochester's reality is 'like a cold dark dream' (p. 67). He is associated with England, with London – the city, streets and houses full of people. Antoinette becomes one with the rivers, mountains and sea of her homeland, the intense colours and smells, and, above all, the intense emotions. Rochester is afraid of this intensity, afraid of an environment and feelings he is unable to control. And he is even more afraid of a woman – indeed, what could be described as a whole matriarchal community – over whom he is seemingly powerless.

Rhys uses symbolic inversion to demonstrate the fallacy of a patriarchal mono-dimensional reality. The novel is indeed a 'celebration of the negative'.[24] Just as women have traditionally been associated with lack, with Freudian notions of castration, with silence and absence, so Rhys inverts this experience. It is Rochester who suffers this 'lack', this 'speechlessness': 'As for my confused impressions they will never be written. There are blanks in my mind that cannot be filled up' (p. 64). In so doing, Rhys exposes the logic of patriarchal discourse for what it is. As Dale Spender suggests: 'What we have confidently called logic and believe to be "uncontaminated" by human values, may indeed be culture-specific, arbitrary and inappropriate. We may need to change our ideas of what constitutes logic if we are to come closer to making sense of the world'.[25]

Rhys inverts the patriarchal order, where women are classified as negative, as 'wrong'; their reality invalid. Through *Wide Sargasso Sea*, she exposes the other side of the coin. Displaced from his own, male-dominated, 'orderly' society, Rochester comes face to face with the 'wild zone' of female experience: 'It was a beautiful place – wild, untouched, above all untouched, with an alien, disturbing, secret loneliness. And it kept its secret. I'd find myself thinking "What I see is nothing – I want what hides – that is not nothing."' (p. 73). Rochester is simultaneously afraid and curious, torn between frustrated disbelief and the compulsion to discover the 'secret'. Yet he is also incapable of acknowledging the validity (even the superiority) of this 'other reality'. He is conscious of a terrible sense of lack – 'I want what hides' – but in order to acknowledge Antoinette's reality as valid, he must deny his own status and authority: the power of subscribing to, and controlling, the dominant world-view.

The solution to Rochester's dilemma comes with the discovery of insanity in Antoinette's family, and his suggestion that Antoinette herself might have inherited that insanity. The labelling of the two opposing realities, those of dominant and muted, male and female groups, now moves into the realms of 'sanity' and 'insanity': a classification carrying with it the whole weight of Western 'scientific' judgement. Rochester's growing hatred of Antoinette, owing to his inability to understand or influence her, now finds justification in his discovery of her inherently pathological mind.

Rochester redoubles his efforts to destroy Antoinette's already insecure identification with her adopted Jamaican culture, to destroy that reality in which he has no part. He calls her Bertha, after her 'mad' mother, instead of Antoinette – an act which Antoinette parallels with Christophine's magical powers, so strong is its effect on her self image: 'Bertha is not my name. You are trying to make me into someone else, calling me by another name. I know, that's obeah too' (p. 121). He taunts her as a 'marionette'. He refuses to make love to her, even to speak to her. Having once described her as 'alien', a stranger, Rochester now sees Antoinette as animal-like: savage, wild and unruly, very much like the description of Bertha in *Jane Eyre*. In *Wide Sargasso Sea*, Rochester says:

> Then she cursed me comprehensively, my eyes, my mouth, every member of my body, and it was like a dream in the large unfurnished room with the candles flickering and this red-eyed wild-haired stranger who was my wife shouting obscenities at me. It was at this nightmare moment that I heard Christophine's calm voice. (p. 122)

His description of Bertha in *Jane Eyre* runs: '... and my ears were filled with the curses the maniac still shrieked out; wherein she momentarily mingled my name with such a tone of demon-hate, with such language! – no professed harlot ever had a fouler vocabulary than she...' (p. 335).

Rochester can only complete his suppression of Antoinette by returning with her to England, where he can regain the security of controlling the dominant world-view, where he will be 'sane', his 'reality' 'real', and Antoinette 'insane', living in a dream-world. Phrases like 'law and order' and 'justice' inevitably ring hollow in the primitive, uncultured society of Jamaica. Even God – a symbol of the highest power in the patriarchal hierarchical 'order' – has no jurisdiction in Christophine's matriarchal community. She says: 'This is a free country and I am a free woman' (p. 131).

Just before their return to England, however, Rochester has a moment of remorse through which he suddenly becomes more receptive: 'So I shall never understand why, suddenly, bewilderingly, I was certain that everything I had imagined to be truth was false. False. Only the magic and dream are true – all the rest's a lie. Let it go. Here is the secret. Here' (p. 138). His brief moment of revelation confirms the ironic treatment of his narrative for this whole section of the novel. His acknowledgement of the existence and validity of an alternative reality to his own confirms the positive depiction of this female experience throughout. Yet even here, Rochester's patriarchal discourse is imposed on the enigmatic contrasting reality – a reality which he can never grasp except in terms of 'magic' and 'the secret'. His description moves characteristically to talk of possession and domination: 'Not lost, I had found it in a hidden place and I'd keep it, hold it fast. As I'd hold her' (p. 138), and finally to an analogy with 'treasure' and reference to acquisitiveness: 'But they left their treasure, gold and more gold. Some of it is found – but the finders never tell, because you see they'd only get one third then: that's the law of treasure. They want it all, so never speak of it' (p. 139).

Yet despite his continued need for domination, Rochester is finally receptive to the otherness which he has previously tried to dismiss; to the night and the darkness of which he was previously afraid, and perhaps even to Antoinette herself: 'Blot out the moon, /Pull down the stars. /Love in the dark, for we're for the dark /So soon, so soon' (p. 139). But it is too late, and when he is greeted by the hatred of Antoinette's eyes, the moment passes. His own hatred, humiliation and pride return with a vengeance and the battle of wills continues. But despite his apparently having the upper hand, Rochester can never achieve overall power. Antoinette retains a reserve of female power which Rochester can never destroy, and of which he will always feel the lack: 'Above all I hated her. For she belonged to the magic and the loveliness. She had left me thirsty and all my life would be thirst and longing for what I had lost before I found it' (p. 141). Again, Rhys has inverted one of the fundamental axes of patriarchal discourse. It is Rochester who experiences the lack or 'castration' traditionally associated with women.

The final section of the novel moves to England and Antoinette's imprisonment in Rochester's attic at Thornfield Hall. The fast-moving imagery and impressions contrast the warmth and intensity of Jamaica with the coldness of England. Memories of Jamaica are invited by the flames of the fire, and by the single red dress Antoinette has retained from her previous life. The dress carries all the intense sensuous qualities of Jamaica: the colours, the smells, the spiritual and emotional experiences:

> As soon as I turned the key I saw it hanging, the colour of fire and sunset. The colour of flamboyant flowers. "If you are buried under a flamboyant tree" I said, "your soul is lifted up when it flowers. Everyone wants that..." The scent that comes from the dress was very faint at first, then it grew stronger. The smell of vetivert and frangi-panni, of cinnamon and dust and lime trees when they are flowering. The smell of sun and the smell of the rain. (p. 151)

Thornfield Hall seems to her like 'a cardboard house' – it is not 'reality'. Deprived of light and warmth, she no longer knows where she is. The darkness here is not like that of Jamaica, broken by moon and stars and moonflowers. Here she is imprisoned, denied any identity. She is no longer called Antoinette (Rochester has renamed her Bertha) and she does not possess a mirror in which to 'see herself'.

Yet Antoinette retains some of her strength. Grace Poole describes the Hall as a refuge, a place where, as a woman, she is safe from the patriarchal world outside:

> the house is big and safe, a shelter from the world outside which, say what you like, can be a black and cruel world to a woman. Past the lodge gate a long avenue of trees and inside the house the blazing fires and the crimson and white rooms. But above all the thick walls, keeping away all the things that you have fought till you can fight no more. (p. 146)

The Hall takes on almost womb-like qualities – protective and secure. But, like the red-room in *Jane Eyre*, it is also a prison. Antoinette alone does not feel the benefit of its 'security'. She is still fighting ('she hasn't lost her spirit'): 'living in her own darkness' she remains detached from Rochester's attempts to defeat the 'magic and loveliness' she possesses. The attic thus becomes a 'wild zone' itself, where, through her 'madness', Antoinette is able to defy Rochester's attempts to render her powerless. Her final act of defiance is to destroy Thornfield Hall in a fire whose flames contain an array of images from her Jamaican world.

Jean Rhys has skilfully re-written Brontë's account of the fire at Thornfield Hall so as not to end her own novel with Antoinette's suicidal jump from the flames. The event is described as a premonition, and the novel closes as Antoinette wakes from her dream, steals the key to the attic from Grace Poole and carefully wends her way along the dark passages of Thornfield Hall, lighted by the single flame of the candle she carries. The narrative describing the fire itself is fast-moving and dream-like with its ever-changing scenario: a confusion of impressions of England and Jamaica. Antoinette calls on Christophine for help, deriving her final strength from the other woman's solidarity as well as her magical powers. As the fire gradually spreads, cinematic images of Antoinette's childhood flit one by one across her mind – the grandfather clock, Aunt Cora's patchwork, orchids, jasmine, treeferns, moss, the picture of the Miller's Daughter, the parrot, Rochester ... Finally, she sees Tia, by the pool in Coulibri, and it is towards this image that she jumps to her death.

It is not, ultimately, Rochester who 'breaks' Antoinette. Her self-destruction is a final act of her own will and strength; an escape from imprisonment. And the lighted candle in the culminating sentence would seem to be an image of the retention (or final acquisition) of this strength: Antoinette's independence, her consciousness and spirit which she will not allow Rochester to destroy or overpower:

> Now at last I know why I was brought here and what I have to do. There must have been a draught from the flame flickered and I thought it was out. But I shielded it with my hand and it burned up again to light me along the dark passage ... (pp. 155–6)

Jean Rhys thus establishes the strength of the 'muted group' or feminine discourse. In *Wide Sargasso Sea* that discourse is indeed a 'positive source of strength and solidarity', as Showalter has suggested.

Showalter's cultural model of gynocritics is also a useful structure for analysis of Margaret Atwood's *Surfacing*.[26] The novel takes the form of spiritual quest, in which the female protagonist returns to the natural world in search of mystical vision. Her quest could equally be interpreted as a search for a feminine discourse: her escape from, and challenge to, the patriarchal social order she has previously accepted as the 'norm'.

The text is structured on two different levels. Whilst pursuing her struggle towards self-identity and greater knowledge, the protagonist must simultaneously continue to relate to her three companions (two males, one female). And throughout the novel she is haunted by her memories of her treatment by her ex-lover and the male medical profession who aborted her child. Consequently, there are two discourses working contiguously. On more than one occasion, the protagonist is so far immersed in her search for feminine vision that she can barely remember the language of her companions.[27] The two discourses can be seen to correspond to Showalter's structure of 'muted' and 'dominant' groups. It is therefore possible to analyse the novel in terms of Atwood's 'double-voiced discourse', as she depicts her protagonist gradually becoming 'silenced' in her inability to find expression through the dominant structure of patriarchy.

The novel is set on an island in one of the lakes of Northern Quebec, where the protagonist has returned in search of her father, a lone forester who disappeared about one month previously. She is accompanied by her partner and another married couple, all of them Canadian nationalists who abhor the 'Bloody fascist pig Yanks' (p. 9) for their excessive capitalism and encroachment on Canadian territory, and are yet ill at ease in the wilderness of the natural world. The narrative follows the protagonist's search for her missing father, which serves as a pretext for her search for her inner self: we observe her gradual submersion into nature and towards mystical vision. Her relationship with her lover and her two other companions (and theirs with one another) are played out alongside this search. Through her changing perception, we are gradually offered differing perspectives on those relationships. The third thread of the novel – and an important part of the protagonist's journey towards self-knowledge – is her attempt to come to terms with her abortion: an act which she now sees as murderous. As the novel progresses, she is increasingly able to confront her own memory of the event, but it is only as she completes her spiritual quest that she is finally able fully to accept her own responsibility for evil as well as good.

Throughout the novel, Atwood emphasises the contrast between the natural, primitive world of the countryside and the cultured 'civilised' world of city life. Like Jean Rhys, she draws a parallel between these two worlds and female and male perceptions of reality respectively. By setting the novel in the Canadian wilderness, she is better able to question and challenge the values of the patriarchal social order, as Rhys did against the background of the Jamaican community. And like Rhys, Atwood builds on the two axes of the male/female, culture/nature dichotomy. Despite their abhorrence of all things American, the protagonist's male companions are increasingly associated with American values: the need to conquer and control, the need to destroy. By contrast, the female protagonist finds affinity with the innocent inhabitants of the natural world – the slaughtered heron they find hanging in the undergrowth.[28] She is further associated with the creativity and resourcefulness of that wilderness. Yet she too must bear some responsibility for evil. An important feature of the novel is that the protagonist initially participates in both dominant and muted structures.

It is, for the most part, the sexual relationships between the four main characters in the novel, together with the protagonist's memories of her relationship with her previous partner, that act as the arena for Atwood's examination of the patriarchal social order. Within these relationships, that social order is still apparent despite the different 'order' offered by the natural world. The male need to dominate is the prevailing feature of both relationships. This is especially true of David and Anna, the married couple who accompany the protagonist. She observes: ' ... Anna was more than sad, she was desperate, her body her only weapon and she was fighting for her life, he was her life, her life was the fight ... ' (p. 154). Their fight is vividly depicted when David forces Anna to pose naked whilst he and Joe film her: '"Come on, we need a naked lady with big tits and a big ass", David said in the same tender voice; I recognized that menacing gentleness, at school it always went before the trick, the punchline' (p. 234). The image of Anna 'in the air, upside down over his shoulder, hair hanging in damp ropes' (p. 135) parallels the earlier image of the dead heron they find in the forest 'hanging upside down by a thin blue nylon rope tied round its feet and looped over a tree branch, its wings fallen open' (p. 115). Thus the women are associated with the innocent, natural world, incapable of combating the power of their male counterparts. Like the heron, their only 'defense was flight, invisibility' (p. 135).

The relationship between the protagonist and Joe, her lover, also offers an interesting insight into this male/female dichotomy. The protagonist's acceptance of the partnership is almost fatalistic. She thinks of choosing a man 'like buying a goldfish or a potted cactus plant, not because you want one in advance but because you happen to be in the store and you see them lined up on the counter' (p. 42). She observes Joe's need for greater commitment on her part with a mixture of ironic indifference and dread: 'Prove your love, they say. You really want to marry me, let me fuck you instead. You really want to fuck, let me marry you instead. As long as there's a victory, some flag I can wave, parade I can have in my head' (p. 87). She refuses his offer of marriage, accepting that her refusal will only heighten his need. Despite her fear of the consequences, her search for her missing father and her search for self increasingly offer her the power to resist the oppression inherent in their relationship and to reassess her own need.

Whilst the protagonist attempts to unravel the mystery behind the disappearance of her father, the reader struggles to make sense of the often conflicting strands of her story about her marriage, her husband and her child. At various points in the novel she relates incidents from her past. She remembers her inability to return home after her wedding and keeping her child hidden from her parents. The image of her brother as he nearly drowned recurs – although the incident took place before she was born. She remembers her husband treating her like an invalid – instead of bride – after their wedding ceremony; she feels herself to have been betrayed by him. The incidents do not form a coherent whole because of course she never actually had a child and she is confusing the imagined wedding with the abortion of her child. It is only once the protagonist achieves greater self-knowledge that the picture finally falls into place. As her dual search – her search for her missing father and her search for self – gradually coalesce she acknowledges that it is not her father's death that concerns her as much as her own.

The protagonist observes her own 'death' – her inability to feel – with increasing anxiety:

> In the night I had wanted rescue, if my body could be made to sense, respond, move strongly enough, some of the red light bulb synapses, blue neurons, incandescent molecules might seep into my head through the closed throat, neck, membrane ... I rehearsed emotions, naming them ... what to feel was like what to wear, you watched others and memorized it. (p. 111)

Her lack of feeling is reflected in her cool analysis of her relationship with Joe, and with David and Anna. She observes them all with detached objectivity, distancing herself still further as she immerses herself in the natural world. The only emotion she feels is 'the fear that I wasn't alive' (p. 111). As we learn later, this fear is largely the result of her inability to confront the intense emotions surrounding her previous lover's betrayal of her and her acquiescence in the abortion of her child.

In her article, 'Margaret Atwood: the surfacing of women's spiritual quest and vision', Carol Christ traces the protagonist's journey in *Surfacing* from innocence and assumed powerlessness through the recognition of her complicity in evil to self-knowledge and the sense of power. Christ argues:

> Her association of power with evil and her dissociation of herself from both reflect a typical female delusion of innocence, which hides her complicity in evil and feeds her false belief that she can do nothing but witness her victimization. In order to regain her power the protagonist must realize that she does not live in a world where only others have power or do evil.[29]

Showalter's notion of a 'double-voiced discourse' in Atwood is perhaps evidenced in the protagonist's acceptance of her participation in the masculine world of such power and evil. Carol Christ identifies the sighting of the slaughtered heron as the incident which disillusions the protagonist of her childhood innocence. On seeing the dead heron, she says: 'I felt a sickening complicity, sticky as glue, blood on my hands, as though I had been there and watched without saying No or doing anything to stop it' (p. 130). Other incidents of childhood cruelty flash through her mind, completing her realisation that, as Christ puts it, 'the path to redemption through childhood [was] closed' (p. 321). The protagonist's acknowledgement of some level of personal guilt leads her to the next stage in reclaiming her power to feel and act.

Redoubling her efforts to unravel the mystery of her father's disappearance, she concentrates on increasing her understanding of his obsession with primitive drawings. In search of one such drawing, she dives deep into the lake. But instead of the drawing she is confronted with her father's dead body, and thus a final acceptance of his death. The incident serves to release her own blocked senses. The image of her dead father corresponds to the memories of her nearly drowned brother, the latter of which she suddenly recognises as a substitute for her memory of her aborted foetus. The protagonist can then recall the correct facts surrounding the other incidents. The man she remembers was her lover, not her husband, there was no wedding, no childbirth – only the abortion, which she had had on his instructions.

Confronted with the correct version of events, the protagonist cannot deny her complicity in an act she sees as intensely evil ' ... it was hiding in me as if in a burrow and instead of granting it sanctuary I let them catch it. I could have said no but I didn't; that made me one of them too, a killer' (p. 145). She interprets her newly acquired self-knowledge as a gift from the gods – pantheistic gods who have succeeded for her where Christianity (centred in the myths and legends of patriarchy) has failed: 'I regretted the nickels I'd taken dutifully for the collection plate ... These gods, here on the shore or in the water, unacknowledged or forgotten, were the only ones who had ever given me anything I needed; and freely' (p. 145).

Guided by her search for her father, the protagonist finds herself moving towards the 'wild zone': the place where matriarchal values outweigh the powerful evil of patriarchy. She says of her father: 'He had discovered new places, new oracles, they were things he was seeing the way I had seen true vision: at the end, after the failure of logic' (p. 145). The notion of the 'failure of logic' is an important one. As the protagonist moves farther into that 'wild zone', she becomes increasingly aware of her own inability to express her thoughts and feelings through language. The language system does not belong to her; does not address her perception of reality. When Joe asks her if she loves him, she says: 'It was the language again, I couldn't use it because it wasn't mine. He must have known what it meant but it was an imprecise word ... ' (p. 106). After her visionary experience in the lake, she is still more acutely aware of the obstructiveness of the supposed logic of language: 'Language divides us into fragments, I wanted to be whole' (p. 146). With her new-found vision, she is able to interpret things without the use of that language system, to differentiate objects by their very essence, their shape and form: 'Sight flowing ahead of me over the ground, eyes filtering the shapes, the names of things fading but their forms and uses remaining, the animals learned what to eat without nouns' (p. 150).

The two discourses become increasingly detached from one another, so that the protagonist has to struggle to communicate with her companions: 'I had to concentrate in order to talk to him, the English words seemed imported, foreign ... ' (p. 150). And she is suddenly acutely aware of the facade created by the dominant discourse, the illusion of power created through words and ideology. Moreover, she recognises the falseness of this image. She no longer feels threatened by the men's need for sexual domination. Her description of David from her position inside the 'wild zone' offers a perfect critique of Showalter's dominant group:

> The power flowed into my eyes, I could see into him, he was an imposter, a pastiche, layers of political handbills, pages from magazines, affiches, verbs and nouns glued on to him and shredding away ... He was infested, garbled, and I couldn't help him, scrape down to where he was true. (p. 152)

Having been offered some guidance by her father, it is to another woman, her dead mother, that the protagonist must look for the completion of her vision. Sensing that this guidance will be found in an old scrap book she had made as a child, she opens it to find pictures she had drawn of 'a woman with a round moon stomach: the baby sitting up inside her gazing out' (p. 158). She decides to conceive a child. Having confronted her complicity in death, she now recognises her potential for creativity. She sees that 'nothing has died, everything is alive, everything is waiting to become alive' (p. 159).

Outside, under a full moon, she conceives a child with Joe. She feels that the sexual power is all hers. And she envisages the birth, this time without the interference of male medical technology:

> This time I will do it by myself, squatting, on old newspapers in a corner alone; or on leaves, dry leaves, a heap of them, that's cleaner. The baby will slip out easily as an egg, a kitten, and I'll lick it off and bite the cord, the blood returning to the ground where it belongs; the moon will be full, pulling. In the morning I will be able to see it: it will be covered with shining fur, a god, I will never teach it any words. (p. 162)

The protagonist becomes still further alienated from her friends. In order to pursue her quest to its final fulfilment, she chooses to stay on alone on the island after their departure. Casting rationality aside – 'there are no longer any rational points of view' – she decides to undergo a final transformation so that she can be completely at one with the wilderness. She carries out a ritual destruction of the effects of the civilised world – pots and pans, clothing, books, etc. 'Everything from history must be eliminated, the circles and the arrogant square pages' (p. 176). She then sets out on her final journey into the 'wild zone', the place beyond language, beyond the Symbolic Order where boundaries cease to exist: 'they are against borders' (p. 180), and where, Christ suggests, 'she experiences mystical identification with all forms of life' (p. 324). Atwood's deliberate omission of full-stops in the subsequent sentences serves to reinforce the protagonist's sense of fluidity, her loss of personal identity: 'In one of the languages there are no nouns, only verbs held for a longer moment/The animals have no need for speech, why talk when you are a word /I lean against a tree, I am tree leaning' (p. 181).

Having achieved the sense of her own creativity and power through her affinity with the natural order, the protagonist returns to the cabin and opens a can of beans, symbolising her return to the modern world. Joe returns once more to find her, and she decides to leave the island with him. But she retains the wisdom she has gained from her entry into the 'wild zone'. She will no longer accept a position of powerlessness within the patriarchal social order: 'This above all, to refuse to be a victim. Unless I can do that I can do nothing. I have to recant, give up the old belief that I am powerless and because of it nothing I can do will ever hurt anyone' (p. 191).

III.

As I explained in the first section of this chapter, Showalter's attempt to find a theoretical basis for feminist criticism stems from her desire to analyse the 'difference' of women's writing. This 'difference', she goes on to argue, is the result of the different experience of female authors from that of male authors. Hence the inadequacy of male critical theory which constitutes 'a concept of creativity, literary history, or literary interpretation based entirely on male experience and put forward as universal' (p. 183). Showalter thus challenges the assumptions of patriarchal liberal humanism, which claims that universal truths are evidenced in literature through the privileged (predominantly male) texts which go to make up the canon of great literature. Showalter argues that such gender blindness inevitably fails to address women's experience. Gynocritics fulfils the need for a theory based on women's experience and analysing women's perception of reality.

In *Feminist Practice and Post-structuralist Theory*, Chris Weedon states:

> ... if women's experience is different from the experience of men, it is important to understand why. Either we can see women as essentially different from men or as socially constituted as different and subject to social relations and processes in different ways to men ... Theory must be able to address women's experience by showing where it comes from and how it relates to material social practices and the power relations that structure them.[30]

The way in which experience is formulated is one of the mechanisms that Showalter fails to address. By arguing for a stable female aesthetic, unchanging across time, Showalter overlooks the means by which an individual's experience is structured through language and thereby through the range of different discourses operative during any historical period. Whilst she acknowledges the importance of the linguistic debate within feminism, her theory does not take account of the vital role language plays in constructing our meanings and our experience. Because her model of dominant and muted groups rests on the notion of two different but unchanging perceptions of reality, Showalter fails to question patriarchy itself – the system whereby power is organised on the basis of biological sex. Instead, she accepts biological difference as having inherent meaning, unchanging across time and therefore 'natural'. The woman author's 'femaleness' can thus be identified as the source of her different writing strategies. Moreover, the meaning of the text can also be found through its author's 'femaleness' and her consequent experience of reality: its meaning can be found outside the text itself.

As Chris Weedon argues, a theory such as Elaine Showalter's can only attempt to 'revalue the feminine which patriarchy devalues' (p. 81). There is no questioning within gynocritics of the means by which certain values have become associated with femininity, or the muted group, and others with masculinity and the corresponding dominant group. Post-structuralist theory proposes a notion of gender as socially produced, through language and through the interaction of different discourses. Thus, no meaning is always already there. Similarly, 'masculinity' and 'femininity' do not pre-exist the discursive processes that give them meaning: they are constructed through those processes.

By refusing to address the problem of the production of meaning, Showalter poses difficulties for the feminist critic. Toril Moi points to the discrepancy between Showalter's notion of the 'feminist critique' and its approach to male writing and the notion of gynocritics with its analysis of female writing. Whilst the feminist critique is a 'historically grounded inquiry which probes the ideological assumptions of literary phenomena', Toril Moi notes that 'this sort of "suspicious" approach to the literary text seems ... largely absent from Showalter's second category'.[31] She continues: ' ... if texts are seen as signifying processes, and both writing and reading grasped as textual production, it is likely that even texts written by women will be subjected to irreverent scrutiny by feminist critics' (p. 78). But instead of studying 'textual production', Showalter advocates that the feminist critic spend her time acquiring a 'close and extensive knowledge of women's texts' (p. 203), each of which will, as Toril Moi says, 'become the transparent medium through which "experience" can be seized' (p. 76).

It would be unfair, however, to accuse Showalter of total ignorance of the social construction of gender difference. As I explained, the reason for her choice of a cultural model of gynocritics is that it 'incorporates ideas about women's body, language and psyche but interprets them in relation to the social contexts in which they occur' (p. 197). Her theory also incorporates an awareness of the existence of a variety of discourses at work at any one time: ' ... women's writing is a "double-voiced discourse" that always embodies the social, literary and cultural heritages of both the muted and dominant' (p. 201).

However, the problem with the theory is that it fails to examine these notions further. Showalter would seem to assume that gender difference was culturally produced at some unspecified point in history and has continued to be produced in exactly the same way ever since. Whilst acknowledging the existence of different discourses, she insists on their division into groups – the dominant and the muted, or masculine and feminine. She does not question the means by which these categories are constructed. As Chris Weedon suggests: ' ... the meanings of feminine and masculine vary from culture to culture and language to language. They even vary between discourses within a particular language, between different feminist discourses for instance, and are subject to historical change' (p. 22). Without acknowledging such historical change, the task of identifying a 'female aesthetic' becomes an extremely difficult one.

An additional problem arises from Showalter's tendency to prioritise gender over other differences – class differences, racial differences and differences in sexuality. Her system of binary oppositions – dominant and muted groups – does not provide a forum in which to examine these variations within feminist discourse. In my reading of *Surfacing*, for example, some of the characteristics which Atwood ascribes to the *nationality* of the Americans are adopted as features of the dominant group by extending the binary oppositions – dominant/muted, masculine/feminine, culture/nature, *American/Canadian*. My reading of *Wide Sargasso Sea* contains an even more glaring 'oversight' by conflating British imperialism with masculinity and the dominant group, whilst assigning Antoinette, Christophine and Tia to the muted group regardless of racial difference. Gayatri Spivak stresses the dangers inherent in much Anglo-American feminist criticism of '[reproducing] the axioms of imperialism'. She states:

> A basically isolationist admiration for the literature of the female subject in Europe and Anglo-American establishes the high feminist norm. It is supported and operated by an information-retrieval approach to 'Third World' literature which often employs a deliberately 'nontheoretical' methodology with self-conscious rectitude.[32]

In her own reading of *Wide Sargasso Sea*, she focusses on the distinction between the interests of the white Creole, Antoinette, and those of the 'native', Christophine. Whilst I have located the 'wild zone' of Rhys's novel as the areas of 'female' experience which cannot be expressed, Spivak suggests that is in the native, Christophine, that *Wide Sargasso Sea* marks with uncanny clarity 'the limits of its own discourse' (p. 271). My gynocritical reading subsumes Christophine's difference into the wider arena of *feminine* difference with little reference to her oppression as a Black woman.

Clearly, gynocriticism is severely flawed by its concentration on gender difference alone, to the extent that it could even be argued to encourage 'distorted' readings of women's writing. Nevertheless, Showalter provides the reader with a set of tools with which to work a feminist reading of novels by women. What her theory of gynocritics encourages is that the reader be alert to issues of gender difference whilst carrying out her reading. Perhaps the same discipline can then be applied to the other differences within feminist discourse. As I hope to have demonstrated in my own readings of *Wide Sargasso Sea* and *Surfacing*, the theory facilitates a different approach to a novel than allowed for by, for example, either traditional liberal humanist criticism, or indeed, by authentic realist feminist criticism. There is no doubt that Showalter's model addresses many of the problems central to women writers and to feminist critics, and although there are many stones left unturned, gynocritics offers a serious challenge to traditional male-dominated schools of thought.

NOTES

1. Dale Spender, *Mothers of the Novel* (Pandora, London, 1986), p. 115.
2. Ellen Moers, *Literary Women* (The Women's Press, London, 1977); Patricia Meyer Spacks, *The Female Imagination: A Literary and Psychological Investigation of Women's Writing* (Allen and Unwin, London, 1976); Nina Baym, *Women's Fiction: A Guide to Novels by and about Women in America 1820–1970* (Cornell University Press, London, 1978).
3. Elaine Showalter, 'Feminist criticism in the wilderness', *Critical Inquiry*, Winter, 1981.
4. The reader should note the relationship between this notion and Kate Millet's sexual politics (see Chapter One).
5. Among others, Baym examines the work of Catherine Sedgwick, Maria McIntosh, Susan Warner and Maria Cummins.
6. Ellen Moers, *Literary Women, op. cit.*
7. Willa Cather, *The Song of the Lark* (1915), cited in Moers, *op. cit.*
8. Patricia Meyer Spacks, *op. cit.*
9. In Mary Jacobus (ed.) *Women Writing and Writing About Women*, (Croom Helm, London, 1979) pp. 22–42; and *Critical Inquiry*, Winter, 1981.
10. Sandra Gilbert and Susan Gubar, *The Madwoman in the Attic* (Yale University Press, New Haven 1979). See Chapter Four.

11. See Chapter Five for an examination of the importance of language in discussions of gender.
12. Carolyn Burke, *Report from Paris*, p. 844, cited in Showalter, *op. cit.*, p. 191.
13. Mary Jacobus, 'The difference of view', pp. 10–22, in Jacobus (ed.) *op. cit.*, pp. 12–13.
14. See discussion of Lacanian psychoanalysis in Chapters Five and Six and Glossary for explanation.
15. Nancy Chodorow, *The Reproduction of Mothering: Psychoanalysis and the Sociology of Gender* (1978), cited in Showalter, *op. cit.*
16. Edwin Ardener, 'Belief and the problem of women', in Shirley Ardener (ed.) *Perceiving Women* (Malaby Press, London, 1975).
17. Shirley Ardener (ed.), *Defining Females: The Nature of Women in Society* (Croom Helm, London, 1978).
18. Claude Levi-Strauss, *Les Structures Elementaires de la Parenté* (Mouton, Paris, 1967), cited in Edwin Ardener, 1975, *op. cit.*, p. 5.
19. Showalter's notion of the 'wild zone' clearly bears some resemblance to Kristeva's 'semiotic' – the point into which the feminine is repressed (see Chapter Five). This overlap illustrates the limitations of dividing feminist criticism into categories according to the nationality of the critic. It also reinforces our suggestion in the Introduction that different forms of feminist criticism often relate to rather than compete with other positions.
20. Jean Rhys, *Wide Sargasso Sea* (Penguin, Harmondsworth, 1968).
21. Charlotte Brontë, *Jane Eyre* (Penguin, Harmondsworth 1982).
22. Louis James, *Jean Rhys* (Longman, London, 1978), p. 51.
23. See Elaine Millard's discussion of Luce Irigaray's directive that in order to 'access' the feminine it is necessary to disrupt the simple oppositions on which theoretical systems are founded (Chapter Five, p. 159).
24. Barbara Babcock, *The Reversible World: Symbolic Inversion in Art and Society* (Cornell University Press, London, 1978), p. 14.
25. Dale Spender, *Man Made Language* (Routledge and Kegan Paul, London, 1980), p. 97.
26. Margaret Atwood, *Surfacing* (Virago, London, 1984).
27. Lynne Pearce also discusses the protagonist's relation to language and discourse, but from a Marxist–psychoanalytic point of view, in Chapter Six.
28. Atwood's use of the natural world and particularly images of birds to represent women further illustrates Ellen Moers suggestion that these are themes common to much women's writing.
29. Carol Christ, 'Margaret Atwood: the surfacing of women's spiritual quest and vision' in *Signs*, Winter, 1976, p. 320.
30. Chris Weedon, *Feminist Practice and Post-structuralist Theory* (Blackwell, Oxford, 1987), p. 8.
31. Toril Moi, *Sexual/Textual Politics* (Methuen, London, 1985), p. 76.
32. Gayatri Chakravorty Spivak, 'Three women's texts and a critique of imperialism', in Henry Louis Gates (ed.) *'Race', Writing and Difference* (University of Chicago, Chicago, 1985).

4

The Anxiety of Authorship

Sue Spaull and Elaine Millard

Sandra Gilbert and Susan Gubar: *The Madwoman in the Attic*
Susan Gubar: '"The Blank Page" and female creativity'
Angela Carter: *The Magic Toyshop*
Alice Walker: *The Color Purple*

I

Sandra Gilbert and Susan Gubar's study *The Madwoman in the Attic* was first published in 1979.[1] Alongside Ellen Moers' *Literary Women* (1976) and Elaine Showalter's *A Literature of their Own* (1977), it was one of the first major studies of women writers which set the course for Anglo-American feminist criticism, whose main thrust was to be its concern to identify a distinct *female* literary tradition. All three works examine the ways in which society shapes women's perspective of the world, together with the style and subject matter of their writing. Yet despite the similarities between these works and with Showalter's later theoretical writing, the theorist's respective approaches to this female literary tradition show many clear divergences and differences from one another.[2] Whilst they all address themselves to the problem of identifying the 'difference' of women's writing, and the social reasons for that difference, the conclusions they reach, or rather, the emphasis within those conclusions, are surprisingly different.

As well as examining Gilbert and Gubar's *The Madwoman in the Attic* in this chapter, we shall be discussing a second article by Susan Gubar called '"The Blank Page" and the issues of female creativity'.[3] In both these works, the authors begin by addressing themselves to a society and culture which are essentially patriarchal.

Within this context, their examination of Western literary history and of men's and women's respective positions in relation to that literary history takes psychoanalysis as its starting point.[4]

The Madwoman in the Attic opens with the question: 'Is a pen a metaphorical penis?' (p. 3). The question is central to Gilbert and Gubar's discussion of feminist poetics. In order to establish the existence of a female literary tradition, the authors first address themselves to the position of women writers *vis-à-vis* their male counterparts. An essential part of this discussion centres on the notion that creativity is inextricably linked with male sexuality. Gilbert and Gubar stress that 'the patriarchal notion that the writer "fathers" his text just as God fathered the world is and has been all-pervasive in Western literary civilization' (p. 4). With supporting evidence from a wealth of male writers and theorists over the centuries, the authors then elaborate the pen/penis metaphor still further. They quote Edward Said's suggestion 'that the unity or integrity of the text is maintained by a series of genealogical connections: author-text, beginning-middle-end, text-meaning, reader-interpretation and so on. Underneath all these is the imagery of succession, of paternity or hierarchy' (p. 5).[5] They argue that the power of a man's pen 'like his penis's power, is not just the ability to generate life but the power to create a posterity to which he lays claim' (p. 6). So the writer, through writing, has a stake in the literary future. And further, as the 'owner' of his text, he is, by extension, the owner of the 'subjects' of the text – the characters, scenes and events that he has created.[6] These notions of paternity, authority and ownership form an essential background to Gilbert and Gubar's ensuing discussion of female creativity.

Extending their original question, they ask: 'If the pen is a metaphorical penis, with what organ can females generate texts?' (p. 7). They argue that it has been no accident that the pen has been defined as a male tool, encouraging, and even perhaps establishing the notion that it is both *physiologically* and sociologically impossible for women to write. If creativity is an extension of male sexuality, then clearly women do not possess the power to write.

Gilbert and Gubar argue that women have been forced into a position where they must remain passive. They 'exist only to be acted on by men' (p. 8). Returning to notions of ownership and authority, Gilbert and Gubar stress the power of language and the printed word: '[The male author's] literary creations are his possessions, his property. Having defined them in language and thus generated them, he owns them, controls them, encloses them on the printed page' (p. 12). Other men can challenge this 'authority' by generating their own fictions – by 'talking back' with a different version of 'reality'. Gilbert and Gubar accept Harold Bloom's psychoanalytic theory as a useful model of this process.[7] Bloom compares the relationship between the male author and his precursors with the father-son relationship as defined by Freud. Every writer must take part in a literary Oedipal struggle in order to overcome the power of his forefathers, ' ... a man can only become a poet by somehow invalidating his poetic father' (p. 47). But women, it has been argued, lack the power – the pen/penis – to challenge the fictions of their male precursors. There is no place for women in this Freudian power struggle. Hence the images of women created by male writers have taken on greater 'authority'; their female successors unwilling or unable to challenge them.

Reworking Harold Bloom's ideas still further, Gilbert and Gubar identify Milton as the poet who has the supreme power in this patriarchal literary order. They suggest that: 'In an extraordinarily distinctive way, therefore, Milton is for women what Harold Bloom ... calls "the great Inhibitor, the Sphinx who strangles even strong imaginations in their cradles"' (p. 191). It is Milton, then, in *Paradise Lost*, who 'most notably tells to women ... the story of [her] secondness, her otherness, and how that otherness leads inexorably to her demonic anger, her sin...' (p. 191).

Gilbert and Gubar argue that 'women in patriarchal societies have historically been reduced to mere properties, to characters and images imprisoned in male texts because generated solely ... by male expectations and designs' (p. 12). Male writers have thus 'enclosed' women on the printed page. Elaborating this metaphor, Gilbert and Gubar continue:

> As a creation 'penned' by man ... woman has been 'penned up' or 'penned in'. As a sort of 'sentence' man has spoken, she has herself been 'sentenced': fated, jailed for he has both 'indited' her and 'indicted' her. As a thought he has 'framed', she has been both 'framed' (enclosed) in his texts, glyphs, graphics, and 'framed-up' (found guilty, found wanting) in his cosmologies. (p. 13)[8]

This notion that women are forced into a position of passivity in the process of literary production is also the theme of Susan

Gubar's article '"The Blank Page" and issues of female creativity'. She argues that 'female sexuality is often identified with textuality' (p. 294) and further that:

> [The] model of the pen-penis writing on the virgin page participates in a long tradition identifying the author as a male who is primary and the female as his passive creation – a secondary object lacking autonomy endowed with often contradictory meaning but denied intentionality. Clearly this tradition excludes women from the creation of culture, even as it reifies her as an artifact with culture. (p. 295)

In both the *Madwoman in the Attic* and '"The Blank Page" and issues of female creativity', Gilbert and Gubar compare the male act of imprisoning the female in his writing with the act of killing. He both silences the female, and 'stills' her – in essence, he 'kills' her (MW, p. 14). Gilbert and Gubar suggest that this proves a further link between the pen and 'maleness', just as the human male's superiority over the female has traditionally been linked to his ability to hunt and kill. They further suggest that woman has been 'killed into a "perfect" image of herself' by successive male authors (p. 15). That perfect image is, in effect, a male dream of female perfection. As such, Gilbert and Gubar argue, it represents 'the most pernicious image male authors have ever imposed upon literary women' (p. 20). It is the image of the Angel which Gilbert and Gubar find proliferating in male writing, together with its 'necessary opposite and double' – the image of the monstrous woman (p. 17). Both images, it will be shown, are used to a similar end by male writers. And the profound effects of these images on women and their writing are central to Gilbert and Gubar's analysis of the female literary tradition.

The images of Angel and Monster have both been used, Gilbert and Gubar argue, to further the male writer's attempts to *control* the female subjects of his texts, and, by conclusion, women themselves (including women writers). Many feminists and anthropologists have shown that the male need to control women arises from his fear of her 'Otherness'.[9] Denied a position within the social order, denied the autonomy and the subjectivity represented by the pen, Gilbert and Gubar stress that woman inevitably achieves a position of symbolic ambiguity. She is excluded from culture and because of her consequent 'difference', she 'becomes herself an embodiment of just those extremes of mysterious and intransigent Otherness which culture confronts with worship or fear, love or loathing. As "Ghost, fiend, and angel, fairy, witch and sprite, she mediates between the male artist and the Unknown. . ."' (pp. 19–20).[10]

Gilbert and Gubar trace the image of the Angel from the Middle Ages through Dante, Milton and Goethe. As the Angel, woman is wholly passive and essentially self-less: a complement and comfort to man. The image reaches its most extreme form in nineteenth century literature, where the association between man's writing and the act of killing is particularly appropriate: '. . .in the severity of her selflessness, as well as in the extremity of her alienation from ordinary fleshly life, this nineteenth century angel-woman becomes not just a memento of otherness but actually a memento mori . . . an "Angel of Death"' (p. 24).[11]

At the opposite extreme is the image of the Monster. Frequently, the two images may exist within one character: 'the monster may not only be concealed *behind* the angel, she may actually turn out to reside *within* (or in the lower half of) the angel' (p. 29). These contradictory images of woman created by man encapsulate his ambivalence towards female sexuality. They represent the 'mythic masks' he has 'fastened over [woman's] human face to lessen [his] dread of her "inconstancy"' (p. 17). The images also represent man's ambivalence towards his own physicality, and Gilbert and Gubar reiterate Simone de Beauvoir's suggestion that: '. . . woman has been made to represent all of man's ambivalent feelings about his inability to control his own physical existence, his own birth and death. As the Other, woman comes to represent the contingency of life that is made to be destroyed' (p. 34).[12]

Just as the passivity of the image of the Angel, devoid of generative power, must inevitably act as a deterrent for women wishing to write, so too the image of the Monstrous woman, incorporating as it does the male dread of female autonomy, serves to reinforce the notion that creativity is the domain of men: '. . . as a representative of otherness, [woman] incarnates the damning otherness of the flesh rather than the inspiring otherness of the spirit, expressing what . . . men consider the angelic humility and "dullness" for which she was designed' (p. 28). Thus, the female freak becomes a 'powerfully monitory' image for any woman wishing to write.

It is against this background that women have attempted to find their position in the literary order. Returning to Harold Bloom's

Freudian model of literary paternity, it becomes clear that women's position *vis-à-vis* literary history is very different from that of their male counterparts. From a feminist perspective, Bloom's model raises more questions than it answers. The question Gilbert and Gubar confront is 'where does a woman writer "fit in" to the overwhelmingly and essentially male literary history Bloom describes?' (p. 48). The answer, of course, is that women do *not* 'fit in'. And it is this problem which forms the centre of Gilbert and Gubar's discussion of feminist poetics. How do women negotiate their position within (or outside) the male literary tradition? And what is their relationship with their female precursors?

Having established that a woman writer's position in relation to her male precursors is a very different one from that of her male counterpart, Gilbert and Gubar go on to examine the nature of that difference. They describe a man's reaction to his forefathers as an 'anxiety of influence': in order to establish his own position as a writer, he must first do battle with his literary fathers; he must assert his 'authority' over their achievements; his style and subject matter over theirs. They then describe a woman writer's reaction to literary history not as an 'anxiety of influence' but as an 'anxiety of authorship'. Because she has been 'enclosed' by male definitions of herself and her own potential, the woman writer doubts not only *what* she writes, but her ability to write at all.

For twentieth century women writers, the position is somewhat easier. Gilbert and Gubar suggest that contemporary writers will usually seek out a *female* precursor in order to overcome the worst effects of the patriarchal literary tradition against which they are defined. However, even in doing so, twentieth century women must come to terms with the 'anxiety of authorship' imbibed in the writing of their 'motherly precursors'. Gilbert and Gubar argue, therefore, that before any woman can write, she must first come to terms with these male images of herself: 'Before the woman writer can journey through the looking glass toward literary autonomy ... she must come to terms with the images on the surface of the glass' (p. 16). A woman must therefore struggle against her own socialisation, she must 'battle not against her [male] precursor's reading of the world but against his reading of *her*' (p. 49).

Because of this struggle, the 'anxiety of authorship' is, Gilbert and Gubar argue, one of the hallmarks of female creativity. In our reading of *The Color Purple*, we will examine Alice Walker's work in relation to Harriet Beecher Stowe's novel, *Uncle Tom's Cabin*, in an attempt to demonstrate Walker's use of her female precursors, because, as Gilbert and Gubar argue, women will frequently find a female precursor in order to validate their own artistic endeavours. Yet, despite this, Gilbert and Gubar suggest that all women writers are likely to have a negative experience of their own gender, experiencing it as a 'painful obstacle, or even a debilitating inadequacy' (p. 50). Gilbert and Gubar's theory of the 'difference' of women's writing – their 'feminist poetics' – centres on the 'inferiorization' shared by all women writers. Women's creativity is profoundly affected by a variety of factors: their alienation from their male precursors, their need to find their female precursors, their 'dread of the patriarchal authority of art', and inherently 'unfeminine' nature of creativity (p. 50). Gilbert and Gubar stress that whilst positive role models may have helped many contemporary women writers, their eighteenth and nineteenth century predecessors had to undertake an enormous struggle in order to overcome their anxiety of authorship. Hence, 'women writers participate in a quite different literary subculture from that inhabited by male writers' (p. 50).

In examining the female literary subculture further, Gilbert and Gubar make a number of observations. Virginia Woolf argued that before women could write they must 'kill' the 'angel in the house' – and, by extension, the angel's opposite – the monster.[13] For, 'whether she is a passive angel or an active monster ... the woman writer feels herself to be literally or figuratively crippled by the debilitating alternatives her culture offers her' (p. 57). But what Gilbert and Gubar observe is the way in which women frequently 'use and misuse' male literary traditions (p. 80). Far from destroying the male images of themselves, those images of angels and monsters proliferate in writing by women too. Yet the important difference lies in the messages conveyed by their texts:

> Women from Jane Austen and Mary Shelley to Emily Brontë and Emily Dickinson produced literary works that are in some sense palimpsestic, works whose surface designs conceal or obscure deeper, less accessible (and less socially acceptable) levels of meaning. Thus these authors managed the difficult task of achieving true female literary authority by simultaneously conforming to and subverting patriarchal literary standards. (p. 73)

It was in this way women were to overcome their 'anxiety of authorship'. But a further characteristic of their writing has been their obsessive interest in the limited options offered them by society. Gilbert and Gubar thus describe the 'oddity' of women's writing as the result of their struggle to transcend the anxiety of authorship. By working within a male literary tradition, yet working to subvert it, Gilbert and Gubar argue that women are 'enacting a uniquely female process of revision and redefinition that necessarily caused them to seem "odd"'. (p. 73)[14]

One of the most important assertions of Gilbert and Gubar's feminist poetics is that most women's writing contains a hidden story, and that that hidden story represents 'woman's quest for self-definition' (p. 76). They argue that 'in publicly presenting acceptable facades for private and dangerous visions, women writers have long used a wide range of tactics to obscure but not obliterate their most subversive impulses' (p. 74). In '"The Blank Page" and the issues of female creativity', Susan Gubar examines one such story. Gubar's article is centred around a discussion of Isak Dinesen's short story, 'The Blank Page'. Gubar summarises the story thus: a Carmelite order of nuns grow flax to manufacture the most exquisite linen in Portugal. The linen is so fine it is used for bridal sheets in neighbouring royal houses. After the wedding night, the sheet is publicly displayed to attest to the virginity of the princess. It is then reclaimed by the convent where the central piece of stained sheet 'which bore witness to the honour of a royal bride' is mounted, framed and hung in a long gallery with a plate identifying the name of the princess. Female pilgrims who journey to the convent view these sheets. But they are especially interested by one blank, snow white sheet with a nameless plate.

Commenting on this story, Gubar makes several points which are pertinent to the ideas behind the feminist poetics she and Gilbert develop in *The Madwoman in the Attic*. One of the most important is the link between female sexuality and textuality. Just as women are imprisoned by male images of themselves in men's writing, so here there is little distinction between woman and the text; she has used her own body in the creation of art. Gubar argues that the framed, bloodied sheets in the gallery illustrate two important points about the links between the female anatomy and creativity. The first is that many women experience their own bodies as the only available medium for their art, inheriting that part of a male literary tradition which has focussed on women as its primary subject matter.[15] The second is that 'one of the primary and most resonant metaphors provided by the female body is blood' (p. 296). This latter point is clearly linked to the notion that women are 'killed' into art by male writers. Again, Isak Dinesen has accepted part of the tradition of male literature. Like her male precursors, her work 'feels like the destruction of the female body' (p. 302). Gubar argues: 'If artistic creativity is likened to biological creativity the terror of inspiration for women is experienced quite literally as the terror of being entered, deflowered . . .' (p. 302). Further, the sheets acknowledge and accept woman's passivity. The bloodstains, by attesting to the princesses' virginity, affirm that the women are valuable objects for exchange between father and husband: 'The framed stained sheets imply, then, that all the royal princesses have been "framed" into telling the same story, namely the story of their acquiescence as objects of exchange' (p. 301).

But more important than the bloodied sheets in the nuns' gallery is the single blank sheet. It is through this blank sheet that Dinesen is able to subvert the patriarchal literary order, overturning the traditional association of women with blankness, nullity and absence. Gubar states that: '. . . in terms of the patriarchal identification of women with blankness and passivity . . . Dinesen's blank page becomes radically subversive. . . . Not a sign of innocence or purity or passivity, this blank page is a mysterious but potent act of resistance' (p. 305). She argues that the fact that the sheet has been displayed means that the anonymous princess has forced some sort of acknowledgement of her act, of her autonomy. Significantly, the absence of any blood on that sheet – on a literal level – 'may mean any number of alternative scripts for women' (p. 305). Within Dinesen's story it raises the questions: was the princess not a virgin? did she run away and retain her virginity? was her husband impotent? and so on. Hence, 'the interpretation of the sheet seems as impenetrable as the anonymous princess herself' (p. 305). What is important is not that the mystery of the blank sheet be unravelled, but precisely that it refuses explanation and therefore refuses enclosure. Gubar says '. . . the blank page contains all stories in no story, just as silence contains all potential sound and white contains all colour' (p. 305).

By refusing to write what she is expected to write, woman can 'make her statement'. In 'The Blank Page' that statement is particularly bold since Dinesen chooses to expose one of the fallacies of patriarchy, namely that woman is a 'lack' or an 'absence'. In Dinesen's short story, Gubar argues, 'blankness ... is an act of defiance, a dangerous and risky refusal to certify purity' (p. 306).

If we return to *The Madwoman in the Attic*, we can see that there too Gilbert and Gubar focus on women's 'refusal to certify purity' as an essential feature of the female literary tradition. In *The Madwoman in the Attic*, the authors continue to stress the way in which women writers 'have been especially concerned with assaulting and revising, deconstructing and reconstructing those images of [themselves] inherited from male literature ...' (p. 76). The dual images of angel and monster thus become important as an analogy for the contradiction between the 'publicly acceptable facade' presented by women and their 'private dangerous visions' (p. 74). Through their writing, women express their frustration at the limited roles assigned them by society. Gilbert and Gubar argue that they 'almost obsessively create characters who enact their own, covert authorial anger' (p. 77). By re-writing the monstrous image of themselves created by their male precursors, women thus give expression to feelings central to the female experience. 'It is significant, then, that when the speaker of "The Other Side of a Mirror" looks into her glass the woman that she sees is a madwoman, "wild/With more than womanly despair", the monster that she fears she really is rather than the angel she has pretended to be' (p. 77).

One story particularly illustrative of Gilbert and Gubar's theory of feminist poetics is Charlotte Perkins Gilman's short story 'The Yellow Wallpaper'.[16] Gilbert and Gubar claim that Gilman's story 'seems to tell *the* story that all literary women would tell if they could speak their "speechless woe"' (p. 89). The story, written in 1890, describes the experiences of a woman suffering from a 'severe postpartum psychosis', or nervous breakdown. Her husband, who is also her physician, is treating her with methods used by the famous nerve specialist, S. Weir Mitchell, in treating Gilman herself. He has confined her to a large garret room in an 'ancestral hall' he has rented and forbidden her to read or write until she recovers. The cure worse than the disease, the protagonist's condition can only decline. She comments that she feels it would help her to write something, but locked away in a room that was once a nursery 'she is literally locked away from creativity' (MW, p. 90).

The most important feature of the nursery room is its wallpaper: sickly yellow paper with an asymmetric pattern which both disgusts and fascinates the woman. Gilbert and Gubar suggest that the paper 'surrounds the narrator like an inexplicable text, censorious and overwhelming as her physician husband, haunting as the "hereditary estate" in which she is trying to survive' (p. 90). Underneath the pattern there lies a further formation: the wallpaper is barred, and trapped behind these bars is a woman desperate to escape. Gilbert and Gubar suggest that the figure is 'concealed behind what corresponds . . . to the facade of the patriarchal text'. They argue that as the narrator 'sinks more deeply into what the world calls madness', the 'terrifying implications' of both the figure and the wallpaper begin to haunt the ancestral mansion. The 'yellow smell' of the paper begins to permeate the whole house and so too the trapped woman begins to creep through the house into the garden and along the road (p. 90).

Gilbert and Gubar argue that the figure creeping behind the wallpaper 'is both the narrator and the narrator's double' (p. 91). By the end of the story, the narrator facilitates the figure's escape from behind the wallpaper – her escape from her 'textual/architectural confinement'. And Gilbert and Gubar stress that there is clearly more to the tale than mere madness. 'More significant are the madwoman's own imagining and creations, mirages of health and freedom with which her author endows her like a fairy godmother showering gold on a sleeping heroine' (p. 91). The figure from behind the wallpaper creeps away to freedom. The protagonist notes 'I have watched her sometimes a way off in the open country creeping as fast as a cloud shadow in a high wind'. Gilbert and Gubar compare the movement of that cloud with 'the progress of nineteenth century literary women out of the texts defined by patriarchal poetics into the open spaces of their own authority' (p. 91). For the woman writer, and for Gilman in particular, it represents the 'flight from dis-ease into health' (p. 91).[17]

Their reading of Charlotte Perkin Gilman's story illustrates the essential characteristics which Gilbert and Gubar locate in much women's writing and which, they argue, form the basis of a female literary subculture. Just as Gilman's protagonist and her trapped double express Gilman's own frustration and anger at the ways in which patriarchy stifles women's creativity, so too many other women writers 'reflect the literal reality of their own confinement. Recording their own distinctively female experience, they are secretly working through and within the conventions of literary texts to define their own lives' (p. 87).

II

Sandra Gilbert and Susan Gubar focus their attention on nineteenth century women writers, for whom, they suggest, the 'anxiety of authorship' is particularly acute. *The Madwoman in the Attic* contains a number of readings of nineteenth century novels by women. In each reading, they demonstrate the way in which the female author has 'used and misused' male literary traditions. If we turn to Angela Carter's novel, *The Magic Toyshop*, it is quite possible to work a similar analysis, despite the fact that the novel – whose first publication date was 1967 – falls outside the period studied by Gilbert and Gubar.[18] Angela Carter almost certainly uses male writing strategies more self-consciously than her nineteenth century precursors. She writes: 'Reading is just as creative an activity as writing and most intellectual development depends on new readings of old texts. I am all for putting new wine in old bottles, especially if the pressure of the new wine makes the old bottles explode'.[19] Yet there are obvious similarities between their respective modes of expression. The notion of 'putting new wine in old bottles' is clearly analogous with Gilbert and Gubar's idea that women enact 'a uniquely female process of revision and redefinition' (MW, p. 73) and that they are 'especially concerned with assaulting and revising, deconstructing and reconstructing those images of women inherited from male literature' (MW, p. 76).

Angela Carter has described herself as being in the 'demythologizing business' (NFL, p. 70). Many of her novels, especially her early novels, including *The Magic Toyshop*, are steeped in mythology, and have a strong psychoanalytic bent. Carter has suggested that 'the literary past, the myth and folklore and so on, are a vast repository of outmoded lies' (p. 74). In other words, they serve to reinforce existing patriarchal structures. Pauline Palmer suggests that Carter, in *The Magic Toyshop*, uses mythology and psycho-analytic materials to 'represent the self-perpetuating and closed nature of patriarchal structures and institutions'.[20] To a large extent, then, Carter is using the tools of a male literary tradition in order to represent woman's imprisonment within that patriarchal structure. She attempts to subvert traditional patriarchal themes and imagery in fairly subtle and covert ways.[21]

The novel can be compared in a variety of ways with the nine-teenth century stories of 'enclosure and escape' discussed by Gilbert and Gubar. The setting itself resembles the confines of Bluebeard's castle, an impression reinforced when Melanie discovers a severed hand in the kitchen drawer. The 15-year-old girl's first sighting of the house and shop places it firmly in a nightmare world of myth and folklore.

> Between a failed, boarded-up jewellers and a grocer's ... was a dark cavern of a shop, so dimly lit one did not at first notice it as it bowed its head under the tenement above. In the cave could be seen the vague outlines of a rocking horse and the sharper scarlet of its flaming nostrils... (p. 39)

Here Melanie, like her Aunt Margaret, is to remain trapped, notching off the weeks by the appearance of the green banded china each Sunday, and on Monday wishing she could use the little bridge on her willow-patterned plate to 'run away from her Uncle Philip's house to where the flowering trees were' (p. 74). And not only are Melanie and Margaret physically trapped: they are also spiritually trapped into conventional female roles.

The most significant image in *The Magic Toyshop* is that of the puppet: an image especially pertinent to a feminist analysis of the novel. Within the power structure of the toyshop, women's position is equal to that of the puppets. Uncle Philip, the toymaker, takes on the role of a particularly despotic patriarch, whilst Melanie, his orphaned niece, and Margaret, his wife, are reduced to positions of terrified powerlessness whenever he is present (and usually when he is not).

In addition, throughout the novel visual images of the women are particularly important. In the opening section, before the death of her parents, Melanie spends hours posing in front of the mirror:

> She also posed in attitudes, holding things. Pre-Raphaelite, she

combed out her long, black hair ... *À la* Toulouse Lautrec, she dragged her hair sluttishly across her face ... she contrived a pale, smug Cranach Venus with a bit of net curtain. ... After she read Lady Chatterley's Lover, she secretly picked forget-me-nots and stuck them in her pubic hair. (p. 2)

Significantly, the poses she takes up are derived from male images of women. Her subjectivity has been shaped by those images. The novel traces Melanie's awakening sexuality along with her adolescent yearnings: 'Since she was 13, when her periods began, she felt she was pregnant with herself bearing the slowing ripening embryo of Melanie-grown-up inside herself for a gestation time the length of which she was precisely not aware' (p. 20).

Her quest for self-definition is at the centre of the novel. Yet that quest is strictly limited by the roles and potential assigned to her by her cultural heritage, her socialisation and the overbearingly patriarchal world she inhabits. Looking into the mirror, the images she sees are those previously inscribed there by male authors, painters and women's magazine writers. The boundaries of Melanie's adolescent imaginings are thus marked by thoughts of her future roles as lover, wife and mother.

Immediately she enters the confines of her uncle's house, Melanie's loss of autonomy becomes apparent. Recognising her powerlessness, she feels herself to be like one of her uncle's puppets: 'She was a wind-up putting-away doll, clicking through its programmed movements. Uncle Philip might have made her over, already. She was without volition of her own' (p. 76). Her feelings of powerlessness intensify, in relation to both her Uncle Philip and her cousin Finn. She no longer has a mirror in which to see herself, a further factor contributing to her loss of subjectivity. 'She was seized with panic, remembering that she had not seen her own face for so long' (p. 103). Control of her identity is taken over by Finn and Uncle Philip. She begins to see herself as she is seen by others. Discovering the spy-hole into her room from Finn's, she realises that 'all the time, someone was watching her' (p. 109). Later, she sees the picture Finn has painted of her through the spy-hole, undressing: an image of an idealised, pale, pure virginal girl, which is how he sees her and 'not precisely as she saw herself' (p. 154). She recognizes herself, uncannily, in one of her uncle's toys on her first day in the shop: '... a sylphide in a fountain of white tulle. She had long, black hair down to the waist of her tight bodice' (p. 67). Finally, she must literally fit the image Uncle Philip has of her, forced to take part in one of his puppet shows alongside his puppets. He complains: '"I wanted my Leda to be a little girl. Your tits are too big"' (p. 143). Melanie is thus denied her own sexuality. She must taken on the role of angel – passive and virginal.

Examining the 'cultural production of femininity', Palmer states that Carter focusses on 'one of the roles conventionally allocated to woman in a patriarchal culture – object of exchange' (p. 183). Within the patriarchal social order, women become tokens in the battle for power between men. The patriarchal world of the toy-shop is essentially violent. Uncle Philip himself exudes violence: 'His authority was stifling', 'His size shocked her...', 'How could she, Melanie, have ever guessed that her Uncle would be a monster with a voice so loud she was afraid it would bring the roof down and bury them all?' (p. 77). Carter's analysis of the struggle for power between the younger male, Finn, and the older patriarch is clearly Freudian: Finn undertakes an Oedipal struggle in an attempt to displace Uncle Philip's authority. The struggle is inherently violent, culminating in Philip angrily sending Finn crashing down onto the stage from the heights of the puppet theatre during one of his performances. But the most important manifestation of male violence is in relation to women and particularly in acts of sexual violence.

Melanie becomes the 'object of exchange' in the power struggle between Philip and Finn. Throughout the novel, there are a number of 'rape' scenes and violent sexual acts. One of Melanie's first encounters with Finn is heavy with sexual overtones. 'She could see the pointed tip of his tongue between his teeth' (p. 45), and she is immediately aware of the predatory threat encapsulated in his maleness: 'He was a tawny lion poised for the kill – and was she the prey?'. On both this occasion and later in the pleasure garden when Finn first kisses her, Melanie's romantic notions of heterosexual love rapidly vanish in the face of the harsh reality of the inherently destructive nature of male sexual desire: 'She remembered the lover made up out of books and poems she had dreamed of all summer; he crumpled like the paper he was made of before this insolent, off-hand, terrifying maleness, filling the room with its reek' (p. 45).

The scene in the pleasure garden is indeed a 'rape' scene, during which Finn's sexual desire is clearly part and parcel of his desire to submit Melanie entirely to his will. Her reaction, far from sexual arousal, is one of disgust and horror: 'Finn inserted his tongue between her lips, searching tentatively for her own tongue inside her mouth. The moment consumed her. She choked and struggled, beating her fists against him, convulsed with horror at this sensual and intimate connection, this rude encroachment on her physical privacy, this humiliation' (p. 106).

The final rape scene is Uncle Philip's show of Leda and the swan. This is preceded by the 'rehearsal' which Philip suggests Finn should carry out with Melanie. Carter's use of the Leda story once again demonstrates her awareness of mythology's role in reinforcing patriarchal structures and the conventional relationship between the sexes. In accordance with the female literary tradition outlined by Gilbert and Gubar, Carter reworks patriarchal mythology in order to illustrate her female character's repression. In the two Leda scenes – the rehearsal and the final performance – both the men participate in attempts to 'rape' Melanie. During the first of these, where Finn takes the part of the swan, Melanie awaits Finn's action passively, with bated breath, emotionless and utterly subdued: 'They lay together on the bare, splintered boards. There was no time any more. And no Melanie, either' (p. 149).

It is Finn who prevents intercourse taking place; significantly not out of consideration for Melanie, but because of his realisation that Uncle Philip has orchestrated the whole situation: it is his will that he, Finn, should rape Melanie. 'He's pulled our strings as if we were his puppets, and there I was, all ready to touch you up just as he wanted' (p. 152). The sexual act is thus even further removed from Melanie's wild romantic imaginings. She is once again forced to shift her level of consciousness to acknowledge that Finn's act would have been one of power and violence, not one of love and tenderness. She is forced to accept his displacement of her notion of 'making love' with the aggressive act of 'fucking'.

The second Leda scene is far more violent, symbolising Uncle Philip's continuing position as the supreme patriarch. The swan he has created, whilst absurd and cumbersome, is also terrifyingly phallic with its 'long neck made of rubber' which 'bent and swayed with an unnerving life of its own' (p. 167). Far from having to act the part of Leda, Melanie is indeed subsumed by the huge swan which 'made a lumpish jump forward and settled on her loins ...

The gilded beak dug deeply into the soft flesh.... The obscene
swan had mounted her' (p. 167).

In further defiance of Philip, Finn destroys the swan during the
night. Melanie's position is thus a contradictory one. Whilst she
feels superior to Finn and repulsed by him, she is also grateful for
the protection he offers her from her uncle. As Pauline Palmer
points out: 'As is typical of woman in patriarchal society, she is pres-
sured to seek refuge from one man in the arms of another' (p. 187).
Melanie thus gradually resigns herself to the prospect of sex and
marriage with Finn: she accepts the roles of lover, wife and
mother assigned her by society. Melanie's enclosure within patriarchal structures is thus complete, and Finn has finally 'won' her
from his Uncle Philip. In Carter's vision of this patriarchal nightmare world, it would appear that there is no escape.

> She knew they would get married one day and live together all their
> lives and there would always be pervasive squalor and dirt and mess
> and shabbiness, always, forever and forever. And babies crying and
> washing to be done and toast burning all the rest of her life. And
> never any glamour or romance or charm. (p. 177)

But finally, we must turn our attention to the second woman in
the novel – Philip's wife, Margaret. Margaret's position is an
important one in Carter's analysis of women's submissiveness in
the face of men's assertive power. The metaphor of the puppet as
a representation of women's powerlessness is at its height in
Margaret, for she – like Philip's puppets – is dumb. Margaret thus
epitomises woman's position in the patriarchal social order. In
Susan Gubar's words, she is 'a tabula, a rasa, a lack, a negation, an
absence' (p. 306). To an even greater extent than Melanie, it would
appear that Margaret lost her subjectivity and her autonomy the
day she entered her life with Philip, at which point she also lost her
voice. More completely than Melanie, she appears to submit to
Philip's authority. Dressed in the 'ultimately dejected and miser-
able grey dress' which Melanie decides Philip must have chosen for
her, Margaret is crushed by his presence, '... frail as a pressed
flower' she 'seemed too cowed by his presence even to look at him'
(p. 73). His only communication with Margaret is 'to bark brusque
commands' (p. 124) and his satisfaction in her submissiveness
reaches its height when, on Sundays, she wears the stiff, silver
collar he has made for her. 'The necklace was a collar of dull silver,
two hinged silver pieces knobbed with moonstones which snapped

into place around her lean neck and rose up almost to her chin so that she could hardly move her head' (p. 112). The collar makes it difficult for Margaret to eat, but increases Philip's appetite as he '[gazes] at her with expressionless satisfaction' (p. 113). Just as he expresses displeasure at Melanie's sexual being – her periods and her breasts – so too he does his utmost to stifle Margaret's sexuality and physicality, reducing her literally to the state of her replica in his puppet theatre.

Yet Margaret's silence represents more than her submission to patriarchal authority. It is in Margaret that we should perhaps identify Carter's 'double', her 'covert authorial rage'. Like Bertha, the madwoman in the attic in *Jane Eyre*, it is Margaret who finally challenges the patriarchal order depicted in the novel. And, like Bertha, it is Margaret who is responsible for the fire which destroys the toy shop in the closing scene. Just as in Susan Gubar's analysis of Dinesen's story 'The Blank Page', blankness was shown as 'an act of defiance', so Margaret's silence hides her secret and her ultimate defiance of Philip's authority. From her first night at the toy shop, when she discovers Margaret and her two brothers playing Irish music and dancing in the kitchen, Melanie recognises the vitality of her Irish relatives which seems to survive even the oppressive atmosphere of her uncle's house. They are 'the red people' who, through their magical qualities, are able to ward off the pervasive evil spirits of the patriarchal world. 'Not four but three angels ... All the red people lighting a bonfire for her, to frighten away the wolves and tigers of this dreadful forest in which she lived' (p. 112). The spirit they uphold represents a challenge to Uncle Philip's patriarchal control. Through their secret music-making, they retain their own autonomy and creativity.

But the 'red people' also have demonic qualities, exactly those qualities which Gilbert and Gubar suggest that men associate with women's 'otherness', and which are linked to women's 'speech': '... in patriarchal culture, female speech and female presumption – that is angry revolt against male domination – are inextricably linked and inevitably daemonic' (MW, p. 35). So Carter too links Margaret's defiance of her husband with the male literary images of female anger. Finn's picture of Uncle Philip represents him burning in hell. And the final scene of the novel is of the flames of the burning toyshop as Margaret and her brother Francie are shown about to murder Philip with an iron bar. But before this final scene, the secret behind Margaret's silence is revealed as Melanie and the reader are told of her incestuous relationship with Francie. The relationship is her ultimate defiance of her husband's authority and the rigid, patriarchal structures he upholds; her greatest act of autonomy. Just as 'the blank page contains all story in no story', so Margaret's silence 'contains all potential sound' (Gubar, The Blank Page, p. 305). And at the point when Philip finds her in her lover's arms and discovers her secret, Margaret's voice returns, together with the will to destroy the ogre who has ruled her life: 'Struck dumb on her wedding day, she found her old voice again the day she was freed' (p. 197). Whilst Melanie's escape from the burning house throws her conclusively into her future life with Finn and the implied roles of wife and mother, the novel leaves us guessing as to Margaret's future. What is certain, however, is that she escapes from Philip's despotic rule, either through death in the fire which also destroys him, or into unhindered future autonomy and the choice to live openly with the man she loves.

Like her nineteenth century predecessors, then, Angela Carter's novel is 'marked not only by an obsessive interest in [the] limited options' available to women – writers included – but also by the 'obsessive imagery of confinement' used by many female artists, revealing the ways in which they "feel trapped and sickened both by suffocating alternatives and by the culture that created them"' (MW, p. 64). Carter, too, analyses women's position by revising male genres, including material from mythology and psycho-analysis. In many respects, *The Magic Toyshop* conforms to patriarchal literary standards. Significantly, Carter uses her female character's silence – a characteristic traditionally identified with women by patriarchy – to subvert those literary standards. This technique is echoed in the French feminist critics who take up the Lacanian concept of the lack as the most significant feature of female creativity.[22] Like Dinesen's blank page, Carter's use of Margaret's silence is 'not a sign of innocence or purity or passivity', it is 'a mysterious but potent act of resistance' (The Blank Page, p. 305). Thus, in a fairly subtle and covert way, Carter challenges the patriarchal social order she has conveyed.

In *The Madwoman in the Attic* Gilbert and Gubar suggest that Milton's *Paradise Lost* is an overwhelming literary precursor of nine-teenth century fiction and Milton himself a literary father figure from which, like Satan, the daughter must rebel. This view informs their reading of *Wuthering Heights*:

> The sum of this [*Wuthering Heights*] novel's visionary parts is an almost shocking revisionary whole. Heaven (or its rejection), hell, Satan, a fall, mystical politics, metaphysical romance, orphanhood and the question of origins – disparate as some of these matters may seem, they all cohere in a rebelliously topsy-turvy retelling of Milton's and Western Culture's central tale of the fall of woman and her shadow self, Satan. (p. 255)[23]

In attempting now to use their strategies of detecting the female process of revision and redefinition of woman's self-image in nineteenth century literature, and applying it to a reading a twentieth century Black woman's novel, *The Color Purple*, it seems important to locate a similarly powerful cultural precursor for Alice Walker.[24]

We have shown how Gilbert and Gubar's central argument is that a female tradition of writing developed in the nineteenth century, largely in response to a patriarchal literary order. However, we have further argued that by the 1980s a more self-conscious women's tradition has to be taken into account. Important too, as Cora Kaplan has argued in her essay, 'Keeping the color in *The Color Purple*', is to acknowledge that American literature is the product of a very different culture with an independent literary tradition and markedly different history of racial conflict. Kaplan suggests that Walker must be considered a writer 'explicitly in resistance to existing fictions and politics', particularly White and Black Southern fictions, in order to understand how 'her critique and reconstruction of "family", "community" and "femininity" has been made'.[25] Gilbert and Gubar identify Milton as the most powerful mythologiser of patriarchal values from which nineteenth century writers seek emancipation. In considering the literary precursors of Alice Walker's story of Black family relationships, Harriet Beecher Stowe's *Uncle Tom's Cabin* (1852) will be the text we shall take as of central importance as a precursor. It is a text which James Baldwin has described as a 'cornerstone of American protest fiction'.[26] The story concerns a noble-hearted and deeply religious slave who is sold by the kindly Shelby family when they experience financial setbacks. He is separated from his wife and children and though at first is bought by an idealistic master, indebted to him for saving the life of his little daughter, Eva, he is forced by their deaths into the hands of a brutal plantation owner, Simon Legree, who beats him to death for concealing the whereabouts of two female runaway slaves. Particularly in its emphasis on the interdependence of family and religious values which are embedded in a glorification of passive suffering and self-sacrificing domesticity, it provides themes which are taken up and transformed in Walker's revisionary work.

In their essay on George Eliot, Gilbert and Gubar identify Stowe as an important, if marginalised, alternative to the central female tradition, emphasising the strategy of 'feminine receptivity and nurturance', that enabled her to solve the 'anxiety of authorship' by 'excluding any portrait of herself from the fictional world she created' (p. 483). Later critics, however, have seen an image of self in the central character of Tom, who shares all the characteristics of the vapid, self-abnegating, Victorian heroine. Stowe's novel, as Baldwin stresses, is as concerned as Milton's epic with questions of heaven and hell, damnation and salvation. Stowe's narrative of Black slaves, he suggests, is not a story of individuals, but of symbols or touchstones by which to measure the white community's humanity. In order to win our sympathies, Baldwin continues, the Black characters, George and Eliza, are 'as white as she can make them', bleached to an acceptably hispanic appearance or, if outwardly back or woolly-haired like Tom, so 'phenomenally forbearing' that he is 'robbed of his humanity and divested of his sex' (p. 12). Tom's case is permitted to wring the hearts of white readers because, though Black, he earns redemption through suffering. Blackness, Baldwin argues, is construed as the shadow that lies athwart (American) national life. If, as Gilbert and Gubar claim, Milton's misogyny is a mythology that nineteenth century writers 'covertly reappraise and repudiate by misreading and revising the story of woman's fall' (p. 80), it is the far more overwhelming equation of Black with suffering and damnation that is at the heart of *Uncle Tom's Cabin*. For Stowe the slaves, like souls in hell, have been damned in order that they might be saved and to point others the way to salvation. Significantly, after the self-sacrificing death of Tom, the other slaves escape to Africa to become missionaries, redeeming themselves by converting others to the white man's God, an irony that is picked up and reversed in Nettie's account of the missionary worker she encounters on her journey back from Africa (p. 195).

Alice Walker is engaged in a redefinition of Stowe's mythologising of the suffering, but saintly, oppressed slave. It is an image that lies beneath the dominant 1960s figure of the 'nigger'; one that blames the oppressor for everything. Identified as a sub-species whose humanity has to be battled for by the evangelist, s/he is incapable of taking responsibility for any action.

The reader's 'love' of Uncle Tom is dependent on his protection of both the saintly Little Eva and the runaway female slaves, Cassie and Emmeline, which involves a total abnegation of self. The obverse of this saintliness is, suggests Baldwin, figured in the demoniacal figure of Biggar Thomas, Richard Wright's rapist and murderer, who, in his acceptance of his own dehumanisation, is Uncle Tom's mirror image, a way of expressing the author's rage.[27] The image of the 'nigger' in American literature has under-gone the same polarisation into saint and monster that Gilbert and Gubar uncovered in the male images of women; Medea and Medusa, for example, as opposed to Patmore's Honoria or Dicken's Little Doritt. Just as a masculine fear of female procrea-tion has spawned the monstrous breeding goddesses of Death, Errour and Sin (MW, pp. 33–6), so White male fear of Black male sexuality has created the emasculated Tom or sub-human Bigger. Toni Morrison has shown the results of the internalisation of this process of dehumanisation vividly in her recent novel, *Beloved*.[28] A runaway slave has butchered her own small daughter rather than have her recaptured and grow up in slavery. Witness to the horror of her desperate act, the slavemaster's thoughts run on the animal nature of the slaves:

> See what happened when you overbeat creatures God had given you responsibility of – the trouble it was and the loss. He could claim the baby but who would tend her? Because the woman – something was wrong with her. She was looking at him now, and if his nephew (who was responsible for the beating) could see that look he would learn that lesson for sure: you can't just mishandle creatures and expect success. (p. 150)

His last dismissive thought completes the denial of a common humanity to Black people: 'All testimony to the results of a little so-called freedom imposed on people who needed every care and guidance in the world to keep them from the cannibal life they preferred' (p. 151).

The Color Purple can be read in terms of Gilbert and Gubar's definition of women as revisers of traditional themes, as well as an interrogation of the damaging images imposed on Black family relationships by White Americans which have been reinforced by the evangelical fervour of *Uncle Tom's Cabin*. If the Black women in Stowe's domestic economy are protected from the worst excesses of White exploitation by the interventions of the kindly patriarch, Tom, the obverse is the case in *The Color Purple*. White characters feature in the story and have the power to do enormous damage, as in the oppression of Sophia by the mayor and his wife, but it is, as Celie points out, the fault of Harpo, her husband, that she is trapped into service: 'Oh hold on, hell, I say. If you [Harpo] hadn't tried to rule over Sophia, the white folks would never have caught her./ Sophia is so surprised to hear me speak up she aint chewed for ten minutes./ That's a lie, say Harpo./ A little truth in it, says Sophia' (p. 170). In the event, the White characters' ineffectual dependence on the competent domesticity of their Black servants is set against Sophia's suffering. The myth of the happy house slave willingly dedicating herself to the care of the young master or mistress is ironically mocked in Sophia's final rejection of Miss Eleanor Jane: '"I love children", say Sophia. "But all the colored women that say they love yours is lying. They don't love Reynolds Stanley any-more than I do ... some colored folk so scared of white-folks they claim to love the cotton gin"' (p. 225).

Rather than protect the women from White oppression, it is the Black men in the novel who exploit and abuse them, whether they are fathers, brothers, husbands or lovers. Celie, whose story is confided in letters to God, has been raped at 14 by the man she supposes to be her father and passed on, as damaged goods, to Mr —, whose sole concern is to find a drudge for the house and a 'mother' for his children. Pa recommends her usefulness to him: 'She ugly, Don't even look like she kin to Nettie but she make the better wife. She ain't smart either and you better watch her or she give away everything you own. But she can work like a man' (p. 9). Celie is the author's embodiment of a worthless female self: made monstrous through both her ugliness and the horror of her cir-cumstances. Both the incestuous conception and loss of her children is the source of crushing guilt and loss of self-esteem. She accepts her oppression by her father and her husband because she is convinced she is worth no more. She is unable to confide the horrors of her situation to anyone except God, whom she describes later in the novel to Shug Avery as 'big and old and

graybearded and white. He wear white robes and go barefooted'
(p. 168). Celie's self-denial, dutiful forbearance and domestic
virtue are every bit as striking and angelic as those of Uncle Tom.
These traits leave her defenceless because her anger has been
surpassed as part of her learned Christian dutifulness:

> I can't even remember the last time I felt mad, I say. I used to get mad
> at my mama cause she put a lot of work on me. Then I see how sick
> she is. Couldn't stay mad at her. Couldn't be mad at my daddy cause
> he my daddy. Bible say, Honor father and mother no matter what.
> Then after a while every time I got mad, or start to feel mad, I got
> sick. Felt like throwing up. Then I start feeling nothing at all. (p. 39)

In every aspect of her life she is at the mercy of Mr —. Imprisoned
in domesticity she is powerless to protect herself even from his
children:

> Mr — children all bright but they mean. They say Celie, I want dis
> and Celie, I want dat. Our Mama let us have it. They try to get his
> attention he hide behind a puff of smoke./ Don't let them run over
> you, Nettie say. You got to let them know who got the upper hand./
> They got it, I say./ But she keep on. You got to fight. But I don't know
> how to fight. All I know to do is to stay alive. (p. 17)

In her passivity Celie is the ideal housewife, married to the
home (a feature brought out most strikingly in the Spielberg film
adaptation, where Celie's very presence in the house converts it
from chaos to harmonious cleanliness and domestic comfort). She
is compared favourably by Mr —'s sisters with their brother's first
wife who neglected all such domestic duties. The latter, described
by one sister as a slattern, is the reverse image of Celie's goodness,
the monstrous projection of Alice Walker's suppressed rage
directed at domesticity. She makes it very clear who is to blame for
the state of the hovel in Mr —'s sisters' antithetical scoldings:

> And cook, she wouldn't cook. She act like she never seen a kitchen./
> She hadn't never seen his./ Was a scandal, say Carrie./ He sure was,
> say Kate./ What you mean, say Carrie./ I mean he just brought her
> here, dropped her, and kept on running after Shug Avery. That what
> I mean. Nobody to talk to, nobody to visit. He be gone for days. Then
> she start having babies and she young and pretty. (p. 19)

Child-bearing is, for the monstrous female horrors (Errour and
Sin) created by Spenser and Milton and cited by Gilbert and Gubar
as fearful images of the mother, either a curse or cause of
suffering which none of the female characters can control (p. 33).

To be the angel in the house under these circumstances is shown to be truly monstrous, the projection of self-loathing in response to powerlessness in which the victim acquiesces. In its scornful treatment of Celie's dutiful housekeeping, *The Color Purple* revises the domestic road to salvation that is the 'message' of *Uncle Tom's Cabin*, where, as Gilbert and Gubar point out, 'Christian love resides especially in the powerless' and the female traits of domesticity and self-sacrifice bring eternal life (p. 482). The passive virtues of domesticity are rejected in the novel as a self-inflicted burden, reinforced by the laws of an unsympathetic White man's god who shows no signs of responding to Celie's outpourings despite her uncomplaining goodness. For Alice Walker, the oppressive nature of domesticity is located in the Black woman's subservience to men: a state which is far more crushing than Sophia's relationship with the White racists, because it is less identifiable as oppression. Left to themselves and free to come and go as they please, Shug and Celie transform the suffocating nature of 'woman's work and woman's world' into something more creative:

> Us talk about houses a lot. How they built, what kind of wood people use. Talk about how to make the outside of your house something you can use. I sit down on the bed and draw a kind of concrete skirt. You can sit on this I say, when you get tired of sitting in the house. (p. 178)

In a further process of self-definition, Alice Walker has revised the traditional roles of monster slattern and angel housekeeper to create a new perspective. If, for White culture, the binary division of whore and madonna casts a baleful influence on how women imagine themselves, the split is far more insistent in the contrast of pious downtrodden motherhood embodied in the Black 'mammy' figure, familiar to us, if not from fiction, then from numerous Bette Davis films (where doting Black servants alternately coax and scold recalcitrant Southern belles) and the scandalous figure of the sexually-available Black female blues singer who, it is implied, can only make her way by whoring as well as singing. In Stowe's 'protest novel', the route traced for emancipation is through self-denial and submission; in *The Color Purple* the liberated, non-conformist Shug Avery, embodies the transgressive qualities associated with the female siren. She is, however, at one and the same time Albert's mistress and Celie's mother/lover and in her polymorphous ambiguous sexuality is made to embody all that might be accounted demonic in the asexual evangelical world of *Uncle Tom's Cabin*.

Shug is emblematic of the sexual identity repressed in Celie whose experiences of marriage is of a degrading and loveless 'fucking'. However, Shug is very unlike the madwomen and ghost figures that Gilbert and Gubar have identified as the repressed sexual psyches of nineteenth century heroines. In fact, she is a reversal of the whole angel/monster dichotomy. For Celie, domesticity brings disappointment and suffering, but Shug transforms everything, including housekeeping, through her warm, sweet sexuality that is both sensuous and maternal at the same time. She is the Queen Honeybee of her nickname even though the good women of the community find her scandalous: 'Her mammy say she told her so. Her pappy say, Tramp ... the preacher ... talk about slut, hussy, heifer and street cleaner' (p. 40).

Celie and Shug's well-being seem interdependent. Neglect of domestic virtues brings Shug to Mr — on the point of death. Celie's submissive repression of her sexual needs deny her any life of her own. Celie's domesticity rehabilitates both Albert and Shug while Shug's warm sensuality transforms each of the married pair. In the final pages of the story the three are shown living as a single unit: Shug as a kind of benign Heathcliff figure, taken into the home, rather as if Edgar Linton had consented to share Catherine Earnshaw with his rival. Alice Walker has worked to reconcile the opposition between mistress as sexual object and wife as domestic chattel through the enactment of sexual awakening in which its polymorphous perversity (a non-focussed, pre-genital sexuality) reactivates Celie's childhood longings, enabling her to reconnect her sexuality with comfort and pleasure and allowing the catharsis of all past abuses:

> My mama die, I tell Shug. My sister run away. Mr — come git me to take care of his rotten children. He never ast me nothing about myself. He clam on top of me and fuck and fuck, even when my head bandaged. Nobody ever love me I say. She say I love you Miss Celie. And then she haul off and kiss me on the mouth ... Then I feel something real soft and wet on my breast, feel like one of my little lost babies mouth./ Way after a while I act like a little lost baby too. (p. 97)

There are other aspects of a female self that are mirrored in the other women in the story who also share the quest for an independent female sexual identity. Sophia's way is to confront her oppressor directly: 'You ought to bash Mr — head open, she say. Think about heaven later' (p. 39). Sophia's physical resistance, however awe-inspiring, results only in separation and loss.

Celie's sister Nettie provides a full-blown evangelical alternative to domestic submission. Her letters from Africa offer a further challenge to the version of salvation that has been handed to the Black races by a European church, and they question the easy assumption of an African identity's power to liberate. The movement out of Africa that is the solution to Harriet Beecher Stowe's story is reversed in the homecoming of Nettie, her children and Tashi, the Olinka girl.

Alice Walker has turned the abolitionist's novel on its head, finding an evangelical celebration of self that denies the necessity for sacrifice and locates salvation in sisterhood and co-operation; husband, wife and their common lover stitching pants together. Sentimental perhaps, possibly utopian, but definitely widening the possibility for change in the representation of Black women.

Like the nineteenth century novels examined by Gilbert and Gubar, Alice Walker's interrogation of a split female subject uses the dichotomy of angel and monster, archetypes of male Western culture, in a quest for an emancipated self. Unlike the nineteenth century novel, however, Walker makes fewer concessions to convention in the final resolution of her story and the rebellion is an overt, rather than a covert one. 'Black women write against the erosion and repression of female sexuality as it is channelled by male desire', writes Susan Willis in her discussion of Black women writers.[29] They also write against the double constraints of race and gender and a criticism that concentrates on locating a *female* tradition can only obscure the former.

Gilbert and Gubar's criticism locates recurrent themes and images in the writing of women, noting how they were surprised by the coherence of theme and imagery that they encountered in the works of writers who were often geographically, historically and psychologically distant from each other. They use this unity to identify a distinctive female literary tradition and in reading *The Color Purple* from such a perspective it is possible to concentrate attention on images of passivity, imprisonment, silence and disenfranchisement as representations of the author's view of the female self; locating the difficulties on an individual and sexual level as a response to patriarchy, while obliterating the community experience of memories of slavery or disenfranchisement that has been the Black experience. This is to employ the kind of interpretation that prefers the 'transhistorical and essentialist' meanings that Cora Kaplan suggests lead us to 'teaching and thinking about these texts through an unintentionally imperialist lens, conflating their progressive politics with our own agendas, interpreting their versions of humanism through the historical evolution of our own' (p. 177). Kaplan's own strategy is to look to prior constructions of Black social and sexual relations in black male fictional negative interpretations of womanhood, in a move that is reminiscent of the male precursors sought by Gilbert and Gubar. The difference is that these are seen in their historic specificity, rather than as embodying universal values.

III

The main problem, then, with Gilbert and Gubar's mode of analysis is that it appears to assume a universal archetypal female subject which ignores the changing modes of femininity which become possible at particular historical moments. Thus, Angela Carter, a White English woman writing fiction set in the late 1950s/early 1960s, is made to share the same female literary traditon as Alice Walker – a Black American writer dealing with post-slavery in the American South. Not only this: they would be assumed to be placed in relation to the same literary precursors. This is obviously such a preposterous undertaking that in order to facilitate our own reading of Alice Walker we chose to substitute Beecher Stowe for Milton as Walker's 'authority of influence' because American literature clearly partakes of a different tradition from English literature. We were able to focus on the features in *The Color Purple* that seemed specific to the writing of a Black American only by shifting ground and finding a suitable precursor text. Gilbert and Gubar's prioritisation of Milton in the writing of women makes a watertight argument for oppressive patriarchy, but in effect it imposes a specific frame that moves into a metaphysics of heaven and hell and removes them from a specific historic context. For example, reading Celie's 'ugliness' as a dramatic reversal of the image of the angel in the house, we ignore the specificity of Western social conditioning which works to deny Black women a self-image of physical attractiveness.

The identity of author with character can at first seem superficially attractive: Angela Carter has equated Melanie's adolescent yearnings with her own and Alice Walker claims to be the 'medium' through which Celie and the other characters speak. It would also be possible to argue for the authors' (secret) doubles in the characters of silent Aunt Margaret and sexually liberated Shug Avery. This 'authentic realist' stance reinforces the male critics' assumption of a qualitative difference in the writing of men and women and reduces women's stories to a single narrative of anger and entrapment. Further, there is a contradiction in setting up the female author as the transcendental signified of her text whilst attempting to take a stand against patriarchal authority.[30] In our own reading we were forced to discard the simple analogy of author and character. We were able to adopt a psychoanalytical framework to position these women writers against a male literary tradition, and to seek out the common themes which might place them in a female tradition. But what was omitted was any attempt to use these themes to discuss the psychological states of the authors.

In their discussion of the psychodynamics of female creativity, Gilbert and Gubar make no distinction between female nature and the process that determines the social nature of female subjectivity. They stress the individual psyche at the expense of the community and reinforce the negative conceptualisation of femininity as something dark and self-lacerating, rather than as structured in response to specific contexts. Particularly when reading *The Color Purple*, to search for archetypal representation in the novel is to ignore much of what is important to a Black reader. Cora Kaplan has suggested specific ways in which new writing from Black women: 'dialogises the languages, black and white, in which race, class and gender have been discussed in America' (p. 182). Gilbert and Gubar rarely take account of the fictional nature of the literary text or the specific material conditions under which writers work. In order to facilitate our reading, we have drawn analogies between Angela Carter's self-conscious challenge to patriarchal structures and Gilbert and Gubar's idea that all women's writing is inherently revisionary. In fact, Gilbert and

Gubar suggest that the revisionary process is an essential feature of the woman writer's femaleness and not a conscious political stance.

One feature of *The Madwoman in the Attic* that it is very difficult for another critic to reproduce is the particularities of the writers' style. Gilbert and Gubar themselves are engaged in the revisionary process they describe: large sections of the text are given up to restructuring the plots of the novels under discussion to bring them in line with their stories of entrapment and escape. In doing so, their criticism becomes inextricably bound up in the metaphysical imagery of the master text whose influence they seek to define. For example, the story of the Fall taken from Milton is re-enacted over and over again to the point of tedium, as in the following passage, this time with reference to George Eliot's *Middlemarch*:

> Behind the dream-Casaubon, however, lurks the real Casaubon, a point Eliot's irony stresses from the scholar's first appearance in *Middlemarch*, just as – the Miltonic parallels continually invite us to make this connection – the "real" Milton dwelt behind the carefully constructed dream image of the celestial bard. Indeed, Eliot's real Casaubon, as opposed to Dorothea's idealized Casaubon, is in certain respects closer to the real author of *Paradise Lost* than his dream image is to the Miltonic epic speaker. Like Milton, after all, Casaubon is a master of the classics and theology, those 'provinces of masculine knowledge ... from which all truth could be seen more truly'.(p. 217)

The effect is to reduce each new text to a logic of the same: Milton as Satan, woman writer as Eve! These of course are serious criticisms, but we must not lose sight of the positive contribution made by Gilbert and Gubar to women's studies. *The Madwoman in the Attic* is a pioneering work that provides a framework within which to study the major contribution made by women writers to nineteenth century literature, contrary to their usual positioning as marginal figures in the male 'great tradition'.

NOTES

1. Sandra Gilbert and Susan Gubar, *The Madwoman in the Attic* (Yale University Press, New Haven, 1979); referred to as MW in further references.
2. See discussion of Showalter's work in Chapter Three.

3. Susan Gubar, '"The Blank Page" and the issues of female creativity', *Critical Inquiry*, vol. 8, Winter, 1981; referred to as BP in further references.

4. Gilbert and Gubar's use of psychoanalysis is very different from the French feminists (see Chapter Five) and the two should not be confused. Gilbert and Gubar borrow a variety of concepts and theories from psychoanalysis and use them as a background for their own theory of feminist poetics. That theory is *not*, in itself, psychoanalytical.

5. Edward W. Said, *Beginnings: Intention and Method* (Basic Books, New York, 1975), p. 83.

6. Thomas Szasz has pointed to the power involved in any classification or naming process, by which wo/man can attempt to impose an order on things or people; to control them:

> Classification is not reserved for science or the scientists. It is a fundamental human act. To name something is to classify it. But why do men name things? The answer often is: to gain control over the thing named, and, more generally, over one's power to act in the world ... The act of naming or classifying is intimately related to the human need for control or mastery.

Thomas Szasz, *Ideology and Insanity* (Calder and Boyars, London, 1973), p. 196.

7. Harold Bloom, *The Anxiety of Influence* (Oxford University Press, New York, 1973).

8. Susan Penfold and Gillian Walker argue that certain images of woman recur across time, race and culture and that the consistency of these myths and symbols has led to the belief that they are a universal part of a collective consciousness (or unconsciousness), representing deep and universal truths about the nature of women. See *Women and the Psychiatric Paradox* (Oxford University Press, Oxford, 1984), p. vii.

9. See, for example, Susan Griffin, *Woman and Nature* (The Women's Press, London, 1984); Mary Daly, *Gyn/Ecology* (The Women's Press, London, 1978); Barbara Ehrenreich and Deirdre English, *For Her Own Good* (Pluto, London, 1979).

10. I would suggest that Gilbert and Gubar's use of the term 'Otherness' in relation to women differs from Showalter's use of it in her discussion of the 'wild zone' (see Chapter Three). Showalter recuperates the concept to make positive reference to woman's subjective position, whilst Gilbert and Gubar refer to man's negative classification of woman.

11. For a discussion of women's position in the nineteenth century, with particular reference to the restraints inflicted on upper- and middle-class women, see Barbara Ehrenreich and Deirdre English, *For Her Own Good, op. cit.*

12. Simone de Beauvoir, *The Second Sex* (Knopf, New York, 1953).

13. Virginia Woolf, '*Professions for Women*' – *The Death of the Moth and Other Essays* (Harcourt, Brace, New York, 1942), pp. 236–8.

14. Mary Jacobus has also suggested that women's writing works within

male discourse but works 'ceaselessly to deconstruct it'. See 'The difference of view', in Mary Jacobus (ed.) *Women Writing and Writing about Women* (Croom Helm, London, 1979), p. 13.

15. For further discussion of the relationship between woman's body and her creativity, see Chapter Five on French feminists, whose attitude towards that relationship is far more positive and entirely different from Gilbert and Gubar's.

16. Charlotte Perkins Gilman, *The Yellow Wallpaper* (Virago, London, 1973).

17. For a contrasting feminist reading of *The Yellow Wallpaper* see Chapter Six on Marxist-feminism.

18. Angela Carter, *The Magic Toyshop* (Virago, London, 1982).

19. Angela Carter, 'Notes from the front line', in Michelene Wandor (ed.) *On Gender and Writing* (Pandora, London, 1983), p. 69.

20. Pauline Palmer, 'From "coded mannequin" to bird woman: Angela Carter's magic flight', in Sue Roe (ed.) *Women Reading Women's Writing* (Harvester, Brighton, 1987), p. 183.

21. This is the most significant difference between Gilbert and Gubar and the French feminists, whose concern is with the structure of language rather than representation and myth-making (see Chapter Five).

22. See Chapter Five.

23. For comments on Gilbert and Gubar's reading of *Wuthering Heights*, see Chapter Five.

24. Alice Walker, *The Color Purple* (Women's Press, London, 1983); Harriet Beecher Stowe, *Uncle Tom's Cabin*, 1852.

25. Cora Kaplan, 'Keeping the color in *The Color Purple*', in *Sea Changes* (Verson, London, 1986), pp. 176–187.

26. James Baldwin, 'Everybody's protest novel', in *Notes of a Native Son* (Corgi, London, 1964).

27. Richard Wright, *Native Son* (1940), cited by Baldwin (*op. cit.*) as 'Uncle Tom's descendent, flesh of his flesh, so exactly opposite a portrait when the books are put together'.

28. Toni Morrison, *Beloved* (Chatto and Windus, London, 1987).

29. Susan Willis, 'Black women writers: taking a critical perspective', in Gayle Greene and Coppelia Kahn (eds) *Making a Difference: Feminist Literary Criticism* (Methuen, London, 1986), pp. 211–37.

30. A more detailed discussion of this blind spot in Gilbert and Gubar's work can be found in *Sexual Textual Politics* (Methuen, London, 1985), pp. 57–69, where Toril Moi discusses the 'radical contradictions' revealed between 'feminist politics and patriarchal aesthetics'.

5

French Feminisms

Elaine Millard

Julia Kristeva: *The Kristeva Reader*
Luce Irigaray: *Speculum of the Other Woman*
Emily Brontë: *Wuthering Heights*
Angela Carter: *The Magic Toyshop*

I

The names of the best known French feminists, notably Luce
Irigaray, Hélène Cixous and Julia Kristeva echo in British academic
circles as a mantra to invoke a theoretical position that might
silence the more accessible, but unpalatable, critical works of Anglo-
American feminists. Their names have become the index of a
desirable, but perhaps utopian, quest for a feminist critical practice
that would liberate the theorist from competing ideologies of
establishment versus feminist practices, moving in the direction of
a subjectivity that is no longer dependent on a specific sexual
identity: one that transcends the gender principle.[1]

On the other hand, many other feminists reject what they see
as a new form of biological essentialism that reduces accounts of
woman's language to an inarticulate babbling, and women
themselves to the eternally feminine. Luce Irigaray, in particular,
has aroused the kind of hostility voiced by Monique Plaza: 'Luce
Irigaray closes us in the shroud of our own sex, reduces us to the
state of child woman: illogical, mad, prattling, fanciful ... thus is
woman.'[2] Frequently, it is only the psycho-linguistic catch-phrases
of their discourse that are borrowed to lend a surface erudition to
discussion; terms such as 'semiotic', '*nom-du-père*', 'polymorphous
perversity' appear without any accompanying critique of the

writing in which they are embedded. These French women and their texts have themselves become signs in the encoding of theoretical positions and they have come to occupy the space reserved for the marginality and otherness that their work suggests is the location of the 'feminine' in language.

To understand why their texts should constitute a difficulty for British readers, it is necessary to compare briefly the origins of a feminist critique in France with the way women's studies have developed in the UK and the USA. A contrast that an American reviewer of feminist theory and practice formulated, only half jokingly, as an opposition of 'bluff, blunt Yankees and wanton, witty Gauls'.[3] Anglo-American feminist criticism has developed from courses that concentrated on teaching women's texts, whether this was within the context of university English studies or the expanding discipline of Women's Studies. In America, women who had abandoned education in the 1950s in search of what Betty Friedan described as 'the feminine mystique' ('a world confined to her own body and beauty, the charming of man, the bearing of babies, and the physical care and serving of husband, children and home'), were returning to academia on the waves of the Women's Movement.[4] Together with the new generation of feminists, reading omnivorously as part of a programme of consciousness-raising, they developed the new discipline of Women's Studies to which most of the scholarship can be traced.[5] The teaching strategies involved on such courses can be roughly divided in two: gynocriticism (see Chapter Three) which concentrates on re-covering female literary history through re-reading of the classic writers, such as Jane Austen, the Brontës and Emily Dickinson; and a cultural images model that deals with the constructed and biased nature of representations of women both in literature and popular culture.[6] The basis for both critical positions is the liberal humanist tradition of scholarship, with a tendency to separate out experience from the language that 'embodies' it. A woman's real difficulty in writing 'about' herself is seen, by these critics, as one of access to the means of production, namely, a room of one's own, a sympathetic publisher, a regular writing income and public recognition.

French feminism, on the other hand, like structuralist and post-structuralist criticism in France, grew out of two closely connected, but quite different disciplines: linguistics and psychoanalysis. While Anglo-American critics were busy rebelling against the canon of English literature and the choice of reading lists, and setting up their own presses, the French feminists were part of a much bolder deconstructive enterprise that set out to put in question, through Saussurean linguistics and Lacanian psychoanalysis, the whole philosophical basis of language. Their target, rather than raising questions about the representation of women in writing, was an interrogation of the very nature of subjectivity itself. 'Woman' as sign, they argue, is a fictional construct of patriarchal discourse. One of the major points of difference from Anglo-American criticism is their emphasis on the impossibility of locating a place outside patriarchy from which 'woman' could be articulated.[7]

In order to understand how French feminists sought to redefine this woman-question, it is necessary to describe the Lacanian model, so that the feminist divergence from his 'master text' can be highlighted. In Lacan's readjustment of Freud, patriarchy is shown to be inscribed in the very language through which the child learns to define itself and in which it is confirmed in its gender. According to Lacanians, the child, prior to speech, experiences itself as diffused and undifferentiated from the world. It is an 'hommelette', a 'little man', which, like a broken egg, spills over and spreads itself with no fixed (ego) boundaries. It experiences its being in the world as a flux and is dominated by ever changing drives (these drives Kristeva calls *pulsions*). An important transition stage occurs at about six months when, shown its image in a mirror, it recognises a self, which, because it is founded on an image, is imaginary. This imaginary self is supported by the mother whose gaze confirms the separatedness of the I/thou positions.

It is not, however, until the acquisition of language, when the child can make its desires explicit to another and enter into social exchanges, that this self becomes formulated, that is, named and defined by its entry into the Symbolic Order. The Symbolic is marked by the law of structuration of meanings which Lacan calls the *'nom-du-père'*: the Law of the Father. In order to enter the Symbolic Order, some elements of the Imaginary that cannot be expressed within the Symbolic's formulations are repressed, and effectively silenced. It is at the level of the Imaginary that French feminists locate the feminine. As the child says 'I', it constructs a fiction of selfhood that depends on the syntax of the language it has been born into. The 'I' position carries the authority and self possession which Lacan designates as male. This, for French feminists re-reading Lacan, is the crux of the matter (indeed, what effectively *is* the matter), that the child's sense of identity is filtered through external views of itself formulated in a language where the 'I' position is male. It is Lacan's view that language, shaped through the patriarchal *'nom-du-père'* with which only the boy child can identify himself, reserves the 'I' position for one gender, placing the other in the negative pole. At the point of entry into this realm of the Symbolic, i.e. the acquisition of language, the subject divides, and what of the Imaginary cannot find expression in words is repressed in the unconscious. This repressed 'experience' is a key to understanding what Kristeva terms the 'semiotic' (or the area of the unconscious on which conscious speech depends). In the Lacanian account of language acquisition, the phallus is the master signifier, in the face of which the feminine can be defined only as lack. Woman is a gap, a silence, invisible and unheard, repressed in the unconscious. Kristeva argues that this 'feminine' remains at the level of the 'semiotic', accessibly in patriarchal discourse only at the point of contradiction, meaninglessness and silence.

This is quite a different explanation of woman's disadvantage from Dale Spender's analysis of 'man-made' language, with its suggestion of a patriarchal conspiracy against the feminine which is open to direct challenge.[8] Spender makes the problem a social difficulty that can be seen as temporary and local. Lacan's scheme suggests it is a determined psychological cause: a necessary stage in socialisation. Lacan writes of the subject's relation to language, making its role seem a dominant and inescapable one:

> Thus the subject too if he appears to be the slave of the language is all the more so of a discourse in the universal movement in which his place is already inscribed at birth, if only by virtue of his proper name. Reference to the experience of the community, or to the substance of this discourse, settles nothing. For this experience assumes its essential dimension in the tradition that this discourse itself establishes. This tradition, long before the drama of history is inscribed in it, lays down the elementary structures of culture. And these very structures reveal an ordering of possible exchanges which, even if unconscious, is inconceivable outside the permutations offered it by language.[9]

The subject then is processed by the linguistic categories which structure experience. There can be no possible socialisation outside this structuration so that, in Lacan's schema, a woman who 'refused' to enter the Symbolic Order through language would remain unsocialised, psychotic and autistic. The French feminists whose work I draw on challenge the basic determinism of this Lacanian model, while employing its interrogation of subjectivity to locate the feminine, which has been lost or suppressed in the system. Instead of literary texts, their writing most frequently engages with the major works of Western philosophical thought, from Plato to Freud. These are not explications, but major reworkings of ideas that go unchallenged in the writings of their male colleagues, illustrating the historical processes whereby the feminine has been defined and debased in men's texts. Where literary texts are the object of study, for example, in the criticism of Julia Kristeva, they are examined in terms of a politics of style that reveals the suppressed feminine in male writing, particularly in those whose sexuality places them outside the mainstream of literary conventions, for example, Marcel Proust and Jean Genet. Rather than concerning themselves with the representation of women's 'experience', their texts take issue with a dominant masculine tradition of psychoanalytical analysis that, through the concepts of the Oedipal and castration complexes, locates femininity as lack and a convention of philosophy that is locked into male patterns of discourse.

Julia Kristeva has developed ways of addressing the workings of a text's unconscious by applying Lacan's principle of the split subject and reinterpreting the Imaginary. For Kristeva, at the point where consciousness divides, the feminine is repressed into the 'semiotic'. This is a level of discourse which precedes symbolisation, and the Oedipal structuring of sexuality. Marked by the rhythms and patterns of sound that are the basic pulsions of the oral and anal drives, the semiotic continuum can be read, she argues, as the suppressed feminine. The semiotic is not an *alternative* to the Symbolic Order but a process at work within that structuration.[10] If the symbolic embodies the Law of the Father, then the semiotic is that which may disrupt that order from within; it is as much part of the language of poets and the *avant-garde* as of women.[11] In this sense, Kristeva does not offer a theory of femininity or take up issues which are consciously feminist. When, however, the semiotic and the symbolic are employed by the Marxist-feminist critics discussed in Chapter Six, these terms are placed within a framework that allows the politics of how subjects are engendered to be articulated. It is to Luce Irigaray that I shall now turn for her more contentious desire to interrogate the sign 'woman' and the nature of female sexuality.

Luce Irigaray has aroused more hostility both from her (male) psychoanalyst colleagues and from feminists. Her challenge to the orthodoxies of Freudian and Lacanian theories (or rather non-theories) of femininity in her doctoral thesis, *Speculum de L'Autre Femme*, resulted in her expulsion from Lacan's École Freudienne. In this playful, but ultimately complex and theoretical analysis, she demonstrates how the privileging of what is visible and therefore deemed positive (i.e. the penis elevated to the status of phallus, the master signifier) relegates 'woman' to absence in existing structures of psychoanalytical and philosophical discourse. She describes the feminine as 'interdit' (forbidden), located in between signs, between the realised meanings, between the lines.

> Therefore the feminine must be deciphered as inter-dict; within the signs or between them, between the realised meanings, between the lines ... and as a function of the reproductive necessities of an intentionally phallic currency, which, for the lack of the collaboration of a (potentially female) other, can immediately be assumed to need its other, a sort of negative or inverted alter ego.[12]

Irigaray proceeds to demonstrate how, in psychoanalytic theory, woman is man's 'specularised Other', her function to reflect back man's meaning to himself, becoming the negative of this reflection. Woman is thereby forced into a subjectless position by the patriarchal 'logic of the same'. In reading Freud, she shows, by skilful quotation from his analysis and theorising, that he has modelled his account of the little girl's development on that of the little boy, so that female sexuality is perceived not as something particular to women, but constructed as the negative response to the male's desire. Irigaray questions Freud's account of the seemingly total repression of a little girl's sexual instincts which Freud suggests follows from her acknowledgement of her inferiority to the boy's far superior equipment (his penis). What Freud has ignored, Irigaray shows, is the nature of the girl's first love directed towards the mother. His solution, penis-envy, however, can be seen to have been made in the interests of his own sex.

> When Freud solves this problem by insisting that the girl has always been a boy, and that her femininity is characterised by 'penis-envy', he is obviously defending his male point of view and his wish to perpetuate sexual homogeneity; a non-sex organ, a castrated sex organ or 'penis-envy', does not constitute a sexual heterogene but rather represents a type of negativity that sustains and confirms the homogeneity of masculine desire. (p. 63.)

In reading Freud, she highlights his neglect of pre-Oedipal experience that relegates the girl-child's relationship to the Imaginary, and which therefore can find no expression in the realm of the Symbolic. In this respect a woman, silenced in discourse, is as Irigaray has described elsewhere, in the position of the psychotic: 'Spoken more than speaking, enunciated more than enunciating, the demented person is therefore no longer an active subject of the enunciation ... he is only a possible mouthpiece for previously pronounced enunciations.'[13] Irigaray succeeds in her readings in undermining the neutrality of philosophical/psycho-analytical discourse, revealing the process by which the philosopher/psychoanalyst talks about himself from the security of the subject position. In order to attempt to access the primordial experience of femininity, she suggests it is necessary to work to disrupt the simple oppositions on which theoretical systems are founded:

> We have to reject all the great systems of opposition on which our culture is constructed. Reject, for instance, the oppositions fiction/truth, sensible/intelligible, empirical/transcendental, materialist/idealist. All these opposing pairs function as an exploitation and negation at the beginning and of a certain mode of connection between the body and the word for which we have paid everything.[14]

Having uncovered the impossibility of articulating the feminine in the existing structure of language, she has initiated the search for another form of expression that might claim to be a feminine language. She suggests that 'writing women' will create that which as yet is inexpressible, a female subject with the potential to create its own meanings rather than be caught in the 'masquerade' of femininity. This is, of course, a utopian quest. Because women are both inside and outside a discourse that gives no space to the feminine, the primary task is to disrupt the settled order rather than to define what an other might in fact be(come). It is the possibility of there being something that can be defined, except by reference to the masculine, that is the central concern of Irigaray's psychoanalytical concepts:

> Woman remains that nothing at all, or this all at nothing, in which each (male) one seeks to find the means to re-plenish the resemblance to self (as) to same. Thus she moves from place to place, yet, up to the present it was never she that was displaced. She must continue to hold the place she constitutes for the subject, a place to which no eternal value can be assigned lest the subject remain paralysed forever by the irreplaceableness of his cathected investments. Therefore she has to wait for him to move her in accordance with his needs and desires.[15]

To write the body or *'parler femme'* then is to confront and displace this masculine 'movement', to escape its definitions and confines, to attempt a reformation of the Symbolic. Irigaray does not claim that either to write or *'parler femme'* is easily definable or achievable. In *This Sex Which is not One*, Irigaray deals with the problem of female sexuality and subjectivity not by answering questions, but by a continuing process of interrogation.[16] A dominant theme in this questioning process concerns itself with the (im)possibility of elaborating an alternative concept of femininity, which would be entirely other and not the converse, the negative, the complement of that of man. She argues that there can be no such development if it presupposes disconnecting the feminine from the present-day economy of the unconscious. Her argument is that it is necessary to 'become' a woman; whereas a man is a man from the outset, women can only rely on mimicry of the roles assigned her. One strategy is to take this mimicry to its extremes, miming the role in an abject surrender which undermines masculine rhetoric. A second strategy, demonstrated most forcibly in the style and metaphor of *When Our Lips Speak Together*, is to pursue the relationship between female sexuality and language to create a different Symbolic Order.[17] Irigaray also makes use of metaphors of fluidity to encompass the way her writing flows from a source – decentring and putting all fixed meaning into question. To look for evidence of an *'écriture feminine'* then implies a text that disrupts expectations of form and genre rather than any reflection of woman's experience. It is men who hold mirrors to nature, and the mirror, flat and deceiving, is, argues Irigaray, often woman.

Her concept of 'writing the body' which uses the imagery of

fluidity and flux has precipitated both angry and puzzled responses from feminists, who see Irigaray irresponsibly casting off feminism's hardly-worn gown of academic respectability for a disconcerting 'babble'. A further difficulty for someone attempting to use these concepts as a way into literary criticism is that Luce Irigaray concerns herself more often with a practice of writing than in theorising what is already written, unless of course the work is philosophical. In fact, for this reason, French feminism has had far less impact on literary institutions than Anglo-American revisionist reading. Irigaray's own texts, like those of Roland Barthes, enact the crumbling away of easy distinctions between the critical and the creative, poetry and theory, philosophy and fiction.[18] What I therefore intend in this chapter is to impose fragments of the theoretical insights into the construction of the female subject with a reading of what is both said and left unsaid about the tension between childhood and womanhood in *Wuthering Heights* and *The Magic Toyshop*. It might be argued that this is not a systematic method or, indeed, even possible, given that no unitary position could be assigned to the theorists I claim to be following. I can only reply here as I have argued elsewhere, that it is the nature of feminism to appropriate what it can of the systems of thought available to it at the time.[19] In re-reading D. H. Lawrence, I chose to adapt Roland Barthes' semiotics to insert myself within a male text; now I choose to scavenge the texts of more sisterly writings for a similar purpose. My criteria for choice is that of productivity rather than imitation.

II

Before turning to Angela Carter's *The Magic Toyshop*, I would like to consider Emily Brontë's *Wuthering Heights*, which has already attracted the attention of critics of many different persuasions.[20] It is a central text in Sandra Gilbert and Susan Gubar's *The Madwoman in the Attic*, whose work is discussed in detail in Chapter Three, as the Anxiety of Authorship. This is a work of American feminist scholarship deriving from Women's Studies courses in literature, which attempts to establish a female aesthetic in the face of what they define as patriarchal hostility. Gilbert and Gubar, through a 'mythic' interpretation rather than close analysis, retell the story of the women they designate as Cathy I and II and her lovers, wresting the tale from the grasp of its fictive narrators, Lockwood and Nelly Dean, whose limited perspective ceases to be an issue in the new narrative. In the process, they re-present the author, Emily Brontë, to their own readers as a proto-feminist literary scholar, who was writing against both a literary patriarch, Milton, and her own father, to produce an idiosyncratic version of a master plot *Paradise Lost*, that describes the loss of a fictive feminist Eden. This re-writing is quite deliberate on their part, as the following passage shows:

> Having arrived at the novel's conclusion we can now go back to its beginning and try to summarise the basic story that *Wuthering Heights* tells. Though this may not be the book's only story, it is surely a crucial one. As the names on the window-sill indicate, *Wuthering Heights* begins and ends with Catherine and her various avatars. More specifically, it studies the evolution of Catherine Earnshaw into Catherine Heathcliff and Catherine Linton, and then her return through Catherine Linton II and Catherine Heathcliff II to her 'proper' role as Catherine Earnshaw. More generally, what this evolution and devolution conveys is ... a parodic anti-Miltonic myth.[21]

Gilbert and Gubar, by restructuring the narrative, have imaged for their history of women's literature, a model of the ideal literary woman, specifically engaged with a thematic structuring device located outside her text.

> Given the fact that Brontë never mentions either Milton or *Paradise Lost* in *Wuthering Heights*, any identification of her as Milton's daughter may at first seem eccentric or perverse. Shelley, after all, provided an overtly Miltonic framework in *Frankenstein* to reinforce our sense of her literary intentions. But despite the absence of Milton reference, it eventually becomes plain that *Wuthering Heights* is also a novel haunted by Milton's bogey. We may speculate indeed that Milton's absence is itself a presence, so painfully does Brontë's story dwell on the places and persons of his imagination. (p.252)

The persuasive power of the rhetorical frame of this essay and its obsessive reshaping of each story to fit a new gynocritical canon of a female tradition, as well as making compelling reading, demonstrates how the gaps, the unspoken elements of this text, encourage the reader to rush in with her own desires.

For Gilbert and Gubar, Milton is this text's 'unspoken', but it also has been read as many other things. *Wuthering Heights* is a text which seems to invite this onrush of interpretation, and this is also testified, both by its recurrent fascination for adolescent readers, exemplified in Rachel Brownstein's account of a high-school student's classroom response: 'Gloria has read *Wuthering Heights* sixteen times ... It was the first thing she ever said to me without raising her hand', and by the multiplicity of competing readings available to fill the space that opens under the symbolic codes.[22] Hillis Miller catalogues the variety of interpretations at hand:

> There have been interpretations of *Wuthering Heights* in terms of the fair-haired girl and the dark-haired boy in the Gondal poems; or by way of the motifs of doors and windows in the novel (Dorothy van Ghent); or in terms of the symmetry of the family relations in the novel or Brontë's accurate knowledge of the laws of private property in Yorkshire (C. P. Sanger); or as in more or less orthodox and schematic Freudian terms as a thinly disguised sexual drama displaced and condensed (Thomas Moser); or as a dramatisation of a conflict between two cosmological forces calm and storm (Lord David Cecil); or as a moral story of the futility of grand passion (Mark Schorer) ... or as the expression of a multitude of incompatible partial selves breaking down the concept of a unitary self (Leo Bersani), or in more or less sophisticated Marxist terms (David Wilson, Arnold Kettle, Terry Eagleton).[23]

Miller accounts for this plethora of interpretation as an effect of the reading required by the text. He illustrates the way in which it:

> is made up of repetitions of the same in the other which permanently resist rational reduction to some satisfying principle of explanation. The reader has the experience, in struggling to understand the novel, that a certain number of the elements which present themselves for explanation can be reduced to order. This act of interpretation always leaves something over, something just at the edge of the circle of theoretical vision which the vision does not encompass. This something left out is clearly a significant detail. There are always in fact a group of such significant details which have been left out of any reductions to order. The text is over rich. (p. 52)

There is evidence that this sense of something 'missed out' as a key to understanding has always been the experience of reading the novel. Charlotte Brontë has described its first reviewers as: 'Astrologers, Chaldeans and Soothsayers, gathered before the "writing on the wall" and being unable to read the characters or make known the interpretations.'[24] Competing readings find themselves suspended in the gaps between Nelly and Lockwood's perceptions, searching for clues in words 'detached sentences' and 'faded hieroglyphics', scribbled on the margins of biblical texts, inscribed on lintels and scratched into windowsills, together with confessions whispered into the pillows by Catherine in a fevered delirium. Miller sums up the undecidability neatly thus: 'each appearance is the sign of something absent, something earlier or later or further in' (p. 60).

Post-structuralism has shown us that we produce texts by reading them and that the texts we produce repeat the stories that obsess us. In all the cited readings of *Wuthering Heights*, reader, text and language are caught up in an endless displacement of desire. It is not my intention to add to these competing readings by writing my own version of the novel to set alongside the rest. My purpose is to draw attention to the fragmentation of narration and the mingling of genre, whereby the fantastic and uncanny erupt into the hard realism of the story of a Yorkshire farming family's struggle over inheritance. The text refuses a simple resolution, however much the match between the younger Cathy and Hareton Earnshaw is foregrounded. This elusiveness of meaning is such that the novel conforms to the following description: '. . . [the text] presses the linguistic sign to its limits, the semiotic is fluid and plural, a kind of pleasurable creative excess over precise meaning and it takes sadistic delight in destroying or negating such signs'.[25] I am quoting from Terry Eagleton's account of Kristeva's model which appears in *Literary Theory: An Introduction*. Kristeva's thesis is that these 'meanings' remain as the semiotic, inscribed inside the symbolic as part of the condition of its coherence. It is essential to grasp that the semiotic cannot be separated out from the symbolic but remains as a pressure on language as contradictions, meaninglessness, silence and absence. It works from within signification, indicating what is lacking in codified representation. Tensions between the symbolic surface and its semiotic undercurrents connect the obsessive interest that readers find in this novel with Kristeva's concept of an unconscious present in a text. This unconscious communicates to the reader some idea of a pre-Oedipal oneness, an unnameable unity of being that can only be expressed as a lack in the present or the time of reading. 'Woman', Kristeva has argued, does not exist except as constituted in opposition to the male, that which is other than, rather than a thing in itself. 'In "woman", I see something that cannot be represented, something that cannot be said, something above and beyond nomenclature and ideologies'.[26] And she also says:

If logical unity is paranoid and homosexual (directed by men to men) the feminine demand ... will never find a proper symbolic, will be at best enacted as a moment inherent in rejection, in the process of ruptures, of rhythmic breaks. In so far as she has a specificity of her own, a woman finds it in asociality, in the violation of communal conventions, in a sort of symbolic singularity.[27]

Although in her own literary criticism, such as in her discussion of symbolist poetics, Kristeva works at the level of sounds, repetitions and disruptions of grammar, that is, with writing which interrogates small units of language, rather than larger units of signification, the theoretical basis of her methodology is a productive way in to *Wuthering Heights*. Instead of repetition of sound and description at sentence level, what is at work in this narrative is a disruption of all the 'macro elements' of classic realism. Time is dislocated, narration is fragmented, its narrators presented ironically and shown to be limited in their point of view, genre is disrupted; but above all, the smooth working of binary oppositions is transgressed. These neat dispositions of difference into antithesis are what Roland Barthes has described as 'the very spectacle of meaning' which saturate the classic realist text.[28]

In Romantic texts, reader expectation anticipates an antagonistic opposition of male sexual rivalry, in this case between the legitimised, patriarchal choice, landowner Edgar Linton, and the dark Byronic outsider, Heathcliff. However, neat oppositions break down as the simple divide between true and false lover is negated by Edgar Linton's harshness and Heathcliff's asexual indifference; both fail to satisfy the role of either a Mr Knightley or a Rochester.[29] Oppositions of natural versus civilised, duty set against desire, landowner versus servant, the present with the past, spirituality and materialism, are all productive of meaning. It is, however, round the transgressive figure of Heathcliff that the interpretation of the symbolic codes cluster and meanings proliferate. The reader is as uncertain as the internal narrator, Lockwood, of how to dispose her sympathies. Heathcliff simply resists assimilation into an economic framework that stresses the material struggle. Arriving from nowhere, from no named parentage and bearing no Christian name, 'from the very beginning he bred bad feeling in the house' (p. 49) which pervades the story until he dies, similarly alone, leaving nothing: no child, only a single name and the date of his death recorded on his headstone, which will soon be covered over in lichen and moss.

The character created a scandal in its time, prompting this admission from Charlotte Brontë, supposedly writing to defend her sister's work, in the 1850 preface to the novel, from its critics: '... whether it is right or advisable to create beings like Heathcliff I do not know, I scarce think it is' (p. 40). In every sense Heathcliff's presence in the text is a transgressive and disruptive one.

Similarly, representations of Catherine multiply within the text in a process of dispersal and fragmentation that is marked by a similar fragmentation of signifiers. Her presence cannot be pinned down to a single signifier and her name remains oscillating in the reader's perception no less than that of Lockwood, the narrator:

> The ledge where I placed my candle, had a few mildewed books piled up in one corner; and it was covered with writing scratched on the paint. This writing was nothing but a name repeated in kinds of characters, large and small – Catherine Earnshaw, here and there varied Catherine Heathcliff and again to Catherine Linton. In vapid listlessness I leant my head against the window and continued spelling over. Catherine Earnshaw-Heathcliff-Linton, till my eyes closed; but they had not rested five minutes when a glare of white letters started free from the dark as vivid as spectre – the air swarmed with Catherines. (p. 61).

The attempt to spell out the name results only in further disintegration and displacements. Many commentators have noted that the ghost that haunts the narrative is not that of the young woman, dead in childbirth, but of the adolescent Cathy, lost at the point where she chooses/is compelled, to enter into womanhood, as culturally defined by the society in which she lives and which is symbolised in the constricting clothes she wears on her return to the Heights from Thrushcross Grange:

> ... instead of a wild, hatless little savage jumping into the house and rushing to squeeze us all breathless, there lighted from a handsome black pony a very dignified person with brown ringlets falling from the cover of a feathered beaver, and a long cloth habit which she was obliged to hold up with both hands that she might sail in. (p. 93).

It is the 'girl half savage and hardy and free' to whom Catherine longs to return in her illness and who tries to find her way back into the Heights, who appears in Lockwood's uncannily prophetic dream. Yet the name given is that of the married woman:

> "Who are you" I asked, struggling meanwhile to disengage myself. "Catherine Linton" it replied shiveringly (why did I think of Linton? I had read Earnshaw twenty times for Linton) "I'm come home: I'd lost

my way on the moor!" As I looked I discerned a child's face looking through the window. (p. 67)

A similar misrecognition, or displacement of signifiers, occurs in Chapter XIII when Isabella is brought to Wuthering Heights as Heathcliff's bride. It might be supposed that this would have been the role reserved for Cathy in any conventional Romantic plot. In a letter to Nelly, Isabella gives an account of her cold reception, including a detailed description of how Joseph greets a tantrum in which she dashed a bowl of gruel to the ground with the name of her friend/rival: '"Ech, ech," exclaimed Joseph, "Weel done Miss Cathy! weel done, Miss Cathy. Howsiver t'maister shall tum'le o'er them broken pots; un then we's hear summat; we hears how it's to be"' (p. 180).[30]

A further confusion of identities is created by the confusion of selves experienced by the central characters, given expression by Catherine before her separation from Heathcliff in: 'Nelly, I'm Heathcliff', and his equally emphatic: 'Oh, God, it is unutterable. I cannot live without my soul' (p. 180).

Particular readers may choose to invest the ambiguity thus created with a particular meaning, as Mary Daly does in *Pure Lust*. She writes: 'It is clear enough to viragos from these words that Heathcliff is the disguise of the female Friend of Emily Brontë's dream. "He" feels an identity with Catherine that only another female friend could feel'.[31] For Gilbert and Gubar, the key to understanding the passage and with finding the key to the whole novel is to read the pair as halves of an androgynous whole: 'Together they ... [Cathy and Heathcliff] constitute an autonomous androgynous (or more accurately gyandrous) whole: as a woman's man and a woman for herself in Sartre's sense, making up one complete woman' (p. 295).[32] What, however, seems more important than establishing a particular interpretation is a recognition of the disruption of certainty that has been engendered by the text. However much the narrative

opens itself to the repressed at the same time as it initiates a psychic reorganisation of the individual, thanks to a tremendous loosening of the super-ego. The awakening of pre-genitality follows an attempt to integrate it within genitality. In the aftermath of the oedipal stabilisation, the adolescent again questions his identifications along with his capacities for speech and symbolization.[33]

This identification of the novel with adolescent writing is not intended to imply an immaturity, as it might, directed from an authentic realist position, but to emphasise the openness of the structure to encompass a desire set loose from the rigid structuration of the symbolic. In *Wuthering Heights*, this openness to something that escapes symbolisation accounts for the power the text exercises over readers of different kinds. Its power lies in reactivating the adolescent imagery, with its denial of loss, and phallic affirmation. It gives the adult the right to this state, as reader, spectator or artist of a 'psychic interiority' which Kristeva demonstrates to be a creation of the nineteenth century novel. Kristeva's psychoanalytical account of language development, with its concept of adolescence as an 'open structure', can be used to explore the repression of what, as a feminist, I wish to identify as 'the feminine', some undeveloped potential.

Julia Kristeva's poetics, in their emphasis on textuality rather than the intentions of the author or the experience of the characters as reflections of an external reality, have allowed me as a feminist reader to identify those areas of disjunction, silence or contradiction, as evidence for a suppressed feminine within the text, unable to make itself fully heard, because it cannot be contained within the symbolic order which it threatens to disrupt.

Of further use in this analysis is Kristeva's adaptation of the Bakhtinian concept of polyphony, whereby one might demonstrate the fragmentation and dispersal of the authoritarian authorial voice into the characters of the novel.[34] This would be a productive way of pursuing the ambivalent attitudes that surround any value judgements of the novel's central characters. One might identify the discourse of romantic love, set against the bourgeois negotiation surrounding marital status, or the desires of children set against the demands of the adults. These remain tantalising possibilities which I have not taken up in detail, because Kristeva's use of Bakhtin is ultimately used to defend marginality and subversion (albeit the feminine is subsumed in this category).

Toril Moi's reading of Kristeva's work emphasises its revolutionary potential.[35] She is the theorist with whom Moi chooses to end her own quest for a theoretical position that liberates the critic from humanist and essentialist suppositions. Moi admires, in particular, Kristeva's ability to open up language to the free-play of the signifier:

> Applied to the field of sexual identity and difference, this becomes a feminist vision in which the sexual signifier would be free to move; where the fact of being male or female no longer would determine the subject's position in relation to power, and where, therefore, the very nature of power would be transformed. (p. 172).

There remains in much of Kristeva's writing, however, a feature that I find problematic. Having determined to her own satisfaction that woman 'does not exist' and that speaking as a woman is an impossibility, she then focusses most of her attention on the language of male writers, seeking in them a repressed feminine that is asexual, the badge of marginality and exclusion. Women's writing is neglected except where it is used rather conventionally, as in the case of Sylvia Plath's *Ariel* to demonstrate madness and disadvantage. In setting up 'aesthetic practices' as her major concern, her theory often privileges the textual over the sexual, relegating woman and her texts to the silence and obscurity of indifference. This is a negative feature for my own reading that wishes to situate itself firmly within a feminist frame and foreground woman as the producer rather than the product of writing.[36]

In my next reading, therefore, I want to make use of the more defiantly feminist approach to psychoanalysis and women's sexuality provided by Luce Irigaray; in particular, to make use of her ideas on 'masquerade' of man-defined femininity and the disruptive potential of 'mimicry' as a feminist strategy. By mimicry, I mean Irigaray's method of reproducing the discourse of others, in such a way as to undermine the authority of the original. She sees it as an interim strategy for dealing with patriarchal discourses in which the woman deliberately reveals the mechanisms by which these exploit her. Similarly, a masquerade is a deliberate assumption of the roles assigned to woman in the name of femininity. By adopting a masquerade a woman is able to experience herself as she is positioned by the desire of the masculine.

Angela Carter's first novel *The Magic Toyshop*[37] will seem, to many readers, a far cry from a kind of disruption of language and symbolic representation urged upon the feminine by French feminists. The structure and features of style are disconcertingly conventional and the content of the story, an adolescent girl's rite of passage to womanhood, a staple of romantic fiction. *The Magic*

Toyshop was first published in 1967, and marks a period of a first
questioning of female roles; it stands on the threshold of the
explosion of new fictions that has accompanied the growth of a
feminist consciousness. In this respect it follows much of the 'new'
or (re)newed writing current in the feminist presses. As the essay
on authentic realism has shown (see Chapter Two), such work
concentrates on the essence of feminist difference by reference to
experience, either claiming to 'change lives' like Marilyn French's
The Woman's Room, or obsessively re-examining self in a continuous
process of autobiography, such as that of Maya Angelou.[38]

Rosalind Coward's article, 'This novel changes lives', questions
the 'feminist' import of such confessional modes that in their
preoccupation with sexuality as the most significant aspect of
experience 'might have the effect of confirming woman as bearers
of sentiment, experience and romance (albeit disillusioned)'.[39] In a
similar process, strands of Anglo-American criticism seek to
identify the author of the novel with a character, seeing in the
tracing of a link between fiction and life the essence of feminist
thought. For example, Sandra Gilbert and Susan Gubar read the
female, marginal characters, often madwomen, of nineteenth
century novels as 'in some sense the author's double' (p. 78). Both
fiction and criticism conspire to reinforce what Mary Jacobus, in
her review of *The Madwoman in the Attic*, pinpoints as an
'autobiographical phallacy', a process whereby male critics perceive
women's creativity as an extension of 'self', in which 'the female
text is the author, or at any rate a dramatic extension of her
subconscious'.[40]

Angela Carter has in fact hinted, in an interview given to *The
Observer* prior to the filming of this novel, at an 'autobiographical'
origin for the writing:

> When the book came out in 1967 it was reviewed as a kind of fairy
> story. But when I read it again I was struck with the intense sense of
> adolescent longing in an extraordinary sexual yearning. What it
> reminded me of was endless afternoons alone in a room smelling of
> sun-warmed carpet, stuck in the Sargasso Sea of adolescence when it
> seems you are never going to grow up.[41]

Her story of adolescence, however, is caught up in patterns of
narrative that undo the simplicity of reflected experience by
refracting the characters through the convex mirrors of fantasy
and myth. The writing does not however approach the fluidity or

disruptive power of the semiotic, which Irigaray has suggested characterises the style of French *'écriture feminine*. However, just as Lacan recast Poe's *The Purloined Letter* as an allegory of the signifier, this story can be read as a fable of the crisis of the female subject which is proposed by French psychoanalytic models.[42] Indeed, the reader is confronted by textuality that announces itself in terms of fable. Place is left undefined: an Edwardian house somewhere in the country gives place to a toyshop somewhere in the seedier parts of London, while time schemes are sketchy; things take place 'one night', time is marked out by the changing of seasons and the bizarre cuckoo clock created by the puppet-master from a stuffed bird. The latter as villain of the piece, Uncle Philip, is delineated in the simple terms of a fairy tale ogre:

> Uncle Philip never talked to his wife except to bark brusque commands. He gave a necklace that choked her. He beat her younger brother. He chilled the air through which he moved. His towering, blank-eyed presence at the head of the table drew the savour from the good food she cooked. (p. 124)

The image is further reinforced by references to Bluebeard and comparisons which suggest the puppet maker of the Hoffman story.

If Uncle Philip patterns out every feminist's concept of the patriarch, Aunt Margaret's situation most particularly demonstrates the silencing that the imposition of a male symbolic order forces on the feminine. Dumbness marks Aunt Margaret's entry into the patriarchal home and is broken only when this is threatened with destruction and the spell is broken (p. 197).

The text throws into question those elements of story telling that have become fixed as literary norms. Like other contemporary women writers, including the French feminists I am discussing, Carter chooses myth as the site of entry into a new Imaginary. Alicia Ostriker has described this feature of women's writing as a process of revisionary myth-making that plunders sanctuaries of existing language where our meanings of 'male' and 'female' have been preserved.[43] Carter similarly perceives that some stories carry meanings that threaten but which can be revised for feminism. She claims to be in the 'demythologising business' and is '... interested in myths – though I'm much more interested in folklore – just because they are extraordinary lies designed to make people unfree ... I used bits and pieces from various mythologies quite casually because they were to hand'.[44]

Central also to *The Magic Toyshop* is a revisionary look at the myth of Leda and the Swan, which poets such as Yeats have employed as symbols of a phallic potency which sees rape as the prerogative of male power. Melanie, the central character, is shown to be in quest of a female self which is elusive: 'Since she was thirteen, when her periods began, she felt she was pregnant with herself, bearing the slowly ripening embryo of Melanie-grown-up inside herself for a gestation time the length of which she was precisely not aware' (p. 20). At 15, the security of girlhood has to be disrupted for entry into an adult role that involves coming to terms with her sexuality. The continuing quest for self is shown refracted through a literary and cultural ragbag of images that have created ready-made expectations and possibilities for being. The novel is set in a literary frame by the opening that associates Melanie's awakening adolescent sense of self with the new-found land that is John Donne's America, 'safest when by one man, manned'. Melanie's role models have been shaped not only by the metaphysics of love but also by pre-Raphaelite and Romantic imagination. In these discourses, the image of woman is eternally the model, muse and idealised mistress, simultaneously feared and desired; her role is to be the passive, reflecting Other of the male. This is represented in Irigaray's writing as a protean ability to shape shift:

> Woman is neither open nor closed. She is indefinite, in-finite, form is never complete in her. She is not infinite but neither is she a unit(y), such as letter, number, figure in series, proper noun, unique object (in a) world of the senses, simple ideality in an intelligible whole, entity of a foundation etc. This incompleteness in her form, allows her continually to become something else, though this not to say that she is ever univocally nothing. No metaphor completes her.[45]

In many ways this description resembles the Monster/Angel dichotomy that is at the heart of Gilbert and Gubar's analysis of women writers' ambivalence to images of self (see Chapter Four). In Melanie's musing about the sexual activity of her parents, fragments of Lawrence ('sacrificed to the dark gods') jostle with scraps from letters to women's magazines, and each fragment of disparate discourses reinforces the image of a passive femininity.

Luce Irigaray's challenge to Freud is based on her contention that in considering female sexuality Freud took as his basis the visible difference between the male and female sexual organ. His differentiation depends on speculation: to look at woman is to see nothing that proclaims her sexual difference other than an absence. Using the man as the norm, femininity is then its negation: the sex which does not have a penis. Because the definition always takes as its starting point the masculine, woman is therefore outside representation. Because for Lacan the function of language is not to communicate but to give the subject a place from which to speak, woman is constantly placed in the male view, as forever the object of the male subject, so that there is no place from which she can reflect herself. Toril Moi gives a neat summary of Irigaray's position:

> The woman for Freud as for other Western philosophers becomes a mirror for his own masculinity. Irigaray concludes that in our society representation and therefore also social and cultural structures are products of what she sees as a fundamental hom(m)osexualité. the pun in French is on homo (same) and homme (man): the male desire for the same. (p. 135)

Woman, Irigaray argues, is conceived only as the mirror image of man. As if to exemplify the process whereby this self-definition is effected, in *The Magic Toyshop*, Melanie 'pregnant with herself', poses before the bedroom mirror in roles carefully selected from men's paintings and poetry. These images, the formulations of the masculine Imaginary, serve only to restrict woman's instincts and deny them full development. Irigaray has described this process of assumed but superficial desires thus:

> Is it necessary to add, or repeat that woman's improper access to representation, her entry into a specular and speculative economy that affords her instincts no signs, no symbols, or emblems or methods of writing that could figure her instincts, make it impossible for her to work out or transpose specific representations of her instinctual object-goals? The latter are, in fact, subjected to a particularly peremptory repression and will only be translated into a *script of body language*. Silent and cryptic. Replacing the fantasies she cannot have – or can have only when her amputated desires turn back on her masochistically, or when she is obliged to lend a hand with 'penis-envy'. (p. 124)

It is Melanie's 'improper access to representation', particularly to the allure of images of femininity, which makes her vulnerable to the manipulation of her Uncle Philip. She comes to view herself as the object of his attention, the heroine of his stories: 'She was a wind-up putting-away doll clocking through its programmed movements. Uncle Philip might have made her over already. She was without volition of her own' (p. 76).

Her passage to womanhood seems, in this patriarchal system, to demand a symbolic loss of virginity to an all-powerful phallic male. Rape is sanctioned in the patriarchal structuring of things, where woman is delivered, gift-wrapped in flimsy vestments, both to the male gaze and a castrating power. Melanie's acquiescence in the ritual is prefigured in the first scene of the novel where the fantasies acted out in the wedding dress leave her 'hobbled in yards of satin which would rip and tear and tangle irreparably' (p. 20). Her body is swamped by the wedding garment which chills and constrains her, 'she sweltered and rolled in white satin'. Her surrender to the romantic image suggested by her mother's dress prepares her for the Leda role and submission to the phallic swan: 'Melanie was forever grey, a shadow. It was the fault of the wedding dress-night, when she married the shadows and the world ended' (p. 77). To be swathed in a similar material is a pre-requisite for the Leda role: just as in the return from Thrushcross Grange of a newly grown-up Cathy in *Wuthering Heights*, becoming a woman involves disguise in 'the cover of a feathered beaver and a long cloth habit' (p. 93), Melanie is drawn into another masquerade of femininity:

> One night, Aunt Margaret drew a length of white chiffon out of a paper bag ... She gestured Melanie over to her and draped the material around her shoulders. All at once Melanie was back home and swathing herself in diaphanous veiling before a mirror. But the cuckoo clock poked out its head and called nine o'clock and there she was in Uncle Philip's house.
>   'Your costume', wrote Aunt Margaret on a pad to save herself getting up. 'For the show'
>   'What am I?' asked Melanie
>   'Leda, He is making a swan ... That is how he sees you. White chiffon and flowers in your hair. A very young girl' ... Melanie would be a nymph crowned with daisies once again; he saw her as once she has seen herself. In spite of everything she was flattered. (p. 141)

The acting out of the Leda story parodies the cultural sanctioning of phallic supremacy, an ideology that is internalised by both male subject and woman as object of the desire. In the event, this set piece in the novel is turned into ridiculous *mimicry* both in rehearsal and its final performance. Unlike the awesome bird in the Yeats' poem whose 'shuddering' loins engender the history of Troy, Uncle Philip's marionette is an obvious construct

(p. 165). It is a 'mocked up swan', 'made of hollow wood'. Instead of the grace and power of the assumed shape of the 'heavenly visitant' whose 'beauty and majesty' bear its victim to the ground, it is 'a grotesque parody of a swan; Lewis Carroll might have created it.' It approaches 'dumpy and homely and eccentric', making 'lumbering progress, its feet going splat, splat, splat'.

The text mocks the reverence granted the phallic signifier by juxtaposing Melanie's perception of its clumsiness with the inflated rhetoric of Uncle Philip's narrative. 'Almighty Jove in the form of a swan wreaks his will' is followed by 'the swan made a lumpish jump forward'. The ultimate mockery of the patriarchal exaltation of penis to phallus occurs in Finn's comic account of his disposal of the swan in the remnants of the 'pleasure gardens'.

> And I took this spade with me, to dig a grave for the swan, and I kept dropping the spade. And the swan's neck refused to be chopped up; the axe bounced off it. It kept sticking itself out of my raincoat when I buttoned it up to hide it and it kept peering round while I was carrying it, along with all the other bits of swan and the spade as well. I had my arms full, I can tell you. It must have looked to a passer-by as if I were indecently exposing myself, when the swan's neck stuck out. I was embarrassed with myself and kept feeling to see if my fly was done up. (p. 173)

This technique of quoting from the male ordering of things in order to reveal its flaws is exactly the mode adopted by Irigaray in re-examining the ideas of the Greek philosophers, in particular Plotinus, in *'Une mère de glace'* (pp. 168–179).[46] By mimicking the authorial voice in such a way as to deflate it, her text can challenge the assumptions on which its text rests. In this final section of Angela Carter's novel, masculine fantasy of the phallus has been cut down from the dignity of powerful deity to the squalid exhibitionism of a dirty raincoat. Mimicry has been used, as Irigaray suggests, to discompose an accepted order.

The mythic framework of the novel has attached to it elements of popular fiction, Gothic romance and fairy story, so that the reader is propelled into a world that is a repository of vague, unnameable fears and ever-present threats projected on to otherwise mundane elements, such as Uncle Philip's false teeth. Melanie's uncle's shop is Bluebeard's castle, where the severed hands of small girls can be found in the knife drawer (p. 118) and the strewn limbs of dismembered puppets in the workroom (p. 170). It is both a fox's den, dirty and malodorous, and the puppet master's workshop where male fantasies are put on stage. Running through this dream work, the search for a female identity is repeated and transformed. The women of the story lack wholeness (are all castrated), from Melanie's recollections of a mother whom she cannot imagine naked – her clothed body seems to hide a lack – her aunt struck dumb in the house of the archetypal patriarch and Mrs Rundle, whose married title is an assumed one and whose unmarried state is a sign of incompleteness. Only the small child, Victoria, has a simple wholeness which comes partly from ignorance, partly from her continuing unity with a substituted mother figure. 'Victoria, happy Victoria who still lived in the land of Beulah, where milk and honey flow, an Eden where the snake still slumbers in futurity, mindless Victoria slept like a top' (p. 169).

The story then can be read as a fable of the absence of what can be written of female desire. The pleasure garden to which Finn introduces Melanie is defunct: a wasteland whose queen, slimy and fungus-streaked, has lost her consort. Though Melanie escapes intact from struggles with both the grotesque swan and a defloration by Finn, planned by her wicked Uncle, it is still in the economy of male desires that she must shape her future. At the climax of the adolescent sexual encounter, it is Finn who withdraws himself from the act, not she who rebuts him. Although by such abstinence he is challenging Uncle Philip's patriarchal ordering of things, as male, he denies Melanie her own, very real sexuality. As Finn, enacting the part of the swan in rehearsal, topples her 'in slow motion' to the floor, Melanie waits 'tensely for it to happen' but it is Finn who controls the sexual encounter: '"No," said Finn aloud. "No!" again. The tension between them was destroyed with such wanton savagery that Melanie fell limply back and struggled with tears' (p. 150). She has been delivered from the older patriarch into the arms of a younger one, who is no less in control. Her own destiny is a passive acceptance of the inevitability of the female role – sexuality remains phallocentric. Melanie has a prophetic vision as Finn sits beside her:

> in his outrageous jacket, unclean in the clean sheets, yawning so that she saw the ribbed red cathedral of his mouth and all the yellow teeth like choir boys. She knew that they would get married one day and live together all their lives in dirt and mess and shabbiness,

always forever and forever. And babies crying and washing to be
done and toast burning all the rest of her life. And never any glamour
or romance or charm. Nothing fancy. Only mess and babies with red
hair. (p. 177)

If, on the one hand, the novel's main thrust is against the
falsification of the romantic bridegroom, there remains the
expectation that marriage is an inevitability. No alternative exists.
Woman's desire is as yet unnameable and it is into the keeping of
another male that Melanie's escape from the older patriarch leads.
She is mirrored in Finn's eyes (p. 193) as she is shaped by his
painting into an 'asexual pin-up' which is not precisely how she
sees herself (p. 154). Finn's refusal of Melanie's desire mirrors the
emptiness which Irigaray detects at the centre of masculine
discourse:

> . . . a person who is in a position of mastery does not let go of it easily,
> does not even imagine any other position that would amount to
> getting out of it. The masculine is not prepared to share the initiative
> of discourse. It prefers to experiment with speaking, writing,
> enjoying 'woman' rather than leaving to that 'other' any right to
> intervene, to 'act' in her own interests. What remains most
> completely prohibited is that she should express something of her
> own sexual pleasure.[47]

Melanie's hopeful quest for a new world of womanhood in *The
Magic Toyshop*, suggested by the introductory analogy of the
discovery of America, is thrown in doubt by the final line of the
novel. Having burned the infernal desiring machine of the puppet
master to the ground, the couple 'gaze at each other in a wild
surmise'. The connotations of the speculation which promises a
new beginning for male and female relationships are taken from
John Keats' response to Chapman's Homer.

> Much have I travelled in the realms of gold
> And many goodly states and kingdoms seen;
> Round many western islands have I been
> Which bards in fealty to Apollo hold.
> Oft of one wide expanse had I been told
> That deep browed Homer rules as his demesne;
> Yet never did I breathe its pure serene
> Till I heard Chapman speak out loud and bold:
> Then I felt like some watcher of the skies
> Or like proud Cortez, when with eagle eyes
> He star'd at the pacific – and all his men
> Look'd at each other with a wild surmise
> Silent upon a peak in Darien.[48]

The new world 'imagined' is now even less of a material reality than that promised by John Donne's America of the opening. It remains a utopian possibility, multiply displaced through literary images, whose origin is not located in experience but in textual encounter. The evocation of an ocean, 'one wide expanse', is emblematic of the fluidity and changeability of what might emerge from a reworking of the utopian feminine possibilities inherent in romance.

There is also a possibility of an alternative form of socialisation in the transgressive incestuous sub-culture of the toyshop's kitchen, where Aunt Margaret and her brothers communicate in music and dance, modes of expression that may, by their closeness to 'pulsions', escape the realms of the symbolic ruled by the *nom/non du père*, or in this case Uncle Philip. These possibilities are, however, undeveloped and half rejected by an ending that leaves the survival of Aunt Margaret, her surrogate child, Victoria, and her brother/lover in doubt. By ending with a quotation that resounds enigmatically, she defers the closure of a romance, whilst always leaving this as a possibility, so that the text itself becomes a staging point in a feminist interrogation of the nature of 'woman'.

'Surmise' seems also a wholly suitable word for describing Irigaray's push towards *écriture féminine*. It is a process in the making, not a complete practice. Irigaray is at pains to stress that her work is tentative and questioning. In the Questions section of *This Sex Which is not One*, she describes her work in terms of exploration and process:

> To come back to my work: I am trying, as I have already indicated to go back through the masculine imaginary, to interpret the way it has reduced us to silence, to muteness or mimicry, and I am attempting from that starting point and at the same time to (re)discover a possible space for the feminine imaginary. (p. 164)

Neither the novelist nor the philosopher/psychoanalyst move towards a more positive description of what their new 'realm of gold' might be and in this sense each lays herself open to charges of mystification and ahistorical romanticism. However, both novelist and theorist can be seen in their writing practice to be actively engaged in a process of revisionary questioning of the categories and signs that have constructed what passes under the name of woman. I have found Irigaray's strategies of disclosing masquerades and mimicking masculine discourse useful tools in opening out Carter's novel, to reveal a complex, self-consciously feminist text.

III

This chapter differs significantly from the other chapters in our book in its use of two quite separate theorists rather arbitrarily linked together under the catch-all title of French feminists. As more of the writing of French women theorists becomes available in translation it is increasingly evident that no single position can be assigned to them. Their works are also initially far more daunting than those of Anglo-American writers because of the breadth of the reading that informs their discussions of psychoanalysis and philosophy and the referencing of their work to an alien corpus of writing.

In preparing myself to use French feminisms for the reading of these texts, I found myself caught up in an endless process of displacement, whereby the origin of significance might always be located elsewhere anterior to the text being read, sometimes in male-authored texts, so I returned to Lacan, then Freud, sometimes to a female exegete like Jane Gallop.[49] The latter has written precisely on this process of deferral of meaning in the search for origin, suggesting that it is ever a deferment of desire:

> If the subject's desire comes from the Other, the subject does not know what she desires but must learn it from the Other. The desire to know what the Other knows, so as to know what one desires so as to satisfy that desire, is the desire behind all quests for knowledge.[50]

Jane Gallop links reading with desire, the urge to control, to gain mastery. The overwhelming question which lay across my preliminary reading was, what might I be able to appropriate from the French marriage of masculine theory with the position of a woman reading/revising those theories? In order to begin writing I finally made the decision to limit my own quest/will to knowledge to the most accessible concepts that establish ways of reading and/or writing in the face of male authority.

In reading *Wuthering Heights*, I used Kristeva's categories of the symbolic and semiotic to undercut perfected 'interpretations' of meaning in the novel and point up its indeterminacy as a central feature of a feminist reading. Kristeva's psycho-linguistics allowed a way into locating repressed elements of the text that work to undermine the authority of the symbolic codes in operation.

In suggesting an anarchic disturbance working beneath the surface logic of the narrative, I was able to demonstrate the way in which Emily Brontë's novel had inscribed within its signs a problem as yet without a name. The difficulty, however, with accepting Kristeva's positioning of femininity alongside other radical omissions from representation within the symbolic, is that is seems inevitably to associate femininity with negativity, precipitating a fall into the incoherence of madness when the woman attempts to speak with her own voice.

In the section, 'I who want not to be' in *About Chinese Women* Kristeva discusses the emergence of the semiotic in women's writing as the call of the mother:

> For a woman, the call of the mother is not only a call from beyond time, or beyond the socio-political battle ... this call troubles the word: it generates hallucinations, voices, 'madness'. After the super-ego, the ego founders and sinks. It is a fragile envelope, incapable of staving off the irruption of this conflict, of this love which had bound the little girl to her mother, and which then, like a black lava, had lain in wait for her all along the path of her desperate attempts to identify with the symbolic paternal order. Once the moorings of the word, the ego, the super-ego, begin to slip, life itself can't hang on: death immediately moves in.[51]

She characterises Sylvia Plath as 'one of the women disillusioned with meanings and words' and sees in the rhythms of *Ariel* for 'those who know how to read her, her silent departure from life'. The implicit message seems to be: accommodate to the symbolic, be content with small disruptions or die. Indeed, the end result of a theoretical bid to establish the 'feminine' as co-terminous with dissidence and marginality results in a view of female artists that assumes pain, suffering and imprisonment of hope which can only be escaped through madness or death, both rather self-defeating strategies.

It seemed to me in reading that both Emily Brontë and Julia Kristeva might be caught in the act of obliterating traces of any peculiar identity as a woman, one by the choice of a male nom-de-plume, the other in the adoption of a critical stance that assumes an authority from which to reject other feminists' strategies. Kristeva, as Jane Gallop has pointed out, presumes to know: '[her] assertive style and her mastery of several difficult jargons give the appearance of "knowledge" and authority. Kristeva presumes the right to assert, to speak as if she "knows"'.[52] However, the force of her writing works to deny other women comparable status.

Irigaray is equally 'authoritative' in her skilful deconstruction of those elements of Western thought that have 'framed' women as a mirror image of the male. Her revision of psychoanalytical theories of sexuality are presented far more tentatively and interrogatively than those of Julie Kristeva. She too has a theory of the subject-in-process but concentrates her efforts on an attempt to push towards what 'woman' might be if she were able to follow the movement of a different desire.

I have used her interrogation of the male-centred definitions of female sexuality as a way into reading the tentative moves towards questioning the processes through which a young girl moves towards womanhood in a patriarchal economy. Rather than distinguish fictional from critical text, I have seen both women writers as engaged in a similar process of self-definition. Both work to demythologise the objectification of woman as the 'specular other' of the male and both suggest utopian possibilities.[53]

Critics of Irigaray's writing, who include Chris Weedon, have strongly objected to what they read as Irigaray's argument for an integral relationship between sexuality and language.[54] I would argue that to read Irigaray's metaphors of fluidity and contiguity as essentialism, an acceptance of biology as the most powerful determinant of subjectivity, is to take literally what is offered as analogy, to interpret utopian longings for a description of external reality. I have created an analogy between the way that Angela Carter's text is inserted inside a literary tradition in order to disrupt and unsettle representation and the far more complex disruption of the symbolic and authority brought about by Irigaray's writing. In its tentative questioning of what most have accepted as given both writers have considerable power to disturb and unsettle the reader.

It is, however, left to a Marxist-feminist critique to make explicit the tension between the subject and her insertion in language within a historical framework and to effect a reconciliation between theories of the structure of the psyche and material existence.

NOTES

1. See Julia Kristeva, '*Women's time*', pp. 18–211, in Toril Moi (ed.) *The Kristeva Reader* (Blackwell, Oxford, 1986), p. 209. In this important essay Kristeva outlines two generations of feminists; the first egalitarian movement which sought equality, the second emphasising women's radical difference from men. She posits a third generation whose task is to theorise the reconciliation of these two positions. 'In this third attitude which I strongly advocate – which I imagine? – the very dichotomy man/woman as an opposition between two rival identities may be understood as belonging to metaphysics' (p. 209).

2. Monique Plaza, 'Phallomorphic power and the psychology of women', translated by M. David and J. Hodges, in *Ideology and Consciousness*, vol. 4, Autumn 1978, pp. 5–36. Plaza is anxious to stress the material nature of women's oppression against the purely philosophical and ideological categories employed by Irigaray.

3. See A. Morris, 'Locutions and locations: more feminist theory and practice', in *College English*, vol. 49, no. 4, April 1987, pp. 465–76.

4. Betty Friedan, *The Feminine Mystique* (Penguin, Harmondsworth, 1965), p. 136. See also Chapter 3, 'The crisis in women's identity', pp. 61–70.

5. One development within this era is discussed in Chapter Two.

6. For example, see Patricia Beer, *Reader I Married Him, a Study of the Woman Characters of Jane Austen, Charlotte Brontë, Elizabeth Gaskell and George Eliot* (Macmillan, London, 1974); and Susan Koppelman Cornillon, (ed.) *Images of Women in Fiction: Feminist Perspectives* (Popular Press, Bowling Green, Ohio, 1972). The latter is discussed in detail in Toril Moi, *Sexual/Textual Politics* (Methuen, London, 1985), pp. 42–50.

7. See Chapter Three for an account of women taking on male images of themselves.

8. Dale Spender, *Man Made Language* (Routledge and Kegan Paul, London, 1980).

9. Jacques Lacan, 'The agency of the letter in the unconscious or reason since Freud', in *Écrits: A Selection*, translated by A. Sheridan (Tavistock, London, 1980), p. 148. This essay which has been of powerful significance in theorising the relation of the subject to the Symbolic Order of language poses enormous difficulties for the reader. A useful introduction to Lacan's work is provided by Malcolm Bowie in 'Jacques Lacan', in John Sturrock, (ed.) *Structuralism and Since* (Oxford University Press, Oxford, 1979), pp. 116–53.

10. See also the discussion in Chapter Three of Showalter's notion of the 'wild zone' – a way of defining women's Otherness as a positive subject position; see also Chapter Six where these terms are important.

11. See Julia Kristeva, 'Revolution in poetic language', pp. 89–115, in Toril Moi, (ed.) *The Kristeva Reader (op. cit.)*, in particular pp. 113–15, 'The unstable symbolic: substitutions in the symbolic fetishism'.

12. Luce Irigaray, *Speculum of the Other Woman*, translated by Gillian C. Gill (Cornell University Press, Ithaca, 1985), p. 22. All further references

are given after quotations in the text.

13. Luce Irigaray, *Le Language des Déments* (Mouton, Paris) quoted by T. Moi, 'Patriarchal reflections: Luce Irigaray's looking glass', in *Sexual/Textual Politics, op. cit.*

14. From an interview given to L. Serrana and E. Hoffman in Holmes and Meier, (eds) *Women Writers Talking*, pp. 238–9, quoted in Jan Montefiore, *Feminism and Poetry* (Pandora, London, 1987), pp. 141–3.

15. *Speculum of the Other Woman, op. cit.*, p. 227.

16. *This Sex Which is not One*, translated by Catherine Porter, with Carolyn Burke (Cornell University Press, Ithaca, 1985). See particularly pp. 119–69.

17. Luce Irigaray, 'When our lips speak together' in *This Sex Which is Not One, op. cit.*, pp. 205–19.

18. See Roland Barthes, *S/Z*, translated by Richard Miller (Hill and Wang, New York, 1974). In *S/Z* Barthes analyses a classic realist narrative, 'Sarrasine' by Balzac, through narrative, symbolic and cultural codes. In so doing, he creates a text which is as original as any work of fiction.

19. See Elaine Millard, 'Reading as a Woman' in Tallack (ed.), *Literary Theory at Work* (Batsford, London, 1986), pp. 135–70. In this essay I have appropriated Barthes' methods of textual analysis through a detection and tracing of the cultural codes on which meaning depends, in order to insert myself within the text of a Lawrence novella and break down the way gender is specifically constructed within that text.

20. Emily Brontë, *Wuthering Heights* (Penguin, Harmondsworth, 1965).

21. Sandra Gilbert and Susan Gubar; *The Madwoman in the Attic* (Yale University Press, New Haven, 1979), p. 803. All further references are given after quotations in the text.

22. Rachel Brownstein, *Becoming a Heroine: Reading about Women in Novels* (Penguin, Harmondsworth, 1982), p. 137. Brownstein's argument suggests that there are dangers for feminists in the powers of literary texts to create disenabling role models.

23. J. Hillis Miller, *Fiction and Repetition* (Blackwell, Oxford, 1982), p. 50. All subsequent references will appear after quotations.

24. Currer Bell (Charlotte Brontë), 'Biographical notice of Acton and Ellis Bell, 1850', reproduced in the Penguin edition of *Wuthering Heights, op. cit.*, pp. 30–6.

25. Terry Eagleton, *Literary Theory: An Introduction* (Blackwell, Oxford, 1983). This is an excellent general introduction to new theories of the text although it does not give sufficient attention to the development of a feminist critique within mainstream male theory or to feminist theory itself. This is the province of Toril Moi's *Sexual/Textual Politics* (*op. cit.*), which can in some ways be read as a much-needed supplement.

26. Julia Kristeva, 'La femme ce n'est jamais ça', *Tel Quel*, vol. 59, pp. 19–24, Autumn 1974, quoted by T. Moi in *Sexual/Textual Politics, op. cit.*, p. 163.

27. Julia Kristeva, 'A partir de polylogue'. Interview with Françoise van Rossum Guyon in *Revue des Sciences Humaines*, December, 1979, pp. 495–501.

28. *Roland Barthes by Roland Barthes*, translated by Richard Howard (Hill and Wang, New York, 1977), p. 138.
29. Mr Knightley is the hero of Jane Austen's *Emma* and Rochester is the romantic lover and finally husband of Charlotte Brontë's *Jane Eyre*.
30. In many ways Isabella acts out the Romantic aspirations of the young Cathy in her relationship with Heathcliff, and is another aspect of the possibilities for the lost child. This kind of reading finds not unified characters but fragments of the sign 'woman', and thus contrasts markedly with an authentic realist viewpoint, that might begin to discuss Isabella as a case of wife-beating. See Chapter Two.
31. Mary Daly, *Pure Lust: Elemental Female Philosophy* (The Women's Press, London, 1984), p. 382.
32. See Chapter Two for an example of another cohesive reading from an Authentic Realist perspective.
33. Julia Kristeva, 'The adolescent novel', Warwick conference on Kristeva's work, May, 1987, to be published in *Cultural Critique*.
34. See Mikhail Bakhtin, *Problems in Dostoevsky's Poetics*, translated by Caryl Emerson (Manchester University Press, Manchester, 1984).
35. Toril Moi, 'Marginality and subversions: Julia Kristeva', in *Sexual/Textual Politics*, op. cit., pp. 150–73.
36. See in particular the section entitled, 'Another generation is another space', in 'Woman's time', pp. 209–11, in Toril Moi, (ed.) *The Kristeva Reader, op. cit.*
37. Angela Carter, *The Magic Toyshop* (Virago, London, 1981).
38. Marilyn French, *The Women's Room* (1977); Maya Angelou, *I Know Why the Caged Bird Sings* (1984).
39. Rosaline Coward, 'This novel changes lives: are women's novels feminist novels', in Mary Eagleton, (ed.) *Feminist Literary Theory* (Blackwell, Oxford, 1986), pp. 155–60.
40. Mary Jacobus, review of *The Madwoman in the Attic*, cited by Moi, *Sexual/Textual Politics, op. cit.*, p. 61.
41. From an interview given by Carter to Moira Paterson, 'Flights of fancy in Balham', pp. 42–5, in *The Observer*, November 1986.
42. Jacques Lacan, 'Seminar on *The Purloined Letter*', translated by Jeffrey Mehlman, pp. 38–72, *Yale French Studies*, vol. 48, 1972.
43. Alicia Ostriker, 'The thieves of language: women poets and revisionist mythmakers', *Signs*, vol. 8, no. 1, Spring 1982, pp. 66–78.
44. Angela Carter, 'Notes from the front line', in Micheline Wandor (ed.) *On Gender and Writing*, (Pandora, London, 1983), pp. 69–77.
45. *Speculum of the Other Woman, op. cit.*, p. 229.
46. Luce Irigaray, 'Une mère de glace', in *This Sex Which is Not One, op. cit.*, pp. 168–79.
47. Luce Irigaray, *This Sex Which is not One, op. cit.*, p. 157.
48. John Keats, 'On first looking into Chapman's Homer', in H. W. Garrad, (ed.) *The Poetical Works of John Keats* (Ansen House, Oxford Standard Authors, Oxford, 1956), p. 38.
49. Jane Gallop, *Reading Lacan* (Cornell University Press, Ithaca, 1985).
50. Jane Gallop, *Feminism and Psychoanalysis: The Daughter's Seduction* (Macmillan, Basingstoke, 1982).

51. Julia Kristeva, 'On Chinese women', in *The Kristeva Reader, op. cit.*, pp. 138–60.
52. Jane Gallop, *Reading Lacan, op. cit.*, p. 185.
53. The utopian potential of Angela Carter's writing, particularly in *Nights at the Circus* (1984), is explored in Pauline Palmer, 'From coded mannequin to birdwoman: Angela Carter's magical flight', in Sue Roe (ed.) *Women Reading Women's Writing* (Harvester, Brighton, 1987), pp. 179–205.
54. Chris Weedon, *Feminist Practice and Post-structuralist Theory* (Blackwell, Oxford, 1987).

6

Marxist-Feminism

Lynne Pearce and Sara Mills

The Marxist-Feminist Literature Collective: 'Women's
writing'
Margaret Atwood: *Surfacing*
Charlotte Perkins Gilman: *The Yellow Wallpaper*

I

The relationship between Marxism and feminism has been
described as an 'unhappy marriage', but the liaison between
Marxist–feminism and literary criticism has proved an even more
problematic 'affair', resisting and subsuming all the normal
categories of kinship.[1]

The problem of offering any adequate summary of Marxist-
feminist criticism resides first in the fact that its practice has been
developed more consciously in the social science and cultural
studies arena that in literary criticism *per se*[2]; secondly, and in
paradoxical relation to this first point, there are few feminist
literary studies that have not, to a greater or lesser extent, been
informed by Marxist/Socialist perceptions of the social construction of women and gender. The latter obviously relates directly to
the 'origins' of the modern Women's Movement in the various
New Left Campaigns of the 1960s (see Chapter One and Two).
Indeed, looking back to the chapter on Sexual Politics, the reader
will recall that Millett's definition of politics as 'power-structured
relationships, arrangements where one group of persons is
controlled by another' is potentially Marxist in its articulation,
although, as was also explained, her prioritisation of patriarchy
over capitalism as the nexus of oppression has since been rejected

as a rather crude attempt to 'stand Marxism theory on its head'.[3]

A further problem that is inherent in the notion of 'Marxist-feminism' is the very fact that *it is* a hyphenated concept, continually reminding its practitioners of the uneasy relationship of the one part to the other; is Feminism merely an addition to Marxism or vice versa? This, of course, relates to the larger political argument (again touched upon in Chapter One) of the respective claims of Capitalism and Patriarchy as the fundamental categories of oppression; the one reducing the other to a constituent sub-category. This difficult, and often bitter, debate, which had very practical ramifications for various left-wing organisations in the 1970s, has since been shelved by most involved as a red herring, or at least, a question which is not likely to yield any useful answers. Post-structuralist theory has also enabled literary critics to work with contradictions of this kind far more easily, and to see the relationship between the two parties as mutable, shifting and tangential. As Maggie Humm writes in her chapter on the subject: 'Neither Marxism nor feminism can totally incorporate each other'.[4] It is true, however, (as Humm's subsequent remarks tacitly admit) that much Marxist-feminist literary criticism has taken the form of a simple *modification* of the Marxist paradigms of analysis, which are feminist only because they address issues of gender as well as class. This is a problem we shall return to in the concluding section, but it is proper to introduce it here since it is an issue that relates particularly to our chosen theoretical text and to our subsequent readings.

This tentative problematisation of the concept of Marxist-feminism should already have suggested to the reader that its practice, in literary criticism especially, will be far from monolithic. Here, more than with any of the other theories introduced in this book, we are dealing with an approach which has as many qualities as the contexts in which it has been used. There is no simple answer to question like, 'What is Marxist-feminism?' or 'What elements is a Marxist-feminist reading required to contain?' Beyond an obvious commitment of *relation* to the questions facing women in the 'real world' (understood broadly in the term *materialism*), literary Marxist-feminism will manifest itself in a whole variety of readings, all defining their particular commitment rather differently. Thus, texts as far apart in their theses as Penny Boumhela's *Thomas Hardy and Women* and Terry Lovell's

Consuming Fiction (see Bibliography) may both be held up as examples of texts which describe themselves as 'Marxist–feminist', although one is concerned with the relation of sexual ideology to narrative form, and the other to the conditions surrounding the *production* of the novel and the role of women therein. In addition, there are many other feminist theories, including those introduced in this book, which, as indicated above, were born out of a modern Women's Movement which was itself intimately related to a new socialist consciousness.

Yet while all the theories put into practice in this book may be seen to have their own particular relation to a materialist feminism (in so far as 'Marxism and feminism are both theories about the power of the "real" world and its impact on literary imagination'), none is *systematic* in its application of any particular methodology devised by Marxist-feminists.[5] Here, then, we have chosen one example of literary Marxist–feminist practice and sought to engage with it in our own readings of *Surfacing*, and *The Yellow Wallpaper*. The critical text in question is an article by the Marxist–Feminist Literature Collective (MFLC) of 1978, now regarded as breaking new ground in its practical application of a new synthesis of Marxism, feminism and psychoanalysis.[6] This article, entitled 'Women's writing: Jane Eyre, Shirley, Villette, Aurora Leigh' performs readings of each of the listed texts in turn, concentrating on how their 'not-saids' (explained below) represent the 'deconstruction' of the prevailing ideologies inscribed in their main texts and (since the article is specifically concerned with ideologies relating to gender) constitute their feminism. Although concrete in its application, the theoretical assumptions behind these readings are not made clear in the article and need to be inferred through prior knowledge of Marxist theory. What we shall now do here, therefore, is offer a brief summary of the principles that lie behind the Collective's readings, simultaneously illustrating their application in the article itself. Our own readings that follow will consequently be themselves based on an *inference* of the theoretical assumptions of the article rather than a repetition of the readings it performs. Allowing for a very different choice of texts, the latter would, in any case, be practicably impossible.

Since the late 1970s, the type of Marxism that has been favoured by feminist literary critics is that which comes via writers like Louis Althusser and Pierre Macherey. The attraction of these theorists is that they suggest methods of reading texts which are compatible with the post-structuralist realisation that literature is not simple the *reflection* of the world outside the text. This is in opposition to the type of critical practice offered by earlier Marxist critics like Georg Lukács and Christopher Caudwell, with their preference for Socialist-realist texts. Although Lukács actually argued for the importance of *form* in determining a work's radical potential ('the truly social element in literature is the form'), this was only the case if that form, in some way, exposed or *reflected* the structure of society itself.[7] Thus, the realist novel was seen as a 'bourgeois epic', whose three-part form reflected the profile of a society torn apart by capitalism while straining towards a new resolution or synthesis:

> His fiction thus mirrors, in microcosmic form, the complex totality of society itself. In doing this, great art combats the alienation and fragmentation of capitalist society, projecting a rich, many-sided image of human wholeness.[8]

This model was itself based on what is now popularly known as 'the Marxist dialectic', although the programme of Thesis-Antithesis-Synthesis, as we explained above (see Note 3), actually derived from Hegel. While it is consequently debatable whether the dialectic is an appropriate model for the Marxist literary critic to make use of, we have employed it as a structural device in the reading of *Surfacing* which follows; as an index of transformation against which the changing relationships of the characters to their material circumstances is plotted.

Another way of understanding Lukács' approach and, at the same time, recognising the attractions of Althusser and Macherey for feminist critics, is to consider their contrasting attitudes to the role of 'ideology' in the literary work. While Lukács saw the representation of degenerate late-capitalist ideology as reactionary and unproductive, Althusser's formulation of the complex relationship between 'base and superstructure' lent a new interest to literary texts precisely *because* of their ideological content. In the MFLC article, the writers use Althusser's own definition of ideology as 'a representation of the imaginary relationship of individuals to their real conditions of existence' to define the role of the text itself[9]: 'Literary texts are assumed to be ideological in the sense that they cannot give us a knowledge of the social formation; but they do give us something of equal importance in analysing culture, an imaginary representation of real relations' (p.27). Texts, in other words, reveal to us the workings of the ideologies that they themselves are inscribed by. A useful metaphor here is that of the double mirror which reflects itself to infinity. It will be seen at once that this is a much more satisfactory and enabling view of the text than Lukács' prescription that it simplistically mirror the 'Truth' of reality itself.

But to understand how the Marxist-feminist Literature Collective use Althusser's radical restatement of the relationship between ideology and the economic base, it is first necessary to say a little about the Althusserian source itself. The key text here is Althusser's 'Ideology and Ideological State Apparatuses' of 1971.[10] The essence of the hypothesis is summed up by Chris Weedon in *Feminist Practice and Post-Structuralist Theory*:

> Louis Althusser argues ... that the reproduction of the relations of production, which is central to the maintenance of capitalist social relations, is secured by *ideological state apparatuses* such as schools, the church, the family, the law, the political system, trade unionism, the media and culture, backed by the repressive apparatuses of the police and the armed forces. Each ideological state apparatus contributes to the reproduction of capitalist relations of exploitation in the 'way proper to it' and the means by which it determines dominant meanings is *language*.[11]

What is revolutionary about Althusser's formulation is that it gives the 'superstructure' a role *equal* to that of the 'base' in the perpetration of capitalism. He also provides the literary critic with the extremely useful, related concept of *interpellation*, used to explain how the *individual* is governed by these 'ideological state apparatuses' (ISAs);

> I shall then suggest that ideology 'acts' or 'functions' in such a way that it 'recruits' subjects among the individuals (it recruits them all), or 'transforms' the individuals into subjects (it transforms them all) by the very precise operation which I have called *interpellation* or hailing, and which may be imagined along the lines of the most common everyday police (or other) hailing: 'Hey, you there'. (p. 48)

Interpellation is central to both of the readings performed in this chapter. In the section on *Surfacing* it is related specifically to the heroine's own interpellation by the ideological state apparatus of the family and its attendant agencies (gender difference and romantic love), while the reading of *The Yellow Wallpaper* is concerned both with the interpellation of the protagonist and ourselves as women readers of the text into a particular role: that of the mad woman.

In their readings of Brontë and Barrett Browning, the Collective shows how the texts concerned 'evade and interrogate' Althusser's ISAs in the areas of class structure, kinship and Oedipal socialisation. Just how they 'evade and interrogate' these ideologies necessitates introducing another Marxist concept: the Machereyan 'not-said'. Macherey has been of especial importance to literary critics since, unlike Althusser, his writings practise criticism of particular literary texts.[12] The 'not-said' of a text might be thought of as an 'unspoken sub-text', that, by its very silence, interrogates and undermines what is represented by the 'official discourse'. In other words, a Machereyan reading, like a deconstructive one, is concerned with identifying the 'gaps' in a given text and speculating on what they reveal:

> Criticism, then, does not site itself in the same space as the text itself, allowing it to speak or completing what it leaves unsaid. On the contrary, it installs itself in the text's very incompleteness in order to *theorise* the lack of plenitude – to explain the necessity.[13]

To take just one example of such practice, the MFLC posit that *Jane Eyre* in its very exclusion of kinship relations, is effectively challenging their legitimate existence. Thus, although the main text might be seen to be working towards a reactionary conclusion by restoring the dominant kinship structures (Jane finds her lost family and is married to Rochester), its 'not-said' covertly challenges this status quo:

> *Jane Eyre* does not attempt to rupture the dominant kinship structures. The ending of the novel ('Reader, I married him') affirms those very structures. The feminism of the text resides in its 'not-said', its attempt to inscribe women as sexual subjects within this system. (p. 35)

Such a reading makes explicit connections between this type of Marxist–feminism and a more general post-structuralist resistance to closure and 'inherent' or singular meanings within a text. In the reading of *The Yellow Wallpaper* which follows we argue that it is the text's very refusal to offer a conclusive ending that constitutes its problematisation of madness in materialist terms.

It is necessary to consider finally the way in which the MFLC combine this feminist utilisation of Althusser and Macherey with the psychoanalysis of Lacan and Kristeva. The most obvious point of intersection, and the one we shall ourselves be using in our readings, is that which inheres around the notion of the *imaginary*.[14] Althusser's definition of ideology, as we have already seen, is as the 'representation of the *imaginary* relationship of individuals to their real conditions of existence'. The 'imaginary' here constitutes the failure of individuals to recognise that the ideological forces by which they are interpellated are neither real nor inevitable. They are thus the victims of social relations that they perceive to be natural and determinate, but which are imposed upon them by the State.

This 'mis-recognition' of the imaginary for the real is also at the heart of Lacanian theories of subjectivity. As has already been explained in Chapter Five, the Imaginary is used specifically to describe the pre-Oedipal identification of a child with its mirror-image, before it has acquired language and gendered subjectivity. This is followed by a second split which occurs when the child 'enters language' (the Symbolic Order):

> Just as the infant of the mirror phase misrecognises itself as unified and in physical control of itself, so the speaking subject in the symbolic order misrecognises itself and its utterance as one and assumes that it is the author of meaning.[15]

It will be seen that this second 'misrecognition' has much in common with Althusser's notion of the imaginary as it pertains to the interpellation of the individual by ideology. In both instances, the subject believes in an external truth which *she is the author of*, but which does not really exist. It is just this 'delusion' that allows, on the one hand, for our existence as social beings (without such a misrecognition we could not function effectively in the world), yet on the other, for our manipulation by the forces of the State.

The MFLC illustrate the potential for analogy between these two uses of the 'imaginary' in their reading of *Villette* by postulating that the nun who appears to Lucy Snowe 'banishes the Lacanian "Imaginary" and reinstates the "Symbolic" realm' (p. 41). In Marxist terms, this full entry into the Symbolic Order may be thought of as analogous with the heroine's re-alignment with the Ideological State Apparatuses by which she has been interpellated.[16]

Thus, while until the appearance of the nun, Lucy Snowe's delayed alignment with the Symbolic means that she resists the prevailing ideologies of kinship, class and Oedipal socialisation, the three 'visitations' (all simultaneous with her declarations of love for the male) announce her subsequent interpellation by them. And in Lacanian terms this is possible because she had misrecognised the Other as herself.

Yet while this analogy between a subject's ideological interpellation and her alignment with the Symbolic Order is both simple and suggestive, it is rather the *dislocation* of the two that offers the most potential for the feminist critic. While none of us, as Althusser makes clear, can escape from our position within ideology (individuals are always-already subjects), the difficulty women have in taking up a position within the Symbolic order (conceived by Lacan as an alignment with the Phallic, though not necessarily male, position), often results in their alienation from various social practices, the most obvious being *language* itself. This, in turn, means that women are in a better position to challenge and subvert many of the ruling 'ideological state apparatuses'. The notion of women being in some way 'outside' the patriarchal Symbolic Order is, of course, inherent in both Showalter's 'wild zone' (see Chapter Three) and Kristeva's 'semiotic' (see Chapter Five). In the following readings of *Surfacing* and *The Yellow Wallpaper*, however, we demonstrate the way in which this ostracisation directly undermines the ideological forces by which both heroines are defined. By their temporary exclusion from the Symbolic Order (both through what the patriarchal world would define as 'madness'), they expose the historical and material means of their oppression. However, it is important to make clear the difference between a Marxist–feminist reading, which makes use of this alienation as evidence of the fallibilities and inconsistencies of our ruling ideologies, and those feminist readings (Gilbert and Gubar's, for instance: see discussion in Part II) which *celebrate* 'madness' as a simplistic disruption of the Patriarchal Order *per se*. 'Madness', as the following reading of *The Yellow Wallpaper* will show, cannot be regarded as 'revolutionary' if, for the subject concerned, it is co-terminous with their material oppression.

To summarise then, it is the Marxist-Feminist Literature Collective's engagement with the following that we shall be particularly concerned with in the following readings:

1. The Althusserian formulation of Ideological State Apparatuses and their interpellation of subjects (fictional characters and readers).

2. The Machereyan 'not-said'.
3. The materialist appropriation of psychoanalytic models.
4. The relation of all these theories to issues of gender.

By coincidence, we have found ourselves working with two texts that have in common 'nameless' heroines who are alienated from the social context that has been prescribed for them as women. The two readings, nevertheless, approach the materialist implications of this with two very different sets of hypotheses, and will therefore demonstrate the claims of this introduction that a Marxist-feminist criticism, without a central methodology, is without prescription. The benefits and disadvantages of non-prescriptive feminist theory will be discussed at the end of the chapter.

II

Margaret Atwood's *Surfacing*, like the nineteenth century 'realist' novel that Georg Lukács saw as profiling the rise and fall of capitalist society, is divided into three parts.[17] In order to explore the hypothesis that such a structure may be thought of as analogous to the Marxist dialectic, we have organised the reading under the sub-headings of Thesis, Antithesis and Synthesis, with each 'phase' roughly corresponding to a section of the novel. Within these sub-divisions, we practise readings which derive from the Althusserian and Machereyan theories outline in Part I. As in the Marxist-Feminist Literature Collective's readings of Brontë and Barrett Browning, we have looked for ways in which the text both reflects and interrogates Althusser's Ideological State Apparatuses (ISAs), through the interpellation of the heroine and the other characters.[18] In this analysis, our principal focus is on *the family*, together with its attendant ideological agencies of *gender difference* and *romantic love*.

However, because *Surfacing* must be regarded as a self-consciously political or *interrogative* text, we do not, like the MFLC, attempt to 'discover' its feminist subversion in its 'not-said', except in our closing comments on the problems surrounding its ending.[19] In crude terms, the story is about the heroine making these discoveries herself: coming face to face with her own 'not-said' in the form of the ideologies by which she has been interpellated.

Thus, instead of searching for the 'not-said' we have chosen to perform a reading which explains this process of self-discovery in terms of the heroine's changing relation to the Lacanian Symbolic Order. Our contention is that it is the very *dislocation* between her ideological interpellation and her psychological subjectivity (see Part I above) that enables her to challenge 'her imaginary relationship' to her 'real conditions of existence'. Thus, as the narrative moves through the dialectic of Thesis – Antithesis – Synthesis, the heroine's changing position *vis-à-vis* the Symbolic Order may be seen to culminate in a 'revolution' through which she eventually arrives at a 'synthesis' of the different 'stories' she has told from within the ideological structures by which she has been interpellated.

Thesis

In Part One of the novel, it is gradually revealed that the heroine is caught up in what Althusser describes as 'the imaginary distortion of the ideological representation of the real world' (p. 154). 'Distortion' is a key term here, since it describes well the 'false narratives' she uses to tell the story of her life: her 'marriage', her 'child', the 'drowning' of her brother. In these stories, she mixes elements of what 'really happened' with what she believed happened, or what *might* have happened. At various points, she even draws attention to the treachery of 'memory': the discrepancy between what one experiences, and what one learns afterwards. For example, about her childhood in the war, the heroine states:

> Anna was right, I had a good childhood; it was the middle of the war, flecked grey newsreels I never saw, bombs and concentration camps, the leaders roaring at the crowds from inside their uniforms, pain and endless death, flags rippling in time to the anthems. But I didn't know about that till later, when my brother found out and told me. At the time it felt like peace. (p. 18)

This compares to the story she tells, on the very first page of the novel, of an incident that happened to her brother in a restaurant before she herself was born (p. 7); also, to her constant checking and correcting of bits of the narrative: 'That won't work, I can't call them "they" as if they were someone's family: I have to keep from telling that story' (p. 14) and 'The old priest was gone. What I mean is dead' (p. 18). Then, at the very end of Part One, she brings her propensity for distortion to full consciousness, thus preparing for the process of antithesis that occurs in Part Two:

> I have to be more careful about my memories, I have to be sure that they're my own and not the memories of other people telling me what I felt, how I acted, what I said: if the events are wrong the feelings I remember about them will be wrong too, I'll start inventing them and there will be no way of correcting it, the ones who could help are gone. I run quickly over my version of it, my life, checking it like an alibi; it fits, it's all there till the time I left. Then static, like a jumped track, for a moment I've lost it, wiped clean; my exact age even, I shut my eyes, what is it? To have the past but not the present, that means you're going senile. (p. 73)

But what we need to consider here is the *reason* the heroine tells the stories she does. A clue resides in the last quotation in which she refers to 'the memories of other people telling me what I felt'. This, of course, is an excellent paradigm for the functioning of Althusser's ISAs. The stories the heroine tells are the ones her interpellated self deems she should tell. Let us consider some examples.

In Part One of the novel, the heroine may be seen to be conditioned by not one, but *two*, ideologies of the family. The first of these is represented by the pre-war nuclear family, whose traditions and beliefs were largely shared by both French and English speaking Canadians. In the heroine's own story, these two social groups are symbolised respectively by her parents, and by Paul and his wife. The other view of the family by which she has been interpellated is its *partial* disestablishment by the 'new permissiveness' of the 1960s. This is the 'revolution' represented by the heroine's contemporaries: her 'ex-husband', Anna, David and Joe. It is important to note, however, that these factors only represent a partial overthrow of the system. All of them have 'disowned their parents long ago, the way you are supposed' (p. 17), but they still believe in marriage for themselves (Anna and David have been married for several years; Joe wants to marry). Their real difference from their parents is that they no longer believe in the sanctity or exclusivity of marriage; all claim the right to practise adultery and to get divorced.

Around these two models of the family, the heroine constructs two different stories of her past life. In the first of these stories (the one that her parents would have understood), she has been married and had a baby which she subsequently left with her

husband when the marriage failed. In the second (the story of her
'own generation'), she has been married, had a baby, but has also
been divorced. Neither of these stories, as we find out later, is the
'true' one: she was a mistress, not a wife; and instead of a baby, she
had an abortion. For much of the narrative, the difference
between the telling of these two stories is very subtle. In the
following quotation, however, we witness the sort of linguistic
slippage characteristic of her awkward transition from one
cultural stereotype to another:

> My status is a problem, they obviously think I'm married. But I'm
> safe, wearing my ring, I never threw it out, it's useful for landladies. I
> sent my parents a postcard after the wedding, they must have
> mentioned it to Paul; that, but not the divorce. It isn't part of the
> vocabulary here, there's no reason to upset them.
>   I'm waiting for Madame to ask me about the baby, I'm prepared,
> alerted, I'll tell her I left him in the city; that would be perfectly true,
> only it was a different city, he's better off with my husband, former
> husband. (p. 23)

Between 'husband' and 'former husband' is the fine difference of
the two ideologies the heroine has been interpellated by.

The functioning of Althusser's Ideological State Apparatuses,
including the family, depends on the perpetration of a number of
constituent ideologies. The ones we have chosen to consider here
are those relating to gender difference and romantic love. As with
the family, the heroine's interpellation by gender is a mixture of
pre-war and 1960s ideology. Having rejected the 'crinolines and
tulle' (p. 108) femininity cultivated by her Canadian childhood,
she, like Anna, is now a product of 1960s permissiveness.
Although, in Part One of the novel, she reports the sexual politics
of the group with an objectivity which might be seen as critical,
her passive acceptance of David and Joe's sexist authority reveals
that she is not in a position to challenge her interpellation.
Moreover, her accounts of her own past relationships with men
show that she was very much the victim of a crude power game.

If we construct a profile of the heroine's gender development
we can see that her transition from Old Canada to Modern
America did nothing to alter her status as feminised sexual object:
inferior to and dependent upon the male. In childhood she, like
Anna, fed upon the latter-day 'princess in the tower' stories that
she now illustrates:

Ladies in exotic costumes, sausage rolls of hair across their foreheads, with puffed red mouths and eye-lashes like toothbrush bristles: when I was ten I believed in glamour, it was a kind of religion and these were my icons. (p. 42)

Yet the 'liberated' femininity she assumed as an art student was no less the product of patriarchal exploitation. When her tutor became her lover, she surrendered her career potential to his authoritative dismissal of her sex:

For a while I was going to be a real artist; he thought that was cute but misguided, he said I should study something I'd be able to use because there never have been any important women artists. That was before we were married and I still listened to what he said, so I went into Design and did fabric patterns. But he was right, there never have been any. (p. 52)

The final rejoinder here, 'but he was right', also acts as an indicator that in Part One of the novel the heroine is still largely unable to grasp the extent to which she has been manipulated in sexual–political terms. This is reflected both in the way she and Anna perform all the domestic tasks and silently submit to crude sexist remarks, and, more subtly, in her 'subconscious' compliance to Joe's wishes:

He feels me watching him and lets go of my hand. Then he takes his gum out, bundling it in the silver wrapper, and sticks it in the ashtray and crosses his arms. That means I'm not supposed to observe him; I face front. (p. 8)

Where the sexual politics of gender difference relate more specifically to the ideology of romantic love, however, the heroine may already be seen to have assumed an ambivalent position when the novel opens. Her 'divorce' has alienated her from the concept, so that she no longer 'believes' in it:

We begin to climb and my husband catches up with me again, making one of the brief appearances, framed memories he specialises in: crystal clear image enclosed by a blank wall. He's writing his initials on a fence, graceful scrolls to show me how, lettering was one of the things he taught. There are other initials on the fence but he's making his bigger, leaving his mark. I can't identify the date or the place, it was a city, before we were married; I lean beside him, admiring the fall of winter sunlight over his cheekbone and engraved nose, noble and shaped like a Roman coin profile; that was when everything he did was perfect. On his left hand is a leather glove. He said he loved me, the magic word, it was supposed to make everything light up, I'll never trust that word again. (p. 47)

A little earlier, she uses this fact of her 'divorce' to explain her inability to 'love' Joe:

> I'm trying to decide whether or not I love him. It shouldn't matter, but there's always a moment when curiosity becomes more important to them than peace and they need to ask; though he hasn't yet ... I'm fond of him, I'd rather have him round than not; though it would be nice if he meant something more to me. The fact that he doesn't makes me sad: no one has since my husband. A divorce is like an amputation, you survive but there's less of you. (p. 42)

As we shall see in the next section, this 'disbelief' in romantic love is linked explicitly to the heroine's alienation from language. It is, indeed, her first point of dislocation from her interpellation as feminine subject: her first resistance to the ideologies into which she has been born.

Antithesis

In accordance with the dialectical model, Part Two of the novel sees the heroine moving towards a position in which all the ideologies by which she has been interpellated are problematised and finally overthrown by an epiphany analogous to revolution: the discovery of her father's dead body. We will consider this transformation with respect to the triad of family, gender difference and romantic love considered in the first section, and suggest ways in which it is the heroine's changing position to the Symbolic Order that has enabled it.

We begin with the family itself. While still telling the same stories as in Part One, the heroine now militantly rejects the traditional family structure. She consistently presents herself as the 'divorced woman', and names her husband as the accused. In the present, she resists and rejects a 'second marriage' with Joe, and exposes the hypocrisy and degeneracy of Anna and David's relationship. Yet this cannot be considered a fully feminist consciousness, because she is still unable to liberate herself from the lie that she was once married. Her growing cynicism, however, which is ultimately related to her disaffection with romantic love, enables her to perceive the institution of marriage as infinitely corrupt:

> I remembered what Anna has said about emotional commitments: they've made one, I thought, they hate each other; that must be almost as absorbing as love. The barometer couple in their wooden house, enshrined in their niche on Paul's front porch, my ideal;

except they were glued there, condemned to oscillate back and forth, sun and rain, without escape. (p. 138)

Similarly, in her perception of the power politics associated explicitly with gender difference, the heroine presents a new, ironic awareness. The sexual harassment to which she and Anna are subjected throughout the text is now reported with a grim sense of its potential brutality. During this section of the novel, we are presented with three 'surrogate' rapes: of Anna by David when he wants to film her nude; of herself by David; and of herself (after the discovery of the body) by Joe. I quote the latter:

I didn't want him in me, sacrilege, he was one of the killers, the clay victims damaged and strewed about him, and he hadn't seen, he didn't know about himself, his own capacity for death ... 'What's wrong with you?' he said, angry; then he was pinning me, hands manacles, teeth against my lips, censoring me, he was shoving against me, his body insistent as one side of an argument. (p. 147)

As with her rejection of the romantic love ideology, moreover, this new consciousness is part and parcel of the heroine's new awareness of language. Reporting on David's 'rape' of Anna she reflects:

'Come on, we need a naked lady with big tits and a big ass' David said in the same tender voice; I recognised that menacing gentleness, at school it always went before the trick, the punchline. (p. 147)

Even before she discovers her father's body, the heroine has become aware of the 'double-speak' that separates her own linguistic field from that of the others. She continuously talks at cross-purposes with them, in words they fail to understand:

I said, 'I think men ought to be superior'. But neither of them heard the actual words; Anna looked at me as though I'd betrayed her and said, 'Wow, are you ever brainwashed,' and David said 'Want a job?' and to Joe, 'Hear that, you're superior'. (p. 111)

By failing to hear the 'ought' that qualifies the heroine's statement, Anna and David display their respective inscription by discourses that she herself now stands outside of.

To understand more clearly how the heroine arrives at this antithetical relation to these dominant ideologies, we shall now focus again on the institution of romantic love. The linguistic alienation that we have witnessed operating in her relation to the other ideologies may be seen to stem from this fundamental dislocation. Indeed, Part Two of the novel is full of instances of her antagonism to the ruling discourses. The crisis of her relationship with Joe, for example, hinges on their communication problem in this area:

> It was the language again. I could not use it because it wasn't mine. He must have known what he meant but it was an imprecise word; the Eskimos have fifty-two words for snow because it is important to them, there ought to be as many for love.
> 'I want to,' I said. 'I do in a way.' I hunted through my brain for any emotion that would coincide with what I'd said. I did want to, but it was like thinking God should exist and not being able to believe. (pp. 106–7)

In Lacanian terms, this alienation from the 'official discourse' may be read as the heroine's regression from the Symbolic Order in which, as a woman, she had only ever been imperfectly integrated. At the beginning of Part Two she records significantly:

> I was seeing poorly, translating badly, a dialect problem, I should have used my own. In the experiments they did with children, shutting them up with deaf and dumb nurses, locking them in closets, depriving them of words, they found that after a certain age the mind is incapable of absorbing any language; but how could you tell that the child hadn't invented one, unrecognisable to everyone but itself? (p. 76)

The allusion here to the heroine using a 'dialect' of her own prepares the way for her full regression to the 'semiotic' in Part Three.[20] In Part Two, her 'translation problem' is further evidenced by her misrecognition of her father's scientific papers. Instead of his cave drawings, she sees images of her own aborted child; instead of him being mad (estranged from the conventions of 'normal society'), it is herself. Throughout this section, however, delusion and illumination mix, and she *understands* the dislocation of her language even as she sinks deeper into it: 'The secret had come clear, it had never been a secret, I'd made it one, that was easier. My eyes came open, I began to arrange' (p. 103).

According to Lacanian analogy, meanwhile, the discovery of her father's body may be read as the heroine coming literally face to face with the Symbolic (The-Law-of-the-Father); that is, recognising it for what it is, while situating herself outside of it.[21] In the final pages of Part Two, we see the semiotic consciousness repossess the heroine to the point where she can barely understand the language of those about her, and yet she sees through the 'ideology' of their language as though instinctively: 'I had to concentrate in order to talk to him, the English words seemed imported, foreign; it was like trying to listen to two separate conversations, each interrupting the other' (p. 150). This psychological dislocation, moreover, is concomitant with the heroine's realisation of the fraudulent ideologies espoused both by herself and those around her. Of David, she remarks:

> The power flowed into my eyes, I could see into him, he was an imposter, layers of political handbills, pages from magazines, *affiches*, verbs and nouns glued onto him and shredding away, the original surface littered with fragments and tatters ... Second-hand American was spreading over him in patches, like mange or lichen. He was infested, garbled, and I couldn't help him: it would take such a time to heal, unearth him, scrape down to where he was true. (p. 152)

With this new 'meta-consciousness' she begins to see through the distortions of her past stories and to correct them: she had never been married, had had an abortion instead of a wedding, had never ever had a brother.

Synthesis

Part Three of *Surfacing* follows the heroine's complete re-possession by the semiotic through to her re-alignment with the Symbolic following her identification with the ghost of her dead father. In terms of the Hegelian dialectic, they may be seen as the passage from antithesis, through revolution, to a new 'transcend-ant' synthesis. But before drawing some conclusions from these final transactions, it is worth first considering their implications in terms of the heroine's ideological interpellation that we have followed throughout this reading.

The reader will probably have noticed already that in the movement from 'thesis' to 'antithesis' there was a visible conflation of the three ideologies identified at the outset of the novel, with the heroine's alienation from the discourse of romantic love gradually infecting her relation to the sexual politics of gender difference, and simultaneously undermining both 'versions' of the family as Ideological State Apparatus. Similarly, in the 'semiotic' phase of Part Three, to reject one of these ideologies is to reject them all: a summation which links with the more anthropological readings of the text (see Chapter Three), which interpret this phase of the novel simply as a rejection of 'Culture' *per se*. In so far as culture may be seen to relate to industrial capitalism, this wholesale rejection of the trappings of civilisation is certainly of interest for a Marxist–feminist reading: the point at which capitalism can be seen to subsume patriarchy as the greater evil. Indeed, the heroine herself generalises, by subsuming her previous problematisation of gender difference in her larger rejection of the capitalist forces: 'But then I realised it wasn't the men I hated, it was the Americans, men and women both. They'd had their chance but they'd turned against the gods' (p. 154).

Specifically in terms of her relation to the ideology of the family, Part Three sees the heroine pass through a symbolic 'total rejection' to an equally symbolic 'compromise'. The former is achieved in the context of her ritual destruction of the signifiers of industrial capitalism: her exorcising of all things metal:

> I slip the ring from my left hand, non-husband, he is the next thing I must discard finally, and drop it into the fire, altar, it may not melt but it will at least be purified, and blood will burn off. Everything from history must be eliminated, the circles and the arrogant square pages. I rummage under the mattress and bring out the scrapbooks, ripping them up, the ladies, dress forms and decorated china heads, the suns and the moons, the rabbits and their archaic eggs, my false peace, his wars, aeroplanes and tanks and the helmeted explorers. (p. 176)

This symbolic overthrow of the State Apparatus then gives way, after her realignment with the Symbolic Order, to a rationalisation of both her former positions. Both the stories she had previously told she now recognises to be false. Neither married nor divorced, she realises that her former lover had never been part of any family institution, either conventional or permissive; neither had be been exceptionally good, or exceptionally evil:

> I can remember him, fake husband, more clearly though, and now I feel nothing for him but sorrow. He was neither of the things I believed, he was only a normal man, middle-aged, second-rate, selfish and kind in the average proportions; but I was not prepared for the average, its needless cruelties and lies. (p. 188)

In terms of the heroine's final synthesis of the ideologies surrounding gender differences, meanwhile, it is important to note that her own active revolution begins with her symbolic 'drowning' of 'Random Samples':

> The film coils onto the sand under the water, weighted down by its containers; the invisible captured images are swimming away into the lake like tadpoles, Joe and David beside their deflated log, axemen,

arms folded, Anna with no clothes on jumping off the edge of the
dock, finger up, hundreds of tiny Annas no longer bottled and
shelved. (p. 166)

Besides its obvious revenge for her own abortion (the image of the
bottle foetus recurs throughout the text), the heroine's gesture is
an attempt finally to dissolve the iniquities of gender difference. In
their watery grave, the macho axemen and the pornographic
female body are no more. Similarly, her own journey back to the
semiotic pre-Oedipal stage releases the heroine from her own
interpellation as female subject. During her time in the forest, she
completely loses sense of herself as 'feminine': she is merely
female. Upon her return to civilisation, she regards this ungendered self ironically:

> That is the real danger now, the hospital or the zoo, where we are
> put, species and individual, when we can no longer cope. They can
> never believe it is only a natural woman, state of nature, they think
> of that as a tanned body on a beach with washed hair waving like
> scarves; not this, dirt-caked and streaked, skin grimed and scabby,
> hair like a frayed bath-mat stuck with leaves and twigs. A new kind
> of centrefold. (p. 190)

After the discovery of her father's body, the heroine is also able
fully to perceive her earlier interpellation by the agency of
romantic love. Correcting the earlier story of her 'husband's
declaration of love as he inscribed his name on a fence, she
confesses that he never even wrote letters: 'All I had was the
criticisms in red pencil he paperclipped to my drawings' (p. 148).
Moreover, he declared his love for her only by way of an *apology*:

> He did say he loved me though, that part was true; I didn't make it
> up. It was the night I locked myself in and turned on the water in the
> bathtub and he cried on the other side of the door. When I gave up
> and came out he showed me snapshots of his wife and children, his
> reasons, his stuffed and mounted family, they had names, he said I
> should be mature. (p. 149)

The climax of the heroine's re-possession by the semiotic occurs
in Chapter Twenty-Four when, forbidden contact with all things
civilised and reduced to a naked, 'animal' state, the heroine also
loses all consciousness of language. Not merely does she speak a
different language to that of humans: she has no necessity to
speak at all. She has re-entered a world where the signifier is
continuous with the signified, and being exists only as a *context*:

> In one of the languages there are no nouns, only verbs held for a
> longer moment.
>   The animals have no need for speech, why talk when you are a
> word
>   I lean against a tree, I am a tree leaning
> I break out again into the bright sun and crumple, head against the
> ground   I am not an animal or a tree, I am the thing in which the
> animals move and grow, I am a place (p. 181)

From this primal state, the language of 'the Americans' is only a
senseless noise. The voice of Reason has been rumbled; the
Derridean non-referentiality of the sign that first surfaced in the
heroine's response to various road signs and poster in Chapter
One, here culminates in a vicariousness that is also a scathing
indictment of capitalism itself:

> Behind me they crash, their boats crash, language ululating,
> electronic signals thrown back and forth between them, hooo, hooo,
> they talk in numbers, the voice of reason. They clank, heavy with
> weapons and iron plating. (p. 185)

Yet from this fantasy existence, in which she imagines herself to
be outside of language and outside of ideology, the heroine is
forced to return to what is literally 'the material world'. Having
conceived her child on her own terms in a symbolic attempt to win
back the means of reproduction, she has recognised the need to
take possession of the *conditions of production*.[22] This achieved, she
passes through two encounters with the ghosts of her dead
parents which act as her re-entry to the material world, 'to the city
and its pervasive menace' (p. 189). But while the forces which
drive her back may be regarded as ultimately materialist (I can't
stay here forever, there isn't enough food'), it is important to
recognise the prior necessity of the heroine's psychological
realignment with the Symbolic. This is effected by her act of
identification *with* the Father. She takes her place in the world
again by literally 'seeing through her father's eyes':

> I say Father.
> He turns towards me and it's not my father. It is what my father
> saw, the thing you meet when you've stayed here too long alone.
> (p. 187)

This movement is then completed in the final paragraph of the
chapter when the heroine recognises that her father's footsteps
are, in fact, her own.

This is a similar re-alignment to the Symbolic that the Marxist-Feminist Literature Collective identify at the end of *Jane Eyre* and *Villette*. In one sense it, too, reads like a reactionary conclusion. Atwood's heroine, like Brontë's, takes her place again within the standard kinship relations. Yet, in so far as the text is to satisfy a Marxist–feminist commitment to the material conditions of our existence, such re-integration must be seen as necessary. The state of revolution, like the semiotic itself, cannot endure forever, and we are, unless maintaining a false ahistoricity, forced to resume/assume our positions as social beings within the Symbolic Order:

> No gods to help me now, they're questionable once more, theoretical as Jesus. They've receded, back to the past, inside the skull, is it the same place. They'll never appear to me again, I can't afford it; from now I'll live in the usual way, defining them by their absence; and love by its failures, power by its losses, its renunciation. I regret them; but they give only one kind of truth, one hand.' (p. 189)

This recognition of the text's final commitment to a historical and social solution is of vital importance to the Marxist–feminist critic, if she is to postulate an effective alternative to the ahistorical, 'mythological' readings of *Surfacing* which abound. The introduction to the Virago edition by Francine du Plessix Gray is typical of this type of reading, regarding the climax of the text as a mystical and *religious* experience:

> But Atwood's genius rises above these debates. For her naturalistic epiphanies are of a strictly mythic nature and never tend to stereotyping or separatism. The female religious vision that she presents in her utterly remarkable book also marks the surfacing, I believe, of a future tradition of religious quest in women's novels. (p. 6)[23]

Without this final synthesis which sees the heroine preparing to take her place again among the 'cities and factories', the Marxist critic would be justified in regarding the text as an anarchic sell-out. The fact that the 'revolution' effected is itself individual rather than social will, even so, be regarded by many Marxists as an unworkable concept. Such a problematic amalgam of materialism and psychology within the text of course relates to the larger problem to be addressed in Part III, of whether the ahistoricity of psychoanalytic method *can* ever be successfully incorporated into a materialist account of subjectivity.

Yet if we suspend these difficulties temporarily, it will be seen that within the thesis we have been following here, the heroine's re-entry into the Symbolic Order may be seen to effectively complete the dialectical movement of the text as a whole. Marxist and psychoanalytic models would appear to close together in a powerful alliance of their explanations of subjectivity. But what of Feminism? As in the Marxist-Feminist Literature Collective article, the feminism of this reading has not resided in the theoretical models themselves, as much as the gender issues they have been used to uncover. Yet embedded in the last page of Atwood's remarkable text are two sentences in which all the issues raised by this reading are brought to a conclusion that *is* its synthesis; that *does* acknowledge the heroine's re-negotiation of the Symbolic Order; but which also admits for feminists in the material world the *possibility* of change. Beneath its cynicism and probability of failure resides hope. The family, complete with its satellites of gender difference and romantic love, is not what it was; probably we should talk about it:

> If I go with him we will have to talk, wooden houses are obsolete, we can no longer live in spurious peace by avoiding each other, the way it was before, we will have to begin. For us it's necessary, the intercession of words; and we will probably fail, sooner or later, more or less painfully. (p. 192)

Charlotte Perkins Gilman's 'The Yellow Wallpaper' has become increasingly important for many Anglo-American feminists, and it is one which has already been interpreted from various feminist critical positions.[24] Most critics read it as a simple story of a women being driven mad because of her virtual imprisonment by her husband. Because she is forced into inactivity by him, madness is her only escape. Gilman's text is thus often read as radical, which indeed it is, but it is often misrecognised as a reflection of women's experience in the world. One of the most important readings, in this context, is that by Sandra Gilbert and Susan Gubar which Sue Spaull and Elaine Millard have summarised in Chapter Four.[25] There are several ways in which a Marxist-feminist reading would take issue with Gilbert and Gubar's essentialist reading of the short story, and this reaction forms the basis of the following discussion.

First there is the fact that Gilbert and Gubar assume that the author of the text *is* the protagonist. Perkins Gilman and the narrator are often run together as if they were the same person, and the text is therefore read as a straightforwardly autobiographical account of Gilman's experience of madness. This is clearly problematic, since, although a Marxist-feminist position is concerned with the conditions of production of the text, it is in terms of how social forces impinge upon the individual constructing the text, and not in terms of the relations between that subject and the text. As we show later in this section, an autobiographical reading is imposed on the text to resolve it, to give it closure; it is this notion of resolution which a Marxist-feminist reading refuses, preferring to concentrate on the gaps and inconsistencies of the text to highlight the workings of ideology.

Secondly, Gilbert and Gubar call this text 'a paradigmatic tale which ... seems to tell *the* story that all literary women would tell if they could speak their "speechless woe"' (p. 89). Without denying the importance of the text in feminist literary history, within a Marxist-feminist reading, it is necessary to question the fact that a text about a woman's madness, and therefore madness itself, is central to women's literary expression. This is surely accepting the limitations imposed upon women writers by notions of masculine rationality and its polar opposite female sensitivity, intuitiveness and, ultimately, female madness. For Gilbert and Gubar, this woman character's experience can be read as standing for all women's experience under patriarchy, with madness as a potential escape from such oppression. Texts such as Marge Piercy's *Woman on the Edge of Time*, Jean Rhys's *Wide Sargasso Sea*, Toni Morrison's *Beloved* and *Sula* amongst others, tend to pose descent into madness as a potential source of escape: as a haven from which to flee patriarchal oppression. However, feminists such as Gayatri Spivak have worked hard to deconstruct the notion of a unitary female experience – especially one represented by a white middle class woman – and it now seems possible to argue for a re-reading of these 'women and madness' texts to highlight the problems of asserting that madness is liberatory.[26]

Gilbert and Gubar attempt to deny that this is indeed madness, because they term it 'what the world calls madness' (p. 90), implying that there is some 'sense' in this choice by the narrator. Indeed, after Foucault's work on madness and civilisation, it is necessary to be rightly sceptical of the division between insanity and sanity.[27] However, even within the terms of the text, it is difficult to see what happens to the narrator as empowering, except by relying on radical feminist conventions of reading madness as a form of self-expression and power.

Finally, Gilbert and Gubar assume that in some way the woman confined to the house is the same as the women who creep outside since they say: 'And the woman creeps too (like the yellow smell) through the house, in the house, and out of the house, in the garden and "on that long road under the trees"' (p. 90) whereas, in the text, these 'women' are posed as separate from the narrator herself. Yet despite the fact that the narrator explicitly states that 'I think there are a great many women' and she also says, 'Sometimes I think there are a great many women behind [the wallpaper], and sometimes only one' (p. 15), Gilbert and Gubar insist on seeing these numerous women as the narrator: 'Eventually it becomes obvious to both the reader and the narrator that the figure creeping through and behind the wallpaper is both the narrator and the narrator's double' (p. 91). It is true that the narrator later confuses herself with the women in the wallpaper, but it is important that this is read as a *misrecognition*, as an acceptance of madness, rather than as an act of solidarity with other women. Even for the narrator, this identification is not viewed positively: 'Most women do not creep by daylight . . . I don't blame her a bit. It must be very humiliating to be caught creeping by daylight! . . . I always lock the door when I creep by daylight' (p. 16). This statement of identification by Gilbert and Gubar is analogous to their insistence on reading the narrator as Charlotte Perkins Gilman herself, and to reading the narrator as Every-woman, which is helped by the fact that the narrator alone is not named (as in *Surfacing*), and can therefore have a fairly open reference to females in general. This reading is encouraged by the fact that Jenny/Jane, the narrator's sister-in-law, is also caught staring at and touching the wallpaper, thus suggesting a special relationship between women in general and madness. What a Marxist–feminist reading retains is the notion of specificity, both historical and social. This open reference of the text is to be resisted, as we show later.

It is interesting to consider the end of the story, where her husband swoons with horror (or as Gilbert and Gubar put it, with *surprise*) at what she has done to the room:

But John's masculine swoon of surprise is the least of the *triumphs* Gilman imagines for her madwoman. More significant are the madwoman's own imaginings and creations, *mirages of health and freedom* with which her author endows her like a fairy godmother showering gold on a sleeping heroine. The woman from behind the wallpaper creeps away, for instance, creeps fast and far on the long road, in broad daylight. "I have watched her sometimes away off in the open country," says the narrator, "creeping as fast as a cloud shadow in a high wind." Indistinct and yet rapid, barely perceptible but inexorable, the progress of that cloud shadow is not unlike the progress of nineteenth century literary women out of the texts defined by patriarchal poetics into the open spaces of their own authority. (p. 91) [emphasis added]

I have quoted this passage in full as there are several points to be made in the context of a Marxist–feminist reading. Because of the radical feminist and liberal insistence on closure, Gilbert and Gubar are forced to interpret the narrator's crawling over her husband as a triumph, and to view the creeping women positively; otherwise the text would be incoherent. This implies that once the reader has decided that this is a text which has one meaning, then the rest of the text is read to line up with that meaning. However, from a Marxist–feminist position, it is precisely this 'incoherence' this lack of closure which needs to be investigated; analysing the text itself reveals first that the woman's action of creeping over her husband is posited as *both* a triumph and as a defeat; and secondly, that although these 'women' are rather negatively portrayed they are nevertheless something with which the narrator identifies.

Let us consider the ending in some detail to provide evidence for these two claims. The narrator has peeled off most of the wallpaper, she has locked herself in the room and thrown the key out of the window, she has tried to bite the bed because she is so angry, and she has tied herself with a long rope so that she will not be taken outside. Her husband has tried to break down the door, and eventually she tells him that she has thrown the key outside the window. When he enters she reports:

'What is the matter?' he cried. 'For God's sake, what are you doing?' I kept on creeping just the same, but I looked at him over my shoulder. 'I've got out at last,' said I, 'in spite of you and Jane. And I've pulled off most of the paper, so you can't put me back!'
Now why should that man have fainted? But he did, and right across my path by the wall, so that I had to creep over him every time! (p. 19)

As I mentioned earlier, most readings of the text interpret the ending as a triumph of the narrator over her husband, since she creeps *over* him, and she explicitly states, 'I've got out at last'. However, the position mapped out for the reader to adopt in this last section is not a comfortable one; the reader cannot necessarily assume that the narrator is in a position of 'truth', that the information given her is unmediated, nor that she is to view the narrator crawling around the room positively. In some sense at least, although the reader is not expected to take John's position unproblematically either, his fainting leads us to question the notion that this is a scene of triumph. The central figure is left crawling round the room, one imagines interminably, until her husband recovers. There is no suggestion that she has any escape from this crawling, for she says, 'I had to creep over him every time' (p. 19). Thus, she may have 'got out' of the wallpaper but she certainly has not got out of the room; the bars of the wallpaper no longer restrain her, but the bars of the room do. She has 'escaped', but the reader is not sure what exactly she has escaped *into*.

Thus, although the ending of the story only 'makes sense' if we read it as a triumph, in a Marxist–feminist reading, it is this 'making sense' which is to be resisted; instead it is the contradictions, which are ignored in other readings, which are concentrated upon.

Similarly, with the 'women' outside and behind the wallpaper, the fact that the 'women' *creep* (not a particularly positive term), should be enough to signal to the reader that they are not creatures to be admired. The reader is left unsure as to the exact nature of these 'mirages of health and freedom' which the 'women' offer. Consider, for example, the end of the story where the narrator says, 'I don't like to *look* out of the windows even – there are so many of those creeping women, and they creep so fast' (p. 18), and later, when she says, 'I don't want to go outside ... For outside you have to creep on the ground, and everything is green instead of yellow' (p. 18). Clearly, here, creeping is portrayed negatively and not as a positive escape route. However, the narrator *does* identify with the women finally, and is not able to distinguish herself from them, nor from the 'woman' behind the wallpaper; first, because she herself begins to creep, and secondly, because she states that John and Jane 'can't put me back' behind the wallpaper (p. 19), which suggests that she thinks she *is* the 'woman' she discovered in the wallpaper.[28] However, the portrayal of this identification is full of contradictions and cannot be read as straightforwardly positive; for example, she describes the figure behind the wallpaper as a 'strange, formless sort of figure that seems to skulk about behind that silly and conspicuous front design' (p. 8).

As we noted in the introduction to this chapter, a Marxist–feminist reading is concerned with the gaps and contradictions of a text; the places where ideology is attempting to bring the story to a neat close, but where because of the nature of ideology, closure is only partial. It is in analysing the ending of this story that we see where other readings are forced to attempt to recuperate the protagonist's final surrender to madness as triumph. For example, Gilbert and Gubar state: 'That such an escape from the numb world behind the patterned walls of the text was a flight from dis-ease into health was quite clear to Gilman herself' (p. 91). However, even within the terms of the text it is unclear whether the final fall into madness is such a positive one. Clearly, the life behind the wallpaper is negatively portrayed, as is the life that the central figure leads, confined in isolation. Yet can the so-called escape ('a flight from dis-ease into health') really be regarded as positive? It would seem that there are little grounds in the text for imagining that the narrator *escapes* into the haven of insanity from the hell of patriarchal insanity.

This is essentially the major problem of the ideology of the 'woman and madness' text, and one which this text highlights. It is precisely because it is impossible to resolve a text which poses madness as a form of escape that the ending is contradictory or confusing. What can the woman who is now mad go on to do? What exactly has she escaped into? There are very few strategies for resolving this type of text. Once madness has been posed as an escape, little detail can be given of the exact nature of the escape; in Marge Piercy's *Woman on the Edge of Time*, the heroine escapes into a utopia of her own imaginings, but it is difficult to articulate such an alternative 'reality' given the constraints on madness within Western society. What Perkins Gilman has done here is to leave the text unresolved, and we should not see this as a failure in the plot, but rather indicative of the problems with the ideology concerning women and madness.

However, the text *has* been resolved, in the Virago edition at least, by placing after it a text by Gilman called 'Why I wrote *The Yellow Wallpaper*'. It should be remembered that this short text was not included with the short story until 15 years after its first publication. Gilman calls it 'the story of the story' (p. 19), and most critics read it as a 'key' to the story – a way of relating the story to the life of Gilman herself, and to women in general. However, it can be read as *another* story about the story, a further attempt to make an incoherent text make sense. In this 'afterword', Gilman states that she herself suffered from 'a severe and continuous nervous breakdown tending to melancholia – and beyond' (p. 19) and the way that she recovered sanity was by refusing the rest cure and plunging into 'work, the normal life of every human being' (p. 20). The difference between the two texts is often blurred, so that we assume that the protagonist of the first text overcomes madness just as Gilman did.[29] This blurring of the difference between 'real life' and 'story' is also encouraged because of the reference to Weir Mitchell in the story, who was the major proponent for the infamous rest cure which Perkins Gilman escaped from. However, although this information is pertinent, it does not allow us to achieve resolution for *The Yellow Wallpaper*. Thus, we can only assume that, rather than being an escape, this type of madness presented here can be read as a symptom and effect of oppression, and can in turn become oppression in its own right. Although it is important to re-value those things which women have created as alternatives to 'male' behaviour, it is dangerous to re-value the very chains which bind us. Madness may equal resistance to and refusal of oppressive ideologies, but it does not indicate escape. Madness itself is ideologically determined.

A further contradiction in the text is the nature of the narrator's voice: the way in which this text is related to us. At first, the reader feels that it is being kept as a diary, since there are entries such as: 'There comes John, and I must put this away – he hates to have me write a word' (p. 5) and 'We have been here two weeks, and I haven't felt like writing before, since that first day' (p. 6). However, throughout the process of developing madness, the style does not vary greatly; the narrator is lucid, and uses well-connected sentences – not at all the conventions which are generally used for representing madness. Perhaps the only element which shows that the narrator is suffering from incipient insanity is the rapid changes of subject, signalled by very short, one-sentence paragraphs. However, it is interesting that some of her most lucid paragraphs are those in which she is describing the growths and changes in the wallpaper, for example:

> The outside pattern is a florid arabesque, reminding one of a fungus. If you can imagine a toadstool in joints, an interminable string of toadstools, budding and sprouting in endless convolutions – why, that is something like it. (p. 12)

The narrator's lucidity remains with her even when she is crawling round the room interminably, and performing strange actions, such as biting the bed, and tying a rope around her. This very control and clarity of the narrator seems at odds with the actions of the character, and with the conventions for the representations of madness; this makes the reader ask where this voice is coming from and question its supposedly biographical reference.

A Marxist–feminist reading is concerned to show that this is a very specific depiction of madness, and that the nature of this type of madness is constructed by patriarchal pressure and by social conventions. Madness is extremely heterogeneous and over-determined, arising from, and caused by, a variety of sources; yet the type of madness portrayed here is clearly constructed, and can clearly be overcome, rather than being accepted triumphantly as a form of feminist liberation. Using psychoanalysis in this context also shows us that this is not liberation: the physician/husband/father figure of John is portrayed as an embodiment of 'the Law of the Father' (see Chapter Five and Glossary). Indeed, all the male figures in the text are merged: discussing Weir Mitchell, the narrator quotes a friend who had observed, 'He is just like John and my brother only more so' (p. 9). Within this patriarchy the female figure has transgressed the Law, and lapsed into the Imaginary: the pre-Oedipal phase where difference is not as important as sameness. However, as emerged in our reading of *Surfacing*, the Imaginary is only a temporary stage in the child's development, and as a permanent choice, it is essentially a psychotic position: a rejection of the Symbolic Order, and hence of language and meaning.

This lapse into the Imaginary is reinforced by the fact that throughout the text, the narrator is reduced to the status of a baby or child: she is petted by her husband: 'He is very careful and loving, and hardly lets me stir without special direction' (p. 5) and 'Dear John gathered me up in his arms and just carried me upstairs and laid me on the bed' (p. 10). He calls her 'little girl' (p. 11) and says to here 'Bless her little heart! ... She shall be as sick as she pleases!' (p. 12). Also, she is kept in a room which used to be a nursery and she is forced, like a child, to have an afternoon nap. A flight into childhood dependence, or into the Imaginary, is one which the reader is left to feel ambivalent about: the flight into the Imaginary/Wallpaper, where anything and nothing can be seen/read, is to be welcomed and/or rejected as psychotic. Regression into the Imaginary gives the illusion of coherent identity (identification with the other 'women') but it is nevertheless an *illusion*. This is clearly a misrecognition by the central figure of the way that ideological forces have interpellated her. She has been called upon by her husband to misrecognise herself as a child, but this interpellation is not real or inevitable and can be resisted. By the end of the text, this confused position is polarised still further, as I have shown above, since the reader has either to align herself with the Symbolic Order (and John), or with the Imaginary (and the madwoman). Most readers align themselves with the madwoman, but the text does not necessarily offer such an option, since to align with the 'madwoman' is to align with the Imaginary. Yet is it possible to do so, since this 'madness' is related to us in the calm voice of the Symbolic Order?

It is this process of interpellation which is most worrying about this text. The text interpellates women readers into sympathy with the narrator, and thus leads them to recognise within themselves the elements of madness which the protagonist is undergoing. Thus, in reading the text, the connection between madness and womanhood is re-stated, in the same way as patriarchal texts run together these notions of femininity, frailty and madness. It is this false recognition which needs to be challenged and resisted. Centring on the contradictions in the text leads the reader to formulate a position from which to resist this reading. This text is, of course, an *imaginary* representation of the real relations in society, and it would therefore be erroneous to assume, as we are led to believe, that all women are potentially capable of going insane. Yet this is how the text addresses its women readers on the surface at least (but not, it must be noted, its male readers, who have insisted on reading it as 'Gothic horror').[30] There is no inherent link between femaleness and insanity, but, since the nineteenth century, a causal relation has been constructed, as Phyllis Chesler and Elaine Showalter have shown.[31] This link needs to be subjected to a radical critique.

Let us consider how the text goes about getting the reader to collude in this false identification process: the text takes as its motif something which most readers can recognise, that is, staring at wallpaper and following the patterns. This initial recognition is then carried through to a recognition of this as a pre-condition for madness. The story is, after all, called 'The Yellow Wallpaper', as if it were the wallpaper which were the cause of the madness. The diary form and the use of the first person pronoun 'I' makes the reader feel that she is reading a private, personal account, which is reinforced by the fact that on several occasions the reader is directly addressed: for example, 'I think that woman gets out in the daytime! And I'll tell you why – privately – I've seen her!' (p. 15). Thus, the reader is positioned as a confidante to the narrator, and her sympathy is sought. Also, as I noted above, the narrator is not, unlike the other characters in the text, given a name, and this encourages a reading of the character as Everywoman (*all* women), and therefore as potentially having reference to the individual reader herself. However, we need to interrogate the usefulness of a reading strategy that leads the woman reader to assume that the madwoman referred to in the text is none other than herself. Although, as has been shown in Chapter Two, there are occasions when an authentic realist reading is strategically useful, it does not seem useful to recognise madness within oneself, unless it is to question the origin of that madness.

'The Yellow Wallpaper' can be read as a historically specific account of what can induce madness, without being a text which offers coherent solutions to that condition. What needs to be focussed on is the specificity of the conditions which produce madness as described in the text (remembering that all of Freud's female patients suffering from hysteria were from the middle class), rather than assuming that it has universal reference for all women. Indeed, John describes her condition as 'a slight hysterical tendency' (p. 4). The narrator of the text is clearly from the upper middle class: her husband is a doctor, and they are staying in an 'ancestral hall . . . a colonial mansion, a hereditary estate' (p. 3) for the summer. Are we to assume, from the repetitions and rephrasing of this, that the protagonist is trying to make some point about her position in society? She points out that the house is 'quite alone, standing well back from the road ... and there are ... lots of separate little houses for the gardeners and people' (p. 4). From the house, 'I get a lovely view of the bay and a little private wharf belonging to the estate' (p. 7). She is also at pains to point out that, 'My brother is also a physician, and also of high standing' (p. 4); thus, we are not to assume that she has simply married into the upper middle class. The wife is forced to stay at home, without occupying herself with work of any kind; the paradigm of the middle-class housewife since the nineteenth century. Unlike the working-class housewife of the time, the middle-class housewife does not concern herself with the cleaning and cooking of the household, but rather its management by other women. The protagonist's madness is a logical progression or an amplification of this confinement, for eventually, she can no longer act at all: 'I don't feel as if it was worthwhile to turn my hand over for anything' (p. 9). This madness is an intensification of the alienation inherent in the condition of idleness enforced on the bourgeois female at this time, by their husbands and the male work-force.

The cure she is offered is more inactivity: that is, greater alienation. The only cure that the protagonist can offer for her 'illness' is 'more society and stimulus' (p. 4) and to be allowed to write. Perhaps John is right in thinking that this is not the best cure, and even the narrator can see that even though occasionally she feels that 'if I were only well enough to write a little it would relieve the press of ideas and rest me', she can still see that 'I find I get pretty tired when I try' (p. 7). Simply being allowed to write is surely not the cure. She goes on to say:

> I don't know why I should write this. I don't want to. I don't feel able. And I know John would think it absurd. But I *must* say what I feel and think in some way – it is such a relief! But the effort is getting to be greater than the relief. (p. 10)

This 'expression' of her problem in a diary is not perhaps a cure, because it simply describes the symptoms and aggravates them. This obviously does not constitute writing as *work*. In 'Why I wrote "The Yellow Wallpaper"', Gilman notes that what cured her was: 'work, the normal life of every human being; work, in which is joy and growth and service, without which one is a pauper and a parasite' (p. 20). I am not drawing on the Afterword to resolve 'The Yellow Wallpaper' but simply to note that Gilman did not complete the text in the way that she completed the story of her own madness. Thus, the juxtaposition of the Afterword seems to undercut and contradict the readings of 'The Yellow Wallpaper' as a text about escape into madness. However, neither the protagonist nor John can see the structural reason for the protagonist's madness, and that is the fact that she is deprived of involvement with productive work of any sort. Different participants in the reading process assume different reasons for the narrator's madness; the protagonist herself does not give an explanation for it, except to allude to 'nervousness' (p. 6); her husband is content to assume that there is 'no reason to suffer' (p. 6). The reader is led to assume that the reason the woman goes mad is because of her oppressive relation with her husband; however, there is a further reason, and that is her confinement and inactivity which is indicative of a larger social phenomenon affecting middle class women in this period.

In conclusion, a Marxist–feminist reading of 'The Yellow Wallpaper' enables the reader to be critically aware of the type of reading which she has been led to believe is 'natural', and also the way the text 'calls upon' her. Within this type of reading practice, she can centre on the contradictions in the text, rather than having to force the information in the text into a coherent whole, resulting in closure. She can also question the way she is positioned by the text, and become in Judith Fetterley's terms a 'resisting reader'.[32]

III

Several potential problems in the practice of an effective Marxist–feminist criticism were raised in Part I of this chapter, and others will have been seen to emerge in the course of the readings themselves. The principal difficulties that we decided to discuss may be listed under the following headings:

1. Marxist-feminism's lack of a single prescriptive critical model.
2. The tendency for Marxist-feminism to be the simple adaptation of Marxist models to gender issues.
3. The dependence on models that are not primarily literary-critical.

4. The uneasy relationship between Marxist–feminism and psychoanalysis.
5. The place of Marxist-feminism within a more general feminist post-structuralist enterprise.

For the new student or reader coming to a theoretical literary practice for the first time, we recognise that it is the very amorphous nature of the Marxist–feminist model that may well constitute the greatest obstacle. Indeed, the central problem is that there is no *one* model, text, or even group of texts, that can be referred to. As with the French feminisms discussed in the preceding chapter, readings performed under the general auspices of a Marxist–feminist model may be as esoteric as the contexts in which they appear, and without the nominal author-identification of, say, 'Kristeva' or 'Cixous'. Without 'primary texts', as such, Marxist–feminism offers no easy access to the new reader, and the individual must be prepared for a long struggle before she finally works out where she stands politically *vis-à-vis* many diverse theories, and which of those she feels it most useful to appropriate.

This lack of a prescriptive model also relates directly to the second problem we need to consider; that is, the ambiguous relationship of feminism to Marxism. As was indicated in Part I, there is the tendency for Marxist-feminist practice to become the simple adaptation of Marxist models to gender issues. This, essentially, is what the Marxist-Feminist Literature Collective's practice was: using the concepts of Althusser and the reading strategies of Macherey to address 'feminist' issues in their chosen texts. The reading of *Surfacing* that we performed here may be considered an even more blatant exercise of this sort of approach, with the Hegelian and Althusserian theses built into the very *structure* of the reading. The reading was Marxist-feminist only because we chose to address the text in relation to the heroine's interpellation by gender-oriented ideological apparatuses. Had we substituted the 'family' with 'religion' or 'education', the reading would not necessarily have been feminist at all. The text with which this is a problem is debatable, but we can understand that some feminists might be justifiably anxious in adopting a methodology in which the feminist interest is apparently secondary. It returns us, too, to the central dilemma of the materialist feminist of how to negotiate the competing claims of capitalism and patriarchy. The reading of *Surfacing*, for example, demonstrated a shift between the two, as the heroine's oppression was presented sometimes as her position as a woman, sometimes as a subject of American capitalism. While theoretically we might well choose to argue that an effective Marxist–feminism must recognise the inseparability of the one from the other, actual readings often do reveal precedence of the one over the other. Yet it could also be argued that this is the simple cost we have to pay if we are to make readings of texts that are genuinely historically specific. To the extent that women's oppression is *related* to wider economic practices (even if we resist the Marxist inference that it is dominated by them) we have to surrender the idea of patriarchy as the *primal* grievance that Millet postulated it was. The agencies of sexual politics are diverse and variable, and, as we saw in 'The Yellow Wallpaper', the oppression of each subject is bound to be a complex mixture of sex, economic dependency and class. The reading of 'The Yellow Wallpaper' argued strongly that without taking the full materialist circumstances of the protagonist's position into account, madness (*à la* Gilbert and Gubar) might be read as a good thing, forgetful of the fact that it constitutes physical and economic imprisonment. In conclusion, then, we would argue that, for all the difficulty in negotiating its competing demands, feminism cannot afford to forget its implication with attendant Marxist analyses.

Yet even if the feminist reader makes this political commitment to a materialist criticism, there is the further problem that the Marxist models that she is most interested in are not necessarily literary ones. Moreover, their adaptation to critical practice is likely to be problematic, and she will run the risk of producing readings that provoke and/or irritate both Marxists and literary critics. The biggest danger from a post-structuralist position is the realisation that a model such as Althusser's formulation of the Ideological State Apparatuses as an analysis of relations in 'the real world', cannot be directly applied to situations within a text without returning to the Lukácsian hypothesis that literature is in some way a 'reflection of the real world'. Such dangerous over-simplification can, we think, be overcome if the reading continues to remind the reader of its own ideological status throughout (cf. MFLC article, p. 27). While materialist criticism may thus be said to have its *raison d'être* in the fact that it is directed to readings that acknowledge the politics of 'the real world', it does not mean that we can regard the text *as* the real world.

But by far the most contentious aspect of the type of Marxist-feminism that we practised here is its involvement with psychoanalysis. It is important to note that the early dating of the Marxist-Feminist Literature Collective article (1978) means that these connections were forged relatively early in the development of recent feminist literary criticism, and as such (despite the superficial incongruity) cannot be dismissed as marginal or esoteric. Indeed, it could be argued that Marxist–feminism has been informed by psychoanalysis from the start and that this intimate relation is one of the crucial ways in which Marxist-feminism, as such, can be distinguished from straightforward Marxist criticism. For critics like Cora Kaplan, the interest in both Marxism and psychoanalysis has been precisely in the way in which they can be related to one another on the issues surrounding gender and subjectivity.[33] The differences between Marxist and psychoanalytic critics are perceived by the former to be fundamentally ethical. The problem with Freudian and Lacanian models of human development is that they are individualistic and ahistorical, dealing with factors which are seen to be permanent and 'universal'. Thus according to Lacan, every human subject since the world began will have gone through the 'mirror-stage' on her way to the Symbolic, and this is a process that occurs regardless of historical or social context. The real dangers for such an assumption in a reading of a particular text will be that the behaviour of the characters concerned can be 'explained' regardless of their attendant social circumstances, and, even more problematically, *resolved*. Thus, a fully psychoanalytic reading of *Surfacing* might regard the heroine's individual revolution as in some way sufficient and exemplary: through a good bracing dip in the primal waters a woman can come to a new and improved relationship with herself and the world in which she lives! For Marxists, this injudiciously ignores the material conditions of her oppression, and suggests that we all possess within us the means of ameliorating our positions without attending to the social and political forces controlling us. Our reading of *Surfacing*, however, should also have demonstrated how a utilisation of various psychoanalytic models need not necessarily make such assumptions, but can, in fact, be most positively combined with a materialist consciousness. Possibly because, as Marxist–feminists, we address issues of gender and subjectivity, the whole discourse of psychoanalysis has been constantly foregrounded in our theorising, to the extent that it need not be for Marxist critics concentrating on issues like class. Most of us, too, have developed as literary critics within environments exploring various critical positions within which an understanding of psychoanalysis is central. In such circumstances it is therefore hardly surprising that we should have sought ways in which to align the theories to one another. Again, we would suggest that there is a certain puritanism in the traditional Marxist opposition to psychoanalysis which we, as feminists working within an eclectic theoretical environment, have not been oppressed by: because psychoanalysis is traditionally ahistorical, it does not mean that it should continue to be so.

This brings us finally to the practice of Marxist-feminism within a more general post-structuralism. Here we would make the point that it is the post-structuralist critic's ability to work with contradictions and differences that has enabled her to successfully negotiate the tensions inherent in a Marxist–feminist practice. The lack of resolution of the competing claims of patriarchy and capitalism mentioned above are a case in point, as are the potentially antagonistic positions of Marxism and psychoanalysis. Central to the practice of the post-structuralist reader is the notion of mutability and dialogue. Even as Marxist-feminism's purpose, like that of deconstruction, is to read texts 'against the grain', so that the various ideologies which they inscribe (and are themselves inscribed by) are routed out and exposed. This 'subtext' might be an unwitting testimony of patriarchy or the latent feminism unearthed in the Marxist-Feminist Literature Collective's readings of Brontë and Barrett Browning. Yet while born of contradictions and intent on revealing them, it should not be thought that Marxist–feminism is part of the often indulgent relativism that has given much American Deconstruction such a bad name amongst Marxist critics. Behind our 'guerilla' activities, there is a commitment to the reading of literature as a means of understanding more clearly the ideologies that have placed women where they are, and how they have conspired with or actively or silently resisted that determination. This should be seen not merely as a negative activity, moreover, but also as a positive one.

Even as Terry Eagleton has recommended that the time has come for us to re-read texts so that they 'work for socialism' so should we make them work for feminism.[34] With such a wealth of existing theory and criticism available to be adapted to a more materially-conscious criticism, we feel that the Marxist–feminist criticism of the 1990s is in a position to adapt, develop and refine the best of what has been practised, and to move towards a new level of feminist criticism in which 'pluralism' and 'commitment' are not mutually exclusive terms.

NOTES

1. Heidi Hartmann, 'The unhappy marriage of Marxism and feminism: towards a more progressive union', in Lydia Sargent (ed.) *The Unhappy Marriage of Marxism and Feminism: A Debate on Class and Patriarchy* (Pluto, London, 1981). Cora Kaplan uses Hartmann's metaphor to introduce her own problematisation of the relationship in 'Pandora's box: subjectivity, class and sexuality in socialist-feminist criticism', in Greene and Kahn (eds) *Making a Difference* (Methuen, London, 1985).
2. See, for example, Michele Barrett *Women's Oppression Today* (Verso, London, 1985).
3. 'Stand Marxist theory on its head': this metaphor of taking a theory and subverting it to one's own purpose is the one Marx himself used in his appropriation of Hegel's 'dialectic'.

   Since the notion of the dialectic is used in the following reading of *Surfacing*, we offer here a brief summary of the Hegelian model as presented by A. J. P. Taylor in the introduction to *The Communist Manifesto*: like other philosophers, Hegel sought for a world system and claimed to have done better than his predecessors. They had been baffled by the problem that the world would not stand still. No sooner did they devise a universal system than the world changed into something else. Hegel made change itself the heart of his system. Moreover, he laid down how change came about. A principle or idea – the thesis – was challenged by its opposite – the antithesis. From their conflict there emerged not the victory of one side or the other, but a combination of the two – the synthesis. In time this new thesis was challenged by a new antithesis. A new synthesis emerged, and thus mankind rolled forward and upward. This was the Hegelian process of the dialectic.

   Hegel's model, however, was a formulation of the dialectical movement of *ideas*, and failed to offer an account of the external forces which were their motivation. Marx is now understood to have stood the paradigm on its head by postulating that the movement of ideas depended on the changes that took place first on an economic level.

Millett's subsequent replacement of capitalism with patriarchy as the fundamental motivating principle of society may thus be regarded as an inversion similar to Marx's own.

4. Maggie Humm, *Feminist Criticism* (Harvester, Brighton, 1987), Ch. 4, p. 73.

5. Humm, *op. cit.*, p. 73.

6. Marxist-Feminist Literature Collective (MFLC), 'Women's writing: Jane Eyre, Shirley, Villette, Aurora Leigh', *Ideology and Consciousness*, vol. 1, no. 3, Spring, pp. 27–48.

7. Georg Lukács, *The Evolution of Modern Drama* (1909), cited by Terry Eagleton, *Marxism and Literary Criticism* (Methuen, London, 1976), p. 20.

8. Eagleton, *op. cit.*, p. 28.

9. For example, the church preaches a doctrine of brotherly love, yet amasses capital and shows little tolerance for other religions and sects. Brotherly love is here an ideological representation of the real relations.

10. Louis Althusser, 'Ideology and ideological state apparatuses' (often referred to simply as ISAs article), in *Lenin and Philosophy and Other Essays*, translated by Ben Brewster (New Left Books, London, 1971).

11. Chris Weedon, *Feminist Practice and Post-structuralist Theory* (Blackwell, Oxford, 1987), p. 29.

12. See, in particular, Macherey, *A Theory of Literary Production* (Routledge and Kegan Paul, London, 1978).

13. Terry Eagleton, 'Pierre Macherey and Marxist literary criticism', in G. H. R Parkinson (ed.) *Marx and Marxisms*, (Cambridge University Press, Cambridge, 1982), p. 150.

14. Although this intersection of the Althusserian 'imaginary' within Lacan's Imaginary is tremendously suggestive, it is not altogether unproblematic, and care should be taken not to conflate the two out of context. In their respective sources, the Althusserian imaginary and the Lacanian Imaginary possess a whole range of attendant implications which do not relate to one another. However, to the extent that both are concerned with the subject's position within society, the cross-reference is germane. Chris Weedon notes that *historically*, it was Althusser who was indebted to Lacan: 'Aspects of Lacan's analysis of Freudian psychoanalysis have influenced the model of ideology and subjectivity found in Althusserian Marxism and much feminist thinking about language, sexuality, and subjectivity' (p. 51). For further discussion of these terms, see Chapter Five and the Glossary.

15. Weedon, *op. cit.*, p. 52.

16. As well as being a stage in the development of the child, the Imaginary/Symbolic choice is an ongoing one throughout the subject's life.

17. Margaret Atwood, *Surfacing* (Virago, London, 1979).

18. It should be noted that for this reading we have used the term 'heroine' to identify the 'unnamed' central female character. While the connotations of this term are not unproblematic (Pratt uses 'hero' in her reading: see Note 23 below), it does nevertheless distinguish

the central role she plays among the other protagonists.

19. Catherine Belsey uses the notion of the *interrogative text* in *Critical Practice* (Methuen, 1980) to describe a text which is self-consciously aware of problems of its own construction and which, unlike 'seamless' realist texts, seems to invite analysis, because of the way in which it displays its gaps and inconsistencies.

20. For a full explanation of 'Symbolic' and 'semiotic' see Chapter Five and also the Glossary. Kristeva's notion of the semiotic has an advantage over Lacan's Imaginary for feminists, in so far as it does not necessarily constitute a regression or a *lack of language*, but rather the assumption of a certain kind of disruptive language. However, in so far as this reading is specifically linking psychological to materialist 'interpellation' we have reserved the Lacanian model to understand the full measure of the heroine's dislocation.

21. For a definition of Lacan's 'Law-of-the-Father', see Chapter Five and the Glossary.

22. Althusser describes the relation between the means of reproduction and the conditions of production on page 1 of the ISAs article (see Bibliography).

23. Another 'myth' reading of *Surfacing* is performed by Anaïs Pratt in '*Surfacing* and the rebirth journey', in Arnold E. Davidson and Cathy N. Davidson (eds) *The Art of Margaret Atwood: Essays in Criticism* (Anansi, Toronto, 1981), pp. 139–57.

24. Charlotte Perkins Gilman, 'The Yellow Wallpaper' in Ann Lane (ed.) *The Charlotte Perkins Gilman Reader* (Women's Press, London, 1981), pp. 3–20.

25. Gilbert, S. and Gubar, S.; *The Madwoman in the Attic: The Woman Writer and the Nineteenth-Century Literary Imagination* (Yale University Press, New Haven, 1979).

26. Gayatri Spivak, *In Other Worlds: Essays in Cultural Politics* (Methuen, London, 1987).

27. Michel Foucault, *Madness and Civilisation: A History of Insanity in the Age of Reason* (Tavistock, London, 1981).

28. An interesting reading by Pam Slaughter (in press) suggests that 'Jenny/Jane' refers not to her sister-in-law, but in fact to the central figure herself, so that she has been taken over by the 'woman' behind the wallpaper, and it is this 'woman' who speaks at the end.

29. Although even this assumption is difficult, since Gilman is said never to have fully recovered from her nervous breakdown (Ann Lane, *op. cit.*, p. ix).

30. Ann Lane notes that the story was described by H. P. Lovecraft as one of the great 'spectral tales' in American literature (p. xvii).

31. Elaine Showalter, *The Female Malady: Women, Madness, and English Culture 1830–1980* (Virago, London, 1987); Phyllis Chesler, *Women and Madness* (Allen Lane, London, 1974).

32. Judith Fetterley, *The Resisting Reader: A Feminist Approach to American Fiction* (Indiana University Press, Bloomington, 1978).

33. Cora Kaplan, *Sea Changes* (Verso, London, 1986).

34. Terry Eagleton, quoted by Raman Selden in *A Reader's Guide to Contemporary Literary Theory* (Harvester, Brighton, 1985), p. 45.

Conclusion

Sara Mills, Lynne Pearce, Sue Spaull, Elaine Millard

Books take a long time to generate, and collective books perhaps take longer than most. By the time of publication, it will be three years since the idea for this project was first mooted, and even in that time feminist criticism – together with the political and educational context in which it operates – has moved into a new phase. If the early 1980s was characterised by the articulation and consolidation of the ground-breaking work of the 1970s, the late 1980s seems to have admitted a new anxiety. The overwhelming question (spoken and unspoken) that hangs over conference and media reports is, where does contemporary feminism go from here?

In terms of the popular commentaries in newspapers and magazines, the debate has centred around what today's feminist needs from feminism now that her fight for economic independence and market equality has been achieved. Phrased in that way (which it invariably is) such articles have tended towards the conclusion that women in the 1980s do not really need feminism at all; they have become so-called *post-feminists*: women who are the competent, independent equals of men and who therefore no longer need to 'compromise' their femininity or their equally important roles as wives and mothers. The fact that such women are actually a very small middle-class minority within society as a whole is, of course, never said. Similarly, within academic institutions, feminists have watched with mingled satisfaction and doubt, the 'consciousness' for which they have struggled so hard slowly manifest itself in courses, syllabuses and other legislation, only to be told that consequently their case has been won, and they can give up the struggle.

The problem with this supposed post-feminism is, of course, that it is a description of something that does not yet exist and is unlikely to do so in the foreseeable future. Neither the representation of the New Woman in television commercials, nor the English department whose courses include equal quantities of male and female writers, have their representatives in the material world. They are myths; not of something that once happened, but of something that is supposed to have happened: they are the logical conclusion to which liberation should have brought us, rather than a statement of where we actually are.

It is into this most treacherous of historical conjunctures – the moment at which expectation masquerades as reality – that we see a project like *Feminist Readings/Feminists Reading* performing several useful roles. First, as we noted in the Introduction, we are acutely aware that by the 1990s there will be a whole new generation of readers at 20 years' remove from the feminist criticism described, discussed and engaged with in this book: women whose responsibility it will be to carry their legacy forward into the next century, and who, we believe, cannot afford to lose sight of the *circumstances* in which first-generation feminism was conceived. For such women we hope that a book like *Feminist Readings/Feminists Reading* (together with the many other excellent introductory guides referred to throughout this text) will exist as a testament to the roots of modern feminist critical practice; reminding us all of the very real anger and passion that caused women like Millett and Gilbert and Gubar to pick up their pens and begin writing. This last point relates, too, to what we regard as the second, more specific purpose of the volume, and that is to provide new readers – of whatever age, in whatever educational context – with a sense of the rich and complex strands of feminist practice that have brought us to where we are today: a diversity that is not so much pluralist as *multiple* and *interactive*. Like Sue Roe's recent *Women Reading Women's Writing*, we would wish that this collection of readings might generate a sense of the very real pleasure and excitement that can attend the study of women's texts: indeed, in retrospect, we all agree that what survives for us in all the reading positions discussed here, is their enduring impact.[1] Each of the approaches continues to have value in as much as it provides a new way into texts for, and about, women. As teachers, indeed, we depend continuously on the various analyses of women's writing presented here to enable our students to start re-thinking their relation to the literature they have chosen to study, and in this respect Millett's definition of patriarchy or Showalter's 'Gynocriticism' are as useful now as they ever were.

On a theoretical level, moreover, we would like to suggest that the retrospective offered by this collection might be a timely rejoinder to the apparent slide towards the mythical post-feminism alluded to above. While all of us working on this project have identified ourselves as post-structuralists in the sense that we believe the desirable goal of feminist criticism to be a vigorous and complex gender analysis that is not reducible to the biological sex of the author, we are also aware that the utopian conditions for post-feminist scholarship are very far away. While we may welcome the fact the individual males are now eager to address issues of gender, or that occasional courses may choose to include such topics on their syllabuses, we hold that such activity can only be regarded as *supplementary* to the spaces won (at such great expense) to provide courses for, and about, women.[2] For this reason we would suggest that the feminist reader of the 1990s will be obliged to walk the precarious tightrope of increasingly sophisticated theory very carefully indeed. While it might, indeed, appear that the work of the French feminists offers us the most exciting possibilities for a non-essentialist feminist literary practice (i.e., writing that is fully cognisant of 'gender' and 'subjectivity' as social constructs), such a route will be ultimately worthless unless it continues to take account of the fact that in the 'real world' women continue to be treated as if they *were* essentially different.

We would like to offer brief appraisals of each of the six reading positions covered by this book, focussing, in particular, on their relevance for today's feminist reader by revealing what is of enduring value in their formulation, as well as that which might most profitably be adapted and revised.

As a collective, we have agreed that one of the most positive things to emerge from this project has been the re-appraisal of Millett's *Sexual Politics*. Like most feminists, we were all aware of

Sexual Politics as one of the books that 'started it all', and yet we were insufficiently aware of its full potential. For, as Chapter One will hopefully have shown, *Sexual Politics* has far more to offer the present-day reader than its now famous virulent indictment of certain sexist texts by male authors: it also, in its readings of the books of the Sexual Revolution, prepares the way for the complex analyses of the *competing ideologies within texts* which have since become the focus of certain Marxist-feminists. In her inability to decide whether or not the writings of Brontë and Hardy were 'truly revolutionary', Millett revealed both the limitations of her own monolithic patriarchal model and the means by which it might be most usefully adapted. As we went on to show in the Marxist–feminist chapter, female subjects (in 'real life' and in fiction) are not interpellated by one ideology, but many. Thus any text of sufficient complexity is likely to engage with ideologies that both support and oppose the *status quo*. Although Millett's solution – to reconstruct and evaluate the intentions of the authors concerned – now appears naive, she nevertheless helped us to find the way to where the real responsibility lay: not with the individual authors, not with patriarchy *per se*, but with the whole complex matrix of ideologies that have kept women where they are at the same time as providing the means for their resistance. On a more general level it must also be said that the need for 'images of women' criticism is as acute today as it ever was: in a world where our lives are increasingly subject to visual and verbal propaganda, Millett's first anger at the obscene exploitation/ oppression of women must never be forgotton. Just because it is no longer so easy to name names (for example, D. H. Lawrence, Norman Mailer) it does not mean that the crime is any less serious.

Authentic realism, although a problematic reading strategy for many post-structuralist feminists, can be seen to be a useful factor in consciousness-raising. Since so many women read in this way (individually and in groups) and find that it helps them to analyse patriarchy and possible means of resistance, then it cannot be so easily dismissed. In a teaching context authentic realism is also an excellent way to start reading with a group, as long as it can be stressed that this is *one* position amongst many, and that this seemingly 'natural' position is a theoretical position like any other. The very fact of theorising it as a 'common sense' position, rather than simply discarding it, is crucial in the teaching process, in our opinion. But we would stress that this type of reading is perhaps only the first stage in a process of developing other reading strategies. If it is adequately theorised, authentic realism can certainly be a useful reading strategy to describe the way a text speaks to you as a woman. A useful addition might be an analysis of the way that that happens – the way that the reader is addressed, the use of an intimate tone, the 'cultural code' which you are supposed to share and the features of the text which arouse emotion. In the chapter on authentic realism we have tried to emphasise these aspects of the text rather then simply relying on an unproblematised reference to experience. A further area of expansion of the position would be to analyse the pleasure which the reader derives from the text; a certain amount of work has been done in this area, mainly with reference to film theory and the study of women's romance fiction[3], and this can usefully be drawn upon to examine the way in which readers experience emotions and the factors which determine those emotions. A close textual analysis in terms of the theorising of pleasure, and the description of the way a text addresses the reader, mark out new directions for a much-maligned way of reading.

Anyone who makes a choice to read women writers rather than men, or to study a course in women's writing, is declaring an allegiance with the politics behind Elaine Showalter's 'Gyno-criticism'. As a collective we believe strongly that until such a time as women writers have truly equal representation within our educational system, it will remain necessary to follow Showalter's recommendation that feminists construct for themselves an alternative canon of women writers: that after centuries of submitting to the masculine evaluation of 'Great Literature', they begin to redress the balance. The critique at the end of Chapter Three, together with various comments in this Conclusion, will reveal that none of us feel this to be a final solution. Certainly, on a theoretical level, gynocriticism depends upon the untenable assumption that gender is the same as sex-difference. Even though Showalter's cultural model avoids the worst biological essentialism in this respect, it still ignores the fact that women – although subject to different ideological interpellation to men – nevertheless share many experiences with them (and vice versa). Yet, on a pragmatic level, all of us know that the experiences of the sexes do remain different enough for a study of writing by women, for women, to remain both pleasurable and necessary. We feel, too, that the models that Showalter engages to describe the commonality within women's writing, together with their exclusion from certain patriarchal institutions, are accessible and useful. Her utilisation of the Ardeners' concept of the 'muted group' for example, remains an excellent way of beginning discussion about the relation of women to language, and the concept of the 'wild zone' is one that can be used repeatedly to analyse the power women acquire as a result of their marginality. As with several of the theoretical texts dealt with here, we would suggest that articles like 'Feminist criticism in the wilderness' may be of abiding value to new students, providing it is discussed within a wider programme of reading.

We believe that the legacy of Gilbert and Gubar's work on the 'anxiety of authorship' (Chapter Four) is essentially the same as that of gynocriticism. Like Showalter's, Gilbert and Gubar's work has been most important in helping women to establish a new perspective on women's writing in contradistinction to that of men. As a collective we find that while students continue to study a predominantly male canon of literature, Gilbert and Gubar's description of its relation to the work of women authors will need to be discussed. We regard this as a valid activity without necessarily subscribing to the particulars of the Gilbert and Gubar hypothesis, such as the negative inference that women's writing somehow acquired its distinctive quality by default. At the same time – and with some reservations – we would suggest that this model (based on the exclusion of minorities by the dominant social group) could be extended to analyse the way in which certain groups of women writers, such as those who write as Blacks or lesbians, have developed their own alternative feminist aesthetic. Indeed, in their most recent book, *The War of the Words*, Gilbert and Gubar have themselves adapted their earlier monolithic model of an 'essential women's writing' to one where women writers undergo a 'female affiliation complex'.[4] This model admits that not all women are bound to align themselves to a female tradition (i.e., some women writers will identify more with the male mainstream). Those who do, may be seen to have positively affiliated themselves with their sisters, and they can be analysed as significantly different to male-affiliated women writers. We believe that this adaptation may be useful for readers attracted to gynocritical approaches, but who have found its implicit essentialism something of a stumbling block.

French feminist work is a useful way of reclaiming 'feminine' positions as potentially subversive. The terms 'masquerade', '*écriture feminine*' and 'the semiotic' are all connected to the notion of occupying the marginality to which women have been traditionally assigned, in order to celebrate that marginality. At the same time, the mainstream is subverted by mimicry, thus deconstructing the division–centre/margins. French feminisms draw on post-structuralist theory to construct their own positions, and in doing so have made it necessary for feminists of all persuasions to consider the way in which post-structuralist work can be used. However, for many feminists, French feminism presents several problems: firstly because it seems unnecessarily obtuse, and secondly because it can appear ahistorical and tending towards essentialism. It is our view, however, that a sufficiently materialist psychoanalytic model is vital for feminist work, as long as it is sufficiently critical of its own position, and is alert to the importance of historical change. Catherine Clément has recently launched a full-scale attack on the patriarchal assumptions of Lacanian psychoanalysis which some French feminists have worked so hard to recuperate.[5] Perhaps with a more woman-centred psychoanalytic model, these problems could be resolved, or at least more successfully negotiated. Julia Kristeva has started this process by turning to the work of Melanie Klein, and grafting this onto the Lacanian base, so that the role of the mother becomes more central in the Oedipal crisis. This is certainly a direction which it would be useful to follow.

It would also be useful if the example of another less well known French feminist, Monique Wittig, were followed in relation to materialism, since she stresses its importance in any account of women's writing.[6] It is interesting that in Part III of *Revolution in Poetic Language* (this part has not been translated into English), Julia Kristeva details the effects of society on the constitution of the subject and suggests that the structure of the psyche changes according to the social and economic conditions of the time. However, little of this concern with potential change is evident in the readings of French feminism currently available. It is to be hoped that with sufficient attention to the material conditions in which one becomes a subject, it will be possible to move away from potential essentialism.

In the final section of the chapter on Marxist-feminism, we have already dwelt at length on the usefulness of Marxist-feminism for the contemporary reader, and we have stressed its successful adaptation of other theoretical models such as psychoanalysis. One could suggest that Marxist-feminist practice has demonstrated how the best of post-structuralist sophistication can be combined with 'feminism on the ground'. The latter refers, of course, to the awareness of material conditions which is the purpose behind any Marxist reading. Today's Marxist–feminists, while resisting any simplistic equivalence between literature and life, nevertheless believe that we can never afford to lose sight of the social and economic constraints that determine women's existence. We should always be aware of such factors in our readings, even though we may subscribe to the post-Lacanian view that neither gender nor subjectivity is fixed or finite. Marxist–feminism's negotiation of psychoanalytic theory is indeed the supreme testimony to how all that is most compelling in our new complex understanding of the female subject can be linked to the role of that female subject *in society*. And precisely because of the gaps, contradictions and inconsistencies which that relationship exposes, Marxist–feminism also explains why the study of women's writing *per se* must remain part of our commitment. Post-feminism, like a non-class-divided society, is still a long way away: and until such a time that it becomes appreciably closer we must remain faithful to what we are, socialists and feminists.

The theories which we have reviewed here are not static; they have developed over time, and we hope that they will continue to develop, drawing on other positions to supplement them. There is a sense in which we have characterised as fully-fledged theoretical positions what are in fact theoretical tendencies. As we mentioned in the Introduction, it is notoriously difficult to disentangle theoretical positions within feminism, and yet in doing so, and developing a notion of the different practices that these enable, it is then possible to consider the ways in which the tendencies could be aligned in order to deal with current theoretical problems and contexts. We feel that positions such as gynocriticism and French feminism would benefit from a concern with history and materialism; that is not to say that we would like all of the positions to become Marxist–feminist ones, but that each one lacks this sense of the specificity of the historical moment in which the text was produced and received and the constraints on production and reception. A further element which certain of the approaches could benefit from is that of theory itself; for example, authentic realism is a useful position if more fully theorised. Having described this range of feminist positions, it is to be hoped that the reader will be able to choose certain elements which she can use to analyse texts in her particular context; and we hope also that the reader will find feminist theory sufficiently interesting to go on and read some of the more recent theorists through whose work we have been filtering these positions.

The aim of this conclusion, as of the project as a whole, has been to offer our readers *positive* possibilities of how to approach feminist literary practice. As a collective we are aware that what should be the present-day feminist's source of great rejoicing – the very wealth of literature and criticism that has proliferated in the last 20 years – has been in danger of becoming a burden. This, we felt, was especially true for younger women becoming interested in women's writing and feminist criticism for the first time. These readings have shown that, if nothing else, feminist critical practice is accessible to every woman whatever her particular point of interest. Feminist theory, as this volume testifies, is not bound by rules and prescriptions, but remains an open dialogue in which all women are invited to contribute and engage.

NOTES

1. Sue Roe (ed.) *Women Reading Women's Writing* (Harvester, Brighton, 1987).
2. There has been much debate recently about the position of men in feminism, for example, in Alice Jardine and Paul Smith's collection of essays, *Men in Feminism* (see Bibliography). Many feminists feel uncomfortable at male intrusions into what seems to be the one theoretical space which women have mapped out for themselves. We as a group feel that there are spaces and discussions which need to be women-only, for the time being, but we see no reason why that should stop men from becoming interested in feminist theory. Perhaps we would like to ask those men who do become interested to examine their motives in doing so. It is hoped that this book will open up to men possible ways in which they can intervene. Gender

studies, where the construction of femininity and masculinity are considered in similar ways, seems to be an interesting but potentially retrograde move; what is needed is a study which combines some of the insights of feminism together with a continuation of the study of masculinity.

3. Annette Kuhn, *Women's Pictures* (Routledge and Kegan Paul, London, 1982); Tania Modleski, *Loving with a vengeance: Mass-Produced Fantasies for Women* (Methuen, London, 1984),

4. Sandra Gilbert and Susan Gubar, *The War of the Words* (Yale University Press, New Haven, 1988), vol. 1.

5. Catherine Clément, *The Weary Sons of Freud* (Verso, London, 1987).

6. Monique Wittig, 'One is not born a woman', in *Feminist Issues*, vol. 1, No. 2, Winter 1981, pp. 41–8.

Glossary

Some comment is needed on the use of inverted commas throughout this book. In post-structuralist criticism it has become common practice to put within inverted commas those terms which you are treating with a certain amount of suspicion: terms like 'feminine' and 'real', which appear to have a common sense meaning, and which for theoretical and practical reasons need to be questioned.

aesthetic practice a way of describing techniques used in the production of a literary text

alienation a Marxist term used to describe the process whereby the worker gives up his or her labour in exchange for wages and thus becomes an appendage of a machine. Marxist critics, for example Theodor Adorno, stress the alienated nature of reality in contemporary society and argue that the work of art acts within reality to expose its contradictions

Althusserian *see* ISAs

androgynous having characteristics of both sexes. In feminist criticism the concept has been used, particularly by Virginia Woolf, to describe writing which demonstrates both 'male' and 'female' characteristics

anti-theoretical a position which states that it is not drawing on theory, like Authentic Realism described in Chapter Two.

However, that is not to say that it is untheoretical

antithesis the second element in Hegel's dialectical system which is in opposition to the first proposition or thesis (*see* thesis and synthesis)

Anxiety of Authorship this phrase is Sandra Gilbert and Susan Gubar's adaptation of the critic Harold Bloom's concept of 'the anxiety of influence'. Bloom's theory describes the relation of the young poet (ephebe) to his poetic father figure (precursor). The unconscious of the younger poet becomes imprinted by that of the poetic father figure. Only by overturning this influence can the younger poet become free to write. Gilbert and Gubar argue that for the female author a male percursor creates an even more debilitating barrier to creativity. The barrier is so great that she doubts not only what she writes, but her ability to write at all

authentic realist a view of texts which sees them as relating closely to experience, both of the author and of the reader (*see* Chapter Two)

author intentionality *see* intentionality

biological essentialism an assumption that the differences between the sexes are determined by specific biological differences and not socially-constructed gender. Thus women are seen to be essentially different from men

binary opposition an opposition prevalent in Western thought which casts qualities as direct opposites, for example: black/white; male/female; nature/culture. A great deal of feminist and deconstructive work has aimed to show that these terms are not 'true' oppositions, but depend on each other in order to have meaning

canon this is used by theorists as shorthand for that body of literary works and their authors that has become established as the proper texts to study on literature courses. It is marked by a preponderance of what feminists describe as 'dead white men's writing'

castration complex *see* Oedipal phase

classic realism texts which employ various conventions of realism such as particularised description, character development and closure, to create the illusion of 'real life'. The classic realist genre includes many well-known nineteenth century novels such as those by George Eliot and the Brontës

closure the term used to describe resolution, at different levels, at the end of a text. If a text is seen to 'resist closure', this might indicate that it is self-consciously subverting the expectations of much classic realism

confessional a type of writing described by Michel Foucault in *The History of Sexuality* which has interiorised models of behaviour appropriate to the oppressed

consciousness-raising since the 1960s, women have met in groups to discuss patriarchy. For many it was the first time they had discovered that the problems they faced were not individual but suffered by many women. This caused a change of thinking about where the larger structural cause of these problems was located – patriarchy. Women began to identify as a group rather than seeing other women as potential competitors

constitution of the subject many theorists working with an Althusserian or Lacanian model see the acquisition of language as a central element in the forming of the individual

co-terminous two items which have the same meaning or which have the same reference in all their different forms

cultural images also referred to as representation theory; this is primarily British feminist work in cultural studies which examines the practices of representing women; see, for example, Jane Root: *Pictures of Women* and Rosemary Betterton: *Looking On* (*see* Bibliography)

deconstruction this term was originally coined by the French theorist Jacques Derrida to describe a method of reading which focusses on the structure and operation of the text rather than on its content. The method undermines the notion of definite meaning in language, because an examination of any single word or concept reveals that it is only understood in relation to its opposite, or by its difference from other words or concepts. For example, 'darkness' is only understood by comparison and contrast to 'light': we can only understand 'darkness' in terms of the absence, or relative absence, of light. Similarly, 'woman' is understood and defined by the definition of what she is not, i.e., 'man'. Derrida demonstrates the arbitrary nature of the language system, thereby calling into question the meanings it attempts to convey (*see différance*)

determinism a term to describe something preordained; for example, biological determination means that someone behaves in a certain way because of a biological predisposition *différance* a word used by Derrida. His misspelling is deliberate, drawing attention to the written (rather than verbal) nature of language. In French pronunciation the change of vowel goes unnoticed, emphasising writing and textuality at the expense of speech. It is a play on the two meanings of the French verb *différer*: to differ and to defer. Language depends on the difference between signs (words) as the basis of meaning (see below). The sense is deferred as one word refers to another word in the play of meaning, whilst all the time the words are 'standing in' for an object which is not there (we say 'cat' rather than holding up a furry, four-legged animal). Further, the words are always attempting to 'hold down' a meaning which can never be fully expressed

difference this term is used by Saussure to denote the way that meaning depends on the minimal contrast (difference) between words, rather than any correspondence between an object and the word used to name it. Language is not a naming device but a system of differences with no positive terms (i.e., no one term can be singled out to have its meaning in isolation from other words)

discourse a term associated with the theorist Michel Foucault, used to designate established ways of thinking together with the power structures that support them (for example, the 'discourse of science', the 'discourse of patriarchy'. Discourses are the product of social, historical and institutional formations. The existence of 'discursive practices' within a society allows for certain subject positions to be taken up. Modes of discourse are established and modified over time and ideas of class, gender, race, individuality, etc. are determined by them. A discourse depends on shared assumptions, so that a culture's ideology is inscribed in its discursive practices (see below). Discourses embody power relations, and social meaning often arises at the point of conflict between different discourses. For example, concepts of gender result from the struggle between the legitimised discourse of patriarchy with the marginalised discourse of feminism (*see* Macdonnell, Bibliography)

discursive construct an element in a text or 'real life' which is created because of the pressure of the rules of discourse (*see* discourse)

dominant group a term developed by the Ardeners (*see*

Bibliography) to refer to the group in society which controls the way that people in that society view and define themselves through language

double-voiced discourse a discourse which consists of two voices in competition or tension (*see* polyphony)

eclectic using elements from different theories or practices to work out a new position

écriture feminine a type of writing advocated by French feminists which is more fluid and dislocated than classic realism – this experimental writing is seen to be 'feminine', and a form of liberation for women writers

enable used by feminists to refer to a practice which provides you with a set of principles with which to work

epiphany an emotional moment of self-realisation in literature

epistolary a novel written in the form of letters to and from characters

feminine whilst male and female are biological differences, feminine and masculine refer to the way society encourages us to identify in terms of gender. Feminine has also been used by Julia Kristeva to mean a position of marginality, of being outside the mainstream, which is available to both males and females, and from which they can write (*see* masculine and gender)

feminine aesthetic the belief that women's writing is essentially different from writing by men

feminine mystique a concept developed by Betty Friedan (see Bibliography) to describe the way in which women have been restricted to the role of wife and mother. She wishes women to develop their range of choices as individuals

feminist critique feminist analysis of male texts

feminist poetics an analysis of the way texts work from a feminist perspective. Drawing on Jonathan Culler's work in *Structuralist Poetics* (see Bibliography), feminists often use 'poetics' to refer to an analysis which concentrates on the language structures in the text

feminist practice used in the context of this book to describe the activity of performing theoretically-informed feminist readings of literary texts. It is important to realise that in such a practice neither the theoretical nor the literary text is privileged in any absolute way. The final sections of each chapter show how theoretical positions may be challenged/re-defined in the course of reading

first generation feminist those involved in the revived Women's Movement of the 1960s. The problem with the term is that it implies that there were no feminists before; whereas there have been feminists since at least the seventeenth century, for example Mary Astells (*see* Elaine Hobby, Bibliography)

first person narration when the narration is told using 'I', for example: 'I have only lived in this town for two years ...'

foreground a linguistic term which means to place at the centre of attention

foreshadowing when an event which occurs later in a text is alluded to, as an indication of what is to come

French feminism this usually refers to Kristeva, Wittig, Irigaray and Cixous, but there are many other interesting theorists working in France, for example Catherine Clément (see Toril Moi, *French Feminist Thought:* see Bibliography)

gender is a socially-constructed masculine or feminine as opposed to the biologically-determined difference (i.e. sex)

gender studies an analysis of masculinity and femininity as if they were similar constructs (*see* Chapman, Bibliography)

genre a grouping of texts which have similar features; for example, the novel, the drama

gyandry a term which Gilbert and Gubar use as a re-writing of the term 'androgyny' which they feel privileges the male, because of its etymology. See Chapter Four

gynocriticism is a term which refers to the practice of turning away from the analysis of male-authored texts to an analysis of female-authored texts and their specific difference from one another. See Chapter Three

heterogeneous composed of diverse elements

hommelette a term which Jacques Lacan developed to describe the pre-Oedipal psychic condition of the child. He plays upon a pun in French (hommelette=little man and omelette) in that the child is both an adult in the making, with sexual desires, but also a dispersed consciousness which does not distinguish between self and other clearly

homogeneous composed of a single element, unified

ideology a system of beliefs (or illusions) that determines the way in which people live. Ideology is a series of representations and images creating a 'reality' which establishes an imaginary relation of the individual to the world. Ideology presents half truths, glosses over contradictions and is characterised by gaps and omissions, rather than lies. It is not a set of things but an active social practice

images of women this type of criticism concerns itself with analysing the representations of women in visual and verbal texts, often as part of a sexual-political critique. See, for example, Josephine Donovan (see Bibliography)

Imaginary in Lacanian psychoanalytical theory this is a period which roughly corresponds to Freud's pre-Oedipal phase. The child experiences an illusory sense of completeness in which there is as yet no separation from the mother. This unity is broken by the introduction of language which, embodying the Law of the Father, introduces a third term and creates a Symbolic Order in which some of the individual experience of the Imaginary cannot be expressed

intentionality traditional literary criticism proposes that one of the aims of the critic is to recover the aims of the writer. Recent critics like Foucault and Barthes have discussed the problems with this (see Bibliography)

interpellation literally this means 'calling by name'. It is a term taken from the Marxist Althusser, to describe the process by which people are given positions within an ideological frame. The person is constructed in language and individuals recognise (or misrecognise) themselves in the positions assigned them in discourse, i.e., they are 'called' to adopt certain roles and do so unquestioningly

interrogate this term is used to refer to the radical process of questioning carried out by modern literary theory on literary texts rather than simply 'reading' them. It is a more rigorous and 'suspicious' process

interlocutor the person who is addressed by the text

ISA Ideological State Apparatus. This is a term used by Althusser for the educational system, the law, the family, literature, art, the media. All these systems reinforce the dominant ideology of a particular culture and are instrumental in constituting people as subjects (i.e. positioning people within that ideology)

Lacanian psychoanalysis Lacan developed a theory of psychoanalysis based on the work of Freud and Saussure. For an accessible description of his work, see Deborah Cameron's

Feminism and Linguistic Theory and also Malcolm Bowie (see Bibliography)

lack used by Lacanian psychoanalysts to refer to the position allocated to women within the resolution of the Oedipal crisis. Because women subjects cannot identify with the Father, they are left in a position where they cannot experience fullness; this view has been criticised by many feminists

Law of the Father Lacan, in stating that the phallus is the primary signifier, says that this has effect not only in language, but in all institutions and aspects of life. He traces this back to the Oedipal crisis

liberal humanist this term is applied loosely to describe a 'common sense' position where 'man' and his experience are at the centre of interest. Literary texts can be shown to have universal significance, speaking for all time of an unchanging transcendental human nature. The human mind is considered outside of social relations and historical change

logocentrism Derrida uses this term to describe a Western tradition of philosophy that places at its centre the logos, translated as 'word', which also stands for rationality or truth. It is a system of thought that places emphasis on the power of language to deliver the full truth and presence of some external feature. It privileges the spoken over the written word, content above form and implies that meaning is independent of the language that produces it. It assumes an absolute foundation, outside language itself, which 'anchors' or organises language so as to fix particular meanings to particular words. *Différance* is the term that Derrida sets against logocentrism

macro-element a large-scale element in a text or explanation of a text, such as plot or narration

Marxist-feminist a practice or theory which considers both gender and class to be essential components of an analysis

masculine in writing practices, the term is often used to mean that writing which attempts closure and stresses its own authority and rationality (*see* feminine and gender)

masquerade it is similar to mimicry, but is an adoption of the roles assigned to women by men. Irigaray suggests that by adopting these roles it is possible for their flaws to be exploited

materialism or historical materialism is the central tenet of Marxist theory, stressing that wo/man creates social conditions rather than any metaphysical agency (that is: material relations are the primary element and thought or consciousness is secondary to this). It is opposed to idealism, systems of thought based on metaphysics. In literary criticism, the focus is on the modes of literary production and consumption, and social conditions which determine access to these

matriarchal a society where the line of descent is traced through the mother's family, but can be used to refer to a society where women have some power and feminism is no longer necessary

mimicry Irigaray's term for imitating a male model of writing in order to demonstrate its failing. Simply by imitating, mimicry has the effect of subverting the male text

modernist a vague grouping of texts (from a period around 1880–1930) which experiment with language and with form; for example, the writing of Gertrude Stein and Virginia Woolf

muted group groups in society which are relatively inarticulate, because meanings are controlled by the dominant group (*see* dominant group)

narrator the character who tells the story

New Criticism a manner of textual criticism associated with the American academics John Crowe Ransom, Cleanth Brooks and R. P. Blackmur, amongst others. Its emphasis is on the linguistic structure of the work and its verbal complexities as an object in itself without reference to its historical context or the psychology of either the author or the reader

nom-du-père see Law of the Father

not-said this term depends on Pierre Macherey's approach to the literary text, whereby locating the 'lack' in the work, what it cannot articulate, becomes the means of detecting that which threatens and undermines its conscious project. The process whereby the unconscious of a text is formed is directly parallel to the child's entry into the Symbolic Order (language is not capable of expressing everything, so certain thoughts, ideas, feelings, impulses, etc. are left unspoken)

Oedipal phase in Freud's psychoanalytic theory, the point in a child's development where the father enters, forcing the child to give up its unity with its mother and recognise sexual difference. Lacan identifies this point with the child's entry into language, so that as well as recognising sexual difference the child becomes aware that the language system is also based on difference. The male child suppresses his desire for the mother, on realising that he may, like her, be castrated by the Father; he aligns himself therefore with the Father. The female child suppresses her desire for the Father, and aligns herself with the Mother, and the lack she suffers because of castration is filled by having a baby herself. This account is significantly changed in the work of Melanie Klein and subsequently Julia Kristeva (see Bibliography)

the Other this term has multiple meanings in Lacanian psychoanalytical theory. Most simply it means the difference which stimulates desire. It is used to denote that which creates the lack in the subject and initiates desire. The primal Other is the role of the father within the Oedipal triangle. This introduces a gap between desire and its objects that cannot be filled. Lacan suggests that the key discovery of Freud is that we bear this Otherness within ourselves.

the other in the writing of French feminists it is the tendency of Western discourse to posit the feminine as the other in relation to the masculine that is at issue. Thus, the masculine becomes the positive against which the feminine is defined as negative (i.e. not-man)

parler femme see *écriture feminine*

patriarchy is that social organisation which produces and guarantees superior status for the male and inferior for the female. It is a political concept in that it governs power-structured relationships in which one group is controlled by another

penis-envy Freud's much maligned account of the way girls recognise a difference between themselves and their boy-peers (*see* Oedipal phase). Juliet Mitchell suggests that rather than reading Freud's account as the girl's envy for the penis, it is possible for feminists to read it as the girl's envy of the boy's advantages (see Bibliography)

phallogocentrism *see* logocentrism

phallus the symbol of difference at the heart of the language system is the distinction phallus/lack of phallus and from this follow the other differences which form our language system – male/female, head/heart, culture/nature, sane/mad and so on. It is the phallus that can be seen to be the central or primary signifier in the language system, since it is the sign of difference and dominance

pluralism a theoretical position which suggests that more than one position or theory is possible in the reading of a text. It is not necessary to assume that all possible theories or positions are equally valid in all situations, but does not, like traditional criticism, assert that only one view is *right*

polymorphous perversity the sexuality of the child in the pre-Oedipal period. This sexuality is not centred on the genitals but takes pleasure in the anal and oral regions particularly, though pleasure is also experienced over the whole body

polyphony a term developed by Mikhail Bakhtin (see Bibliography) to refer to the many voices which exist in a text. Conventional criticism sees the text as coming from one source, spoken by one voice. Bakhtin, however, sees the text as a collection of voices, competing for dominance or existing in tension

post-feminism a position of having worked one's way through feminist theory to such an extent that the basic tenets of feminism can be taken as read. It can also mean a position where feminism is no longer necessary

post-modernism a vague grouping of texts which experiment with language, and which draw on different styles of writing without wishing to form a unified whole or make specific points by so doing

post-structuralism is used as a general term for recent developments in literary theory. It is the working out in practice of the implications of Derrida's deconstruction, and is marked by a movement away from explanation by examining the author's intentions and the notion of the person as unified subject. It also moves away from an emphasis on the structures which texts share. It encompasses recent applications of psychoanalytic criticism such as that based on the theories of Jacques Lacan, and also cultural and ideological analyses such as those of Michel Foucault and feminists like Luce Irigaray and Julia Kristeva

pre-Oedipal the stage of development of a child before the Oedipal crisis where the child experiences reality as an undifferentiated mass of sensations (*see* hommelette)

prescriptive it is a type of writing which tells you what to do. Prescriptive feminist theory suggests to writers ways in which they might improve their work in terms of gender (*see* Cheri Register, Bibliography)

primary signifier *see* Law of the Father

primary text this is the term generally applied to the literary text under examination. However, as noted in the Introduction, we disagree with the notion of a theoretical text remaining untouched by the reading process. We hold that the theoretical text as well as the literary text is constructed and altered in the process of reading

pro-feminism the position men can adopt if they wish to play a part in the feminist debate. It means that they can show their solidarity with women's work by reading feminist theory etc., while not directly intervening

problematise to call something into question or make problematic

psychodynamics a term used in psychoanalytical readings of literature to describe the way a text is written with reference to psychological predispositions, for example, gender

pulsions Kristeva's term for drives within the pre-Oedipal stage of development of the child. These pulsions move across the child's experiencing of the world; they can be thought of as waves of emotion or sensation which flow through the child in a rhythmic way

reading strategy a way of reading which is used as a tool to the most effective explanation; the reader can adopt different reading strategies according to the text and the situation

recuperate a feminist practice of reading works to fit in with feminist ideas

reflection model a view of texts which sees them as reflecting reality

resisting reader a term developed by Judith Fetterley (*see* Bibliography) to describe the type of strategies which a female reader can adopt when reading a male-authored text. She says that because these texts address us as men, we have to 'side-step' the address, and construct an alternative form of reading or reading practice

role model in authentic realist criticism and images of women criticism, it is thought to be important for women readers to see examples of female characters who are strong. When reading, it is thought that women identify with these characters, and use them as forms of aspiration. Whilst realising the importance of this for many women, it is a term which needs analysis, since this is not the only way women have for constructing a sense of self

romantic friendship a term developed by Lillian Faderman to describe the passionate but hypothetically non-sexual friendship which women have with each other, especially in the nineteenth century (*see* Bibliography)

Saussurean linguistics Ferdinand de Saussure's system of linguistics has been very influential in structuralist and post-structuralist thought. An accessible account of his work is available in Deborah Cameron: *Feminism and Linguistic Theory* (*see* Bibliography) (*see* sign)

secondary text this term is generally applied to theoretical texts, but is one that we have attempted not to use in this book (*see* primary text)

second generation feminist feminists who were not involved in the first wave of the revived Women's Movement in the 1960s, and therefore did not go through the political struggles of first generation feminists, but were nevertheless inspired by feminism

second person address when the text addresses the reader as 'you'

semiotics (semiology) is the science of signs (or, broadly, language) as first proposed by Ferdinand de Saussure.

semiotic Julia Kristeva uses the term to refer to the rhythmic pattern of pulses or 'drives' experienced by a child before it acquires language (i.e. before it enters the 'Symbolic'). The rhythmic pulses are themselves a sort of language which is repressed once the child learns to speak, since our linguistic system is not capable of expressing everything the child experiences. But the semiotic is not totally repressed. It lies beneath the Symbolic Order and can make itself evident in the movement of word play of *avant-garde* or modernist writers marked by rupture, absences and breaks in the symbolic language. Like the feminine, it contains that which cannot find full expression within the Symbolic Order

sexual politics a theory devised by Kate Millett (see Chapter One) which analyses key sections of male-authored texts to show that they portray women as sexual objects

sign is the term used in Saussurean linguistics to describe a unit of language comprised of the concept (the signified) and its form (the signifier, that is the words on the page, or sounds in the air). It is arbitrary and creates meaning in its difference from other such signs rather than by any correspondence to the material world. So, for example, the word 'cat' is used arbitrarily to mean a small, furry animal – there is no actual relationship between the word and the object. We know the meaning of 'cat' because we have not said 'mat' or 'dog'

sisterhood a form of bonding between women, irrespective of race, class or other differences. It is an identifying of one's interests with other women (*see* consciousness-raising, woman-ist and woman-centred)

specularised other the speculum is a curved mirror which reflects back a distorted image. For Irigaray, woman is man's specularised other

split-subject a term used in psychoanalysis in opposition to the idea of the unified subject, that is, the notion that each individual is in control of her thoughts, desires and intentions. In psychoanalysis the subject is the site of conflicting impulses, and is an amalgam of diverse urges, desires and thoughts

structuralism a group of theorists, Levi-Strauss, Barthes, Genette and Propp amongst others, who were interested in analysing the basic components of texts, reducing groups of texts to their lowest common denominator; for example, seeing what all fairy tales had in common in terms of their structure

structuration a term used in psychoanalysis to describe the way that individuals come to see themselves in a way which is determined by ordered forces whose roots are in the psyche. For example, the structuration of desire refers to the fact that desire does not simply spring from the individual 'naturally' but is structured by forces beyond her control

sub-genre a division within genres; for example, feminist detective novels are a sub-genre of the detective genre

subject since most psychoanalysts do not believe in a unified individual consciousness, they use the term 'subject', which does not suggest wholeness or control in the same way as 'individual' does

subjectivity what is involved in becoming a subject, and occupying subject-positions. It is akin to the notion of consciousness, but is less unitary, since one individual occupies several subject positions

Symbolic in Lacanian theory is the stage in the child's development where language is acquired. Language imposes a social order on the child's experience. In the process, some of the child's experience prior to the acquisition of language is lost, because it cannot be expressed in language. The phallus is the 'transcendental signifier' in the Symbolic Order, not because it contains any absolute meaning, but because it marks the child's separation from the Imaginary – it is responsible for introducing sexual difference and the differences on which language is based

synthesis the third element in Hegel's dialectical system, which resolves the conflict between thesis and antithesis (*see* thesis and antithesis)

text a term which can refer to all types of writing, both literary and non-literary

textual determinant there are a variety of factors which can encourage a text to appear in the way it does; one of them is the rules of textual production or textual determinants. For example, a rule of text production for realist texts is that they have closure. This is a textual rule and not a social rule

theory/theoretical a position which provides a way in to a text because of already thought out 'schemas' or models of the way texts work. These models are at a more generalisable level than an intuitive response to individual texts, and are seen to hold true of a range of texts

thesis the first element in Hegel's dialectical system; a first proposition within an argument which is then challenged by its opposition, or antithesis (*see* antithesis and synthesis)

third person narration a novel is told in the third person if the focus of attention is on the actions of 'she' or 'he'; for example: 'She wrote him a brief letter'

un-said *see* not-said

utopian concerned with a depiction of a distant, ideal future world

wild zone a term used by the anthropologists Shirley and Edwin Ardener to describe that section of women's experience which is not available to men. See Chapter Three

woman-centred a text or practice which consciously addresses itself to women and which focusses on women's experience

womanist a term developed by Alice Walker that avoids the race-blindness implicit in the term feminist (since other feminisms need to define themselves as non-white, such as Black feminism). Womanist writing identifies itself as writing to other Black women, and is concerned to focus on their experience. An example of 'womanist prose' can be found in Alice Walker: *In Search of Our Mothers' Gardens* (Virago, London, 1983)

writing the body a form of writing developed by French feminists (*see écriture feminine*) which concentrates on the analogies between the writing process and the functions of the female body

Bibliography

Althusser, Louis, 'Ideology and ideological state apparatuses', in *Lenin and Philosophy and Other Essays*, translated by Ben Brewster (New Left Books, London, 1971).

Atwood, Margaret, *Surfacing* (Virago, London, 1979).

Ardener, Edwin, 'Belief and the problem of women' in Shirley Ardener (ed.), *Perceiving Women* (Malaby Press, London, 1975).

Ardener, Shirley, (ed.), *Defining Females: the nature of women in society* (Croom Helm, London, 1978).

Babcock, Barbara, *The Reversible World: Symbolic Inversion in Art and Society* (Cornell University Press, London, 1978), p. 14.

Bakhtin, Mikhail, *Problems in Dostoevsky's Poetics*, translated by Caryl Emerson (Manchester University Press, Manchester, 1984).

Baldwin, James, 'Everybody's protest novel', in *Notes of a Native Son* (Corgi, London, 1964).

Barrett, Michele, *Women's Oppression Today* (Verso, London, 1985).

Barthes, Roland, *S/Z*, translated by Richard Miller (Hill and Wang, New York, 1974).

Barthes, Roland, *Roland Barthes by Roland Barthes*, translated by Richard Howard (Hill and Wang, New York, 1977).

Barthes, Roland, 'The pleasure of the text', in S. Sontag (ed.), *Barthes: Selected Writings* (Fontana, London, 1982), pp. 404–14.

Barthes, Roland, 'The death of the author', in *The Rustle of Language* (Blackwell, Oxford, 1986), pp. 49–55.

Baym, Nina, *Women's Fiction: A Guide to Novels by and about Women in America 1820–1970* (Cornell University Press, London, 1978).

de Beauvoir, Simone, *The Second Sex* (Knopf, New York, 1953).

Batsleer, Janet, *et al.*, *Rewriting English: Cultural Politics of Gender and Class* (Methuen, London, 1985).

Beer, Patricia, *Reader I Married Him, a Study of the Women Characters of Jane*

Austen, Charlotte Brontë, Elizabeth Gaskell and George Eliot (Macmillan, London, 1974).

Bell, Currer, 'Biographical notice of Acton and Ellis Bell' (1850), reproduced in Penguin edition of *Wuthering Heights* (Penguin, Harmondsworth, 1982), pp. 30–6.

Belsey, Catherine, *Critical Practice* (New Accents, Methuen, 1980).

Berger, John, *Ways of Seeing* (Penguin, Harmondsworth, 1972).

Betterton, Rosemary, *Looking On: Images of Femininity in the Arts and Media* (Pandora, London, 1987).

Bloom, Harold, *The Anxiety of Influence* (OUP, New York, 1973).

Bowie, Malcolm, 'Jacques Lacan' in John Sturrock (ed.), *Structuralism and Since* (Oxford University Press, Oxford, 1979), pp. 116–53.

Boumelha, Penny, *Thomas Hardy and Women: Sexual Ideology and Narrative Form* (Harvester, Brighton, 1982).

Brontë, Charlotte, *Jane Eyre* (Penguin, Harmondsworth, 1982).

Brontë, Emily, *Wuthering Heights* (Penguin, Harmondsworth, 1965).

Brownstein, Rachel, *Becoming a Heroine Reading about Women in Novels* (Penguin, Harmondsworth, 1982).

Butler, Marilyn, 'Feminist criticism, late 80s style', *Times Literary Supplement*, 11–17 March 1988, pp. 283–85.

Cameron, Deborah, *Feminism and Linguistic Theory* (Macmillan, Basingstoke, 1985).

Carter, Angela, *The Magic Toyshop* (Virago, London, 1982).

Carter, Angela, 'Notes from the front line', in Michelene Wandor (ed.) *On Gender and Writing* (Pandora Press, London, 1983), p. 69.

Carter, Angela, Interview with Moira Paterson, 'Flights of fancy in Balham' in *The Observer*, 3 November 1986, pp. 42–5.

Chapman, Rowena, and Rutherford, Jonathan, *Male Order – Unwrapping Masculinity* (Lawrence & Wishart, London, 1988).

Chesler, Phyllis, *Women and Madness* (Allen Lane, London, 1974).

Chester, Gail, and Nielsen, Sigrid, *In Other Words: Writing as a Feminist* (Hutchinson, London, 1987).

Christ, Carol, 'Margaret Atwood: the surfacing of women's spiritual quest and vision', *Signs*, Winter 1976.

Christian, Barbara, *Black Women Novelists: the Development of a Tradition* (Greenwood Press, London, 1980).

Cixous, Hélène, 'The laugh of the medusa', *Signs*, Summer 1975, pp. 875–99.

Cixous, Hélène, 'Sorties', in Elaine Marks and Isabelle de Courtivron (eds), *New French Feminisms* (Harvester, Brighton, 1980) pp. 90–8.

Clément, Catherine, *The Weary Sons of Freud* (Verso, London, 1987).

Cornillon Koppelman, Susan (ed.) *Images of Women in Fiction: Feminist Perspectives* (Popular Press, Bowling Green, Ohio, 1972).

Coward, Rosalind, 'This novel changes lives' in M. Eagleton (ed.), *Feminist Literary Theory: A Reader* (Blackwell, Oxford, 1986), pp. 155–60.

Coward, Rosalind, *Female Desire: Women's Sexuality Today* (Paladin, London, 1984).

Coward, Rosalind, and Ellis, John, *Language and Materialism: Developments in Semiology and the Theory of the Subject* (Routledge and Kegan Paul, London, 1977).

Culler, Jonathan, *Structuralist Poetics* (Routledge and Kegan Paul, London, 1975).

Daly, Mary, *Gyn/Ecology* (Women's Press, London, 1978).

Daly, Mary, *Pure Lust: Elemental Female Philosophy* (Women's Press, London, 1984).

Diamond, Arlyn, and Edwards, Lee R. (eds), *The Authority of Experience: Essays in Feminist Criticism* (University of Massachusetts Press, Amherst, 1977).

Donovan, Josephine (ed.), *Feminist Literary Criticism: Explorations in Theory* (University of Kentucky Press, Lexington, 1975).

Eagleton, Mary, *Feminist Literary Theory: A Reader* (Blackwell, Oxford, 1986).

Eagleton, Terry, *Marxism and Literary Criticism* (Methuen, London, 1976).

Eagleton, Terry, *Literary Theory: An Introduction* (Blackwell, Oxford, 1983).

Eagleton, Terry, 'Pierre Macherey and Marxist literary criticism', in G. H. R. Parkinson (ed.), *Marx and Marxisms* (Cambridge University Press, Cambridge, 1982).

Ehrenreich, Barbara, and English, Deirdre, *For Her Own Good* (Pluto, London, 1979).

Ellmann, Mary, *Thinking about Women* (Harcourt, New York, 1968).

Evans, Mari (ed.), *Black Women Writers* (Pluto, London, 1985).

Faderman, Lillian, *Surpassing the Love of Men: Romantic Friendship and Love Between Women from the Renaissance to the Present* (Morrow, New York, 1981).

Felman, Shoshana, 'Women and madness: the critical phallacy', *Diacritics*, vol. 5, no. 4, 1975.

Fetterley, Judith, *The Resisting Reader: A Feminist Approach to American Fiction* (Indiana University Press, Bloomington, Indiana, 1978).

Foucault, Michel, *The Order of Things: An Archaeology of the Human Sciences* (Vintage/Random, New York, 1973).

Foucault, Michel, *Madness and Civilisation: A History of Insanity in the Age of Reason* (Tavistock, London, 1981).

Foucault, Michel, 'What is an author', in J. V. Harari (ed.), *Textual Strategies: Perspectives in Post-structuralist Criticism* (Methuen, London, 1980), pp. 141–60.

Foucault, Michel, *The History of Sexuality* (Pelican, Harmondsworth, 1981) vol. 1.

Friedan, Betty, *The Feminine Mystique* (Penguin, Harmondsworth, 1965).

Gallop, Jane, *Reading Lacan* (Cornell University Press, Ithaca, 1985).

Gallop, Jane, *Feminism and Psychoanalysis: The Daughter's Seduction* (Macmillan, Basingstoke, 1982).

Gamman, Lorraine, and Marchment, Margaret, *The Female Gaze: Women as Viewers of Popular Culture* (Women's Press, London, 1988).

Gilbert, Sandra, and Gubar, Susan, *The Madwoman in the Attic* (Yale University Press, New Haven, 1979).

Gilbert, Sandra, and Gubar, Susan, *The War of the Words* (Yale University Press, New Haven, 1988), vol. 1.

Gilman, Charlotte Perkins, 'The Yellow Wallpaper', in Ann Lane (ed.), *The Charlotte Perkins Gilman Reader* (Women's Press, London, 1981), pp. 3–20.

Greene, Gayle, and Kahn, Coppelia, *Making a Difference* (Methuen, London, 1986).

Greer, Germaine, *The Female Eunuch* (Paladin, London, 1971).

Griffin, Susan, *Woman and Nature* (Women's Press, London, 1984).

Gubar, Susan, '"The Blank Page" and the issues of female creativity', *Critical Inquiry*, vol. 8, Winter 1981.

Hall, Radclyffe, *The Well of Loneliness* (Virago, London, 1982; first published 1928).

Hardy, Thomas, *Tess of the d'Urbervilles* (Macmillan, London, 1974).

Hartmann, Heidi, 'The unhappy marriage of Marxism and feminism: towards a more progressive union', in Lydia Sargent (ed.), *The Unhappy Marriage of Marxism and Feminism: A Debate on Class and Patriarchy* (Pluto Press, London, 1981).

Haugg, Frigga (ed.), *Female Sexualization*, translated by Erica Carter (Verso, London, 1987).

Hobby, Elaine, *Virtue of Necessity* (Virago, London, 1988).

Humm, Maggie, *Feminist Criticism* (Harvester, Brighton, 1987).

Irigaray, Luce, *This Sex Which is not One*, translated by Catherine Porter, with Carolyn Burke (Cornell University Press, Ithaca, 1985).

Irigaray, Luce, *Speculum of the Other Woman*, translated by Gillian C. Gill (Cornell University Press, Ithaca, 1985).

Jacobus, Mary (ed.), *Women Writing and Writing about Women* (Croom Helm, London, 1979).

James, Louis, *Jean Rhys* (Longman, London, 1978).

Jardine, Alice, *Gynesis: Configurations of Woman and Modernity* (Cornell, Ithaca, 1985).

Jardine, Alice, and Smith, Paul, *Men in Feminism* (Methuen, London, 1987).

Kamuf, Peggy, 'Writing Like a Woman', in S. McConnell-Ginet (ed.) *Women and Language in Literature and Society* (Praeger, New York, 1982), pp. 284–97.

Kaplan, Cora, 'Pandora's box: subjectivity, class and sexuality in socialist-feminist criticism', in Greene and Kahn (eds), *Making a Difference* (Methuen, London, 1985).

Kaplan, Cora, 'Keeping the color in *The Color Purple*', in *Sea Changes* (Verso, London, 1986), pp. 176–87.

Kaplan, Cora, *Sea Changes: Culture and Feminism* (Verso, London, 1986).

Kaplan, Cora, and Light, Alison, 'Feminist criticism in the Eighties', a paper given at *Framing Feminism* at the Institute of Contemporary Art, London, 12 January 1988.

Klein, Melanie, *Envy and Gratitude* (Virago, London, 1988; first published 1975).

Klein, Melanie, in Juliet Mitchell (ed.), *The Selected Melanie Klein* (Peregrine, Harmondsworth, 1986).

Kristeva, Julia, 'La femme ce n'est jamais ça', *Tel Quel*, vol. 59, Autumn 1974, pp. 19–24.

Kristeva, Julia, 'A partir du polylogue', interview with Françoise van Rossum Guyon, in *Revue des Sciences Humaines*, December 1979, pp. 495–501.

Kristeva, Julia, 'Women's time', in Toril Moi (ed.), *The Kristeva Reader* (Blackwell, Oxford, 1986), pp. 188–211.

Kristeva, Julia, 'The adolescent novel' paper presented to the Warwick conference on Kristeva's work, May 1987; to be published in *Cultural Critique*.

Kuhn, Annette, *Women's Pictures* (Routledge and Kegan Paul, London, 1982).

Lacan, Jacques, 'Seminar on *The Purloined Letter*', translated by Jeffrey Mehlman, in *Yale French Studies*, vol. 48, 1972, pp. 38–72.

Lacan, Jacques, 'The agency of the letter in the unconscious or reason since Freud,' in *Écrits: A Selection*, translated by A. Sheridan (Tavistock, London, 1980).

Lovell, Terry, *Consuming Fiction* (Verso, London, 1987).

McConnell-Ginet, Sally (ed.), *Women and Language in Literature and Society* (Praeger, New York, 1982).

Macdonnell, Diane, *Theories of Discourse* (Blackwell, Oxford, 1986).

Macherey, Pierre, *A Theory of Literary Production* (Routledge and Kegan Paul, London, 1978).

Marks, Elaine, and de Courtivron, Isabelle, *New French Feminisms* (Harvester, Brighton, 1980).

Marxist-Feminist Literature Collective, 'Women's writing: Jane Eyre, Shirley, Villette, Aurora Leigh', in *Ideology and Consciousness*, vol. 1, no. 3, Spring, pp. 27–48.

Millard, Elaine, 'Reading as a woman', in Douglas Tallack (ed.), *Literary Theory at Work* (Batsford, London, 1986).

Miller, Hillis J., *Fiction and Repetition* (Blackwell, Oxford, 1982).

Millett, Kate, *Sexual Politics* (Virago, London, 1977).

Mills, Sara, 'Alternative voices to orientalism', *Literature Teaching Politics*, no. 5, 1986, pp. 78–91.

Mills, Sara, '"Going native"? – women's travel writing', in Kowalewski, M. (ed.), *Twentieth Century Travel Writing*, in press.

Mills, Sara, 'No poetry for ladies: Gertrude Stein and Julia Kristeva', in David Murray (ed.) *Theory and Poetry* (Batsford, 1989).

Mitchell, Juliet, *Psychoanalysis and Feminism* (Penguin, Harmondsworth, 1975).

Modleski, Tania, *Loving with a Vengeance: Mass-produced Fantasies for Women* (Methuen, London, 1984).

Moers, Ellen, *Literary Women* (Women's Press, London, 1977).

Moi, Toril, *Sexual/Textual Politics* (Methuen, London, 1985).

Moi, Toril, *The Kristeva Reader* (Blackwell, Oxford, 1986).

Moi, Toril, *French Feminist Thought* (Blackwell, Oxford, 1987).

Moi, Toril, 'Feminism, postmodernism and style: recent feminist criticism in the US' (paper given at Strathclyde University, 1989), *Cultural Critique*, in press.

Monteith, Moira (ed.) *Women's Writing: A Challenge to Theory* (Harvester, Brighton, 1986).

Montefiore, Jan, *Feminism and Poetry* (Pandora, London, 1987).

Morris, A., 'Locutions and locations: more feminist theory and practice', in *College English*, vol. 49, no. 4, April 1987, pp. 465–76.

Morrison, Toni, *Beloved* (Chatto and Windus, London, 1987).

Mulvey, Laura, 'Visual pleasure and narrative cinema, *Screen*, vol. 16, no. 3, 1975, pp. 6–18.

Newton, Judith Lowder, and Rosenfelt, Deborah, *Feminist Criticism and Social Change* (Methuen, London, 1985).

Norris, Christopher, *Deconstructive Criticism* (Methuen, London, 1982).

Olsen, Tillie, *Silences* (Virago, London, 1980).

Ostriker, Alicia, 'The thieves of language: women poets and revisionist mythmakers', *Signs*, vol. 8, no. 1, Spring 1982, pp. 66–78.

Ostriker, Alicia, *Stealing the Language: the Emergence of Women's Poetry in America* (Women's Press, London, 1987).

Palmer, Pauline, 'From "coded mannequin' to bird woman: Angela Carter's magic flight', in Sue Roe (ed.), *Women Reading Women's Writing* (Harvester, Brighton, 1987), p. 183.

Pearce, Lynne, *Women and the Pre-Raphaelite Movement* (Harvester, Wheatsheaf, Hemel Hempstead, in press).

Penfold, Susan, and Walker, Gillian, *Women and the Psychiatric Paradox* (Oxford University Press, Oxford, 1984).

Piercy, Marge, *Woman on the Edge of Time* (Women's Press, London, 1979).

Pinkney, Darryl, 'Black victims: black villains', *New York Review*, 29 January 1987, pp. 17–20.

Plaza, Monique, 'Phallomorphic power and the psychology of women', translated by M. David and J. Hodges, in *Ideology and Consciousness*, vol. 4, Autumn 1978, pp. 5–36.

Pratt, Anaïs, '*Surfacing* and the rebirth journey' in Arnold E. Davidson and Cathy N. Davidson (eds), *The Art of Margaret Atwood: Essays in Criticism* (Anansi, Toronto, 1981), pp. 139–57.

Radcliffe-Richards, Janet, *The Sceptical Feminist: A Philosophical Enquiry* (Routledge and Kegan Paul, London, 1980).

Register, Cheri, 'American literary criticism: a bibliographical introduction', in Josephine Donovan (ed.), *Feminist Literary Criticism, Explorations in Theory* (The University of Kentucky, Lexington, 1975), pp. 1–28.

Rhys, Jean, *Wide Sargasso Sea* (Penguin, Harmondsworth, 1968).

Roe, Sue, *Women Reading Women's Writing* (Harvester, Brighton, 1987).

Root, Jane, *Pictures of Women – Sexuality* (Pandora, London, 1984).

Russ, Joanna, *How to Suppress Women's Writing* (Women's Press, London, 1984).

Said, Edward, *Beginnings: Intention and Method* (Basic Books, New York, 1975), p. 83.

Sargent, Lydia (ed.), *Women and Revolution: The Unhappy Marriage between Marxism and Feminism* (Pluto, London, 1981).

Selden, Raman, *A Reader's Guide to Contemporary Literary Theory* (Harvester, Brighton, 1985).

Showalter, Elaine, *A Literature of their own: British Women Novelists from Brontë to Lessing* (Princeton University Press, Princeton, 1977).

Showalter, Elaine, 'Feminist criticism in the wilderness', *Critical Inquiry*, Winter 1981.

Showalter, Elaine, *The New Feminist Criticism* (Virago, London, 1986).

Showalter, Elaine, *The Female Malady: Women, Madness, and English Culture 1830–1980* (Virago, London, 1987).

Slaughter, Pam, 'Reading between the lines: a Lacanian analysis of "The Yellow Wallpaper"', *Shorter Fiction Studies*, in press.

Smith, Barbara, *Towards a Black Feminist Criticism* (Out-and-out Books, New York, 1980).

Spacks, Patricia Meyers, *The Female Imagination. A Literary and Psychological Investigation of Women's Writing* (Allen and Unwin, London, 1976).

Spence, Jo, *Putting Myself in the Picture* (Camden Press, London, 1986).

Spencer, Jane, *The Rise of the Woman Novelist* (Blackwell, Oxford, 1986).

Spender, Dale, *Women of Ideas and What Men Have Done to Them* (Ark, London, 1982).

Spender, Dale, *Man Made Language* (Routledge and Kegan Paul, London, 1980).

Spender, Dale, *Mothers of the Novel* (Pandora, London, 1986).

Spivak, Gayatri Chakravorty, 'Three women's texts and a critique of imperialism', in Henry Louis Gates (ed.), *'Race', Writing and Difference* (University of Chicago, Chicago, 1985).

Spivak, Gayatri Chakravorty, 'Imperialism and sexual difference', in *Sexual Difference Conference Proceedings* (Oxford Literary Review, Southampton, 1986), pp. 225–40.

Spivak, Gayatri Chakravorty, *In Other Worlds: Essays in Cultural Politics* (Methuen, London, 1987).

Steedman, Carolyn, *Landscape for a Good Woman* (Virago, London, 1986).

Suleiman, Susan (ed.) *The Reader in the Text* (Princeton University Press, New Jersey, 1980).

Szasz, Thomas, *Ideology and Insanity* (Calder and Boyars, London, 1973).

Tallack, Douglas (ed.) *Literary Theory at Work: Three Texts* (Batsford, London, 1986).

Walker, Alice, *The Color Purple* (Women's Press, London, 1983).

Walker, Alice, 'Writing *The Color Purple*', in M. Evans, (ed.), *Black Women Writers* (Pluto, London, 1985), pp. 453–7.

Weedon, Chris, *Feminist Practice and Post-structuralist Theory* (Blackwell, Oxford, 1987).

Widdowson, Peter (ed.), *Re-Reading English* (Methuen, London, 1982).

Williams, Raymond, *Marxism and Literature* (Oxford University Press, Oxford, 1977).

Williamson, Judith, *Decoding Advertisements: Ideology and Meaning in Advertising* (Boyars, London, 1978).

Willis, Susan, 'Black women writers: taking a critical perspective', in Gayle Greene and Coppelia Kahn (eds), *Making a Difference: Feminist Literary Criticism* (Methuen, London, 1986), pp 211–37.

Wittig, Monique, 'One is not born a woman', in *Feminist Issues*, vol. 1, no. 2, Winter 1981, pp. 41–8.

Woolf, Virginia, 'Professions for Women' – *The Death of the Moth and Other Essays* (Harcourt, Brace, New York, 1942), pp. 236–8.

Woolf, Virginia, *A Room of One's Own* (Granada, London, 1977).

Wright, Elizabeth, *Psychoanalytic Criticism: Theory into Practice* (Methuen, London, 1984).

Zimmerman, Bonnie, 'What has never been: an overview of lesbian feminist criticism' in Gayle Green and Coppelia Kahn (eds), *Making a Difference* (Methuen, London, 1986), pp. 177–210.

Index